高级英语选修课系列教材
本成果得到中国人民大学“研究生精品教材建设经费”支持

ESSENTIALS OF CONTEMPORARY WESTERN LITERARY CRITICAL THEORIES

当代西方文艺批评理论要义

（第二版）

陈世丹　史岩林　张东芹　王小会　黄　贺　著

中国人民大学出版社
·北京·

前言

《当代西方文艺批评理论要义》（第二版）（*Essentials of Contemporary Western Literary Critical Theories*）是对20世纪和21世纪初以来陆续出现的每一种西方文艺批评理论的主要思想意义、主要理论主张、主要学术价值的梳理和概述。本书分为上、下两卷，共讨论了18种西方文艺批评理论。上卷包括：1）俄国形式主义；2）英美新批评；3）马克思主义批评；4）心理与精神分析批评；5）神话与原型批评；6）结构主义批评；7）接受美学与读者反应理论；8）后结构主义；9）后现代主义。下卷包括：10）女性主义批评；11）新历史主义；12）后殖民主义研究；13）性别研究；14）文化研究；15）后现代生态文学批评；16）生态后现代主义；17）后现代文学伦理学批评；18）后人文主义。本书英文各章题目如下：

Volume 1

Chapter One　Russian Formalism
Chapter Two　Anglo-American New Criticism
Chapter Three　Marxist Criticism
Chapter Four　Psychological and Psychoanalytic Criticism
Chapter Five　Myth and Archetypal Criticism
Chapter Six　Structuralism
Chapter Seven　Reception Aesthetics and Reader-response Theory
Chapter Eight　Post-structuralism
Chapter Nine　Postmodernism

Volume 2

Chapter Ten　Feminist Criticism
Chapter Eleven　New Historicism
Chapter Twelve　Post-colonial Studies

本书旨在帮助青年读者、学者，特别是高校文学院、外国语学院从事文学批评和理论研究的硕士生、博士生系统地熟悉和把握这 18 种文艺批评理论的核心观念和重要思想，帮助他们恰当地选择合适的理论并将其作为自己学术研究立论的依据、观点的支撑和批判的武器，有助于青年学者在人文社会科学研究中处在学科前沿，不断探索、不断创新。

本书作者除了对每种文艺批评理论做了梳理和概述，还精选、编辑了每种理论学派的代表性理论文献（论文或专著节选）作为选读材料（Selected Readings），供学者们自主阅读和研究使用。作为本书参考教材的《当代西方文艺批评理论选读》（*Selected Readings of Contemporary Western Critical Theories*）已于 2021 年 5 月出版。

本书以专著的形式呈献给读者，但实际上它是在我在中国人民大学自 2004 年秋季学期开始到现在一直承担的英语专业研究生课程“当代西方文艺批评理论”讲义的基础上，经过 19 年的不断扩展、不断修改、不断充实而形成的，由最初的 11 种理论逐步扩展为现在的 18 种理论。逐步增加的理论包括：第九章　后现代主义；第十一章　新历史主义；第十二章　后殖民主义研究；第十五章　后现代生态文学批评；第十六章　生态后现代主义；第十七章　后现代文学伦理学批评；第十八章　后人文主义。

此处要对“第十七章　后现代文学伦理学批评”和“第十八章　后人文主义”做一个特别的说明。对后现代主义文学的批评，国外学者多是从语言、叙事、哲学、政治学、社会学、文化、马克思主义、新历史主义、后殖民主义、女性主义、生态批评等理论视角展开，也有少数学者从伦理学视角讨论后现代主义文学作品。自 20 世纪 90 年代以来，国外虽也出现了齐格蒙・鲍曼、伊曼纽尔・列维纳斯、雅克・德里达、让 – 吕克・南希等哲学家提出的后现代伦理学或后现代伦理思想著述，但一直未见有后现代文学伦理学批评的理论建构。我国学者聂珍钊教授在 2004 年首次提出了文学伦理学批评的理论构想，指出文学的价值就在于它的伦理教诲功能，文学批评不应该有伦理的缺失。他在 2014 年出版了专著《文学伦理学批评导论》，完成了文学伦理学批评理论的建构，产生了巨大影响。该书对我启发很大。我自 1997 年获得第一个国家社科基金项目“美国后现代主义小说主题与艺术手法论”（青年项目，97CWW004）以来，一直从事英美后现代主义小说研究，已出版以及即将出版的专著有《美国后现代主义小说艺术论》（2002）、《虚构亦真实》（2005）、《英美后现代主义小说中的历史与现实》（2023）等 16 部，发表核心期刊论文《论后现代主义小说之存在》（2005）、《代码》（2005）、《后现代文学中的媒介与“再现”和建构》（2012）、

《在虚幻世界反思人类认知能力》(2016)、《西方文论关键词：后人文主义》(2019)、《后人文主义：反思人在世界中的地位》(2021)等100余篇。我在多年的研究过程中发现，作为现代主义思想基础的现代性排斥、拒绝和否定差异，使一切“他者”成为不合法，通过不可能的真理、纯艺术、人性的普遍性来使本来不存在的形而上学的东西在场，把它强加给人们，从而使自己成为可能。现代性对中心性、统一性、整体性、一元性和排他性的追求和强调，导致了普遍主义、绝对主义、一元主义和中心主义的膨胀。而后现代性意指一种强大的变革冲动和创新精神，它要革除现代性对权威、中心和等级的维护，强调承认差异、尊重他者、主张多元性和包容性，是对现代性的批判、否定和颠覆。后现代性试图通过弘扬革新的思想观念，改变和超越现代性或现代精神，建立承认差异、尊重他者、主张多元性和包容性的合理的后现代社会秩序和后现代精神。后现代性是后现代主义的思想基础，也是后现代西方伦理学的思想基础。后现代主义文学消除作者的叙述权威、叙述中心，采用多角度观察、多叙述者、多声音(或复调)、多样杂糅的结构、多元变化的叙事技巧等构成的狂欢化叙事；用平行结构、戏仿、直接引用等构成的互文叙事，即用这种与承认差异、尊重他者、主张多元性和包容性的后现代伦理学一致的后现代伦理的叙事，来表现文学文本中所表现的后现代伦理关系和道德秩序的变化及其引发的各种问题和导致的不同结果，为后现代人类文明进步提供经验和教诲。自2014年起，我根据聂珍钊教授的文学伦理学批评的基本原理，系统研究了齐格蒙·鲍曼、伊曼纽尔·列维纳斯、雅克·德里达、让–吕克·南希等哲学家提出的后现代西方伦理思想，在后现代主义文学研究基础上，尝试建构了“后现代文学伦理学批评理论”。从2015年开始，我在中国人民大学英语专业研究生“当代西方文艺批评理论”课程中增加了“第十七章　后现代文学伦理学批评”。仅在2016—2023年的七个学年内，就有80多名本科生、40多名硕士生和14名博士生用后现代文学伦理学批评理论作为立论依据和批判武器，对英美后现代主义小说、诗歌和戏剧展开研究，撰写学位论文和在学术刊物上发表论文。

自2017年开始，我在后现代文学伦理学批评理论的基础上，增设了“第十八章　后人文主义”。在解构了人的在先性、中心性、绝对性、超验性、自主性等一系列传统人文主义赋予的特权之后，后人文主义宣告了被传统人文主义奉为神明的“人”的死亡。后人文主义思想建立在人类主体伦理道德素质不断提高的基础上，倡导不同种族和不同物种之间的平等和多元化概念，主张开放，倾听一切人的声音，培养“倾听他人”“宽容他人”“尊重他人”的美德——后现代伦理道德，主张多元文化的和谐共存，共建相互依存、包容他者、多元共生的后人类社会。后人文主义也为文学批评提供了一个新的理论视角，它有助于我们揭示后现代主义小说家在作品中所表现的后人文主义主张：1)建构尊重自然、物种间相互依存的生态社会；2)建构造福人类、可持续发展的高科技社会；3)建构人类与赛博格(Cyborg)相互依存、和谐共生，尊重“他者快乐”的后人类社会。后人文主义文学批评揭示了后现代主义作家通过文学创作批判以“人类中心论”和“主客体二元对立”

为基石的传统人文主义思想及其导致的种种现代性危机，同时积极倡导并建构后人文主义和谐社会的思想。仅在 2018—2023 年的五个学年内，就有 40 多名本科生、20 多名硕士生和 8 名博士生从后人文主义批评理论视角对英美后现代主义小说、诗歌和戏剧展开研究，撰写学位论文和在学术刊物上发表论文。

《当代西方文艺批评理论要义》（第二版）（*Essentials of Contemporary Western Literary Critical Theories*）可以用作高校文学专业研究生文学批评和理论研究课程的教材，亦可作为文学、文化、文艺学相关专业的研究生及从事文学批评和理论研究的学者的工具书或参考书。

本书工作量较大，除对每章的理论概述进行系统、全面修改，以及充实、修订外，还要从大量的理论文献中精选与编辑作为学者自主阅读的文献材料。此项工作十分繁重，为了本书顺利出版，我邀请了史岩林、张东芹、王小会和黄贺 4 名英美文学批评、文论研究方向的已毕业博士来协助我完成选读材料的精选和编辑工作。尽管他们各自都很忙，但他们都欣然加入我的工作团队，给予我大力支持。如果没有他们的帮助，这本书的第二版是不可能在计划时间内就得以出版的。因此，我要衷心地感谢他们！

本书写作分工如下：

上卷由陈世丹、史岩林、张东芹编写；下卷由陈世丹、王小会、黄贺编写。

本教材为中国人民大学研究生精品教材建设项目成果，受到中国人民大学 2022 年度“中央高校建设世界一流大学（学科）和特色发展引导专项资金”支持，特向中国人民大学和外国语学院表示衷心的感谢！本书还得到了中国人民大学出版社大众分社的大力支持，也特向中国人民大学出版社大众分社表示衷心的感谢！

陈世丹

2023 年 7 月 20 日

Table of Contents

Introduction

When analyzing a literary text, literary critics ask basic questions such as these about the philosophical, psychological, functional, and descriptive natures of the text itself: 1) Does a text have only one correct meaning? 2) Is a text always didactic; that is, must a reader learn something from every text? 3) Does a text affect each reader in the same way? 4) How is a text influenced by the culture of its author and the culture in which it is written? 5) Can a text become a catalyst for change in a given culture? No matter what question we may ask concerning a literary text, we are participating in an ongoing discussion of the value and enjoyment of a literary work while simultaneously engaging in literary criticism and functioning as practical literary critics. Traditionally, literary critics involve themselves in either theoretical or practical criticism. Theoretical criticism formulates the theories, principles, and tenets of the nature and value of art. By citing general aesthetic and moral principles of art, theoretical criticism provides the necessary framework for practical criticism. Practical criticism (also known as applied criticism) applies the theories and tenets of theoretical criticism to a particular work. Using the theories and principles of theoretical criticism, the practical critic defines the standards of taste and explains, evaluates, or justifies a particular piece of literature. A further distinction is made between the practical critic who posits that there is one theory or set of principles a critic may use when evaluating a literary work—the absolutist critic—and the relativistic critic, one who uses various or even contradictory theories in critiquing a text. The basis for either kind of critic, or any form of criticism, is literary theory. Without theory, practical criticism could not exist. The theories that we are going to study in this course of ours will include "literary theory," "critical theory," and "cultural theory" in a general sense.

Literary theory in a strict sense is the systematic study of the nature of literature and of the methods for analyzing literature. However, literary scholarship since the 19th century often includes—in addition to, or even instead of literary theory in the strict sense—considerations of intellectual history, moral philosophy, social prophecy, and other interdisciplinary themes which are of relevance to the way humans interpret meaning. In humanities in modern academia, the latter style of scholarship is an outgrowth of critical theory and is often called simply "theory." As a consequence, the word "theory" has become an umbrella term for a variety of scholarly approaches to reading texts. Many of these approaches are informed by various strands of continental philosophy and sociology.

Critical theory (or "**social critical theory**") describes the neo-Marxist philosophy of the Frankfurt School, which was developed in Germany in the 1930s. Critical theory maintains that ideology is the principal obstacle to human liberation. Martin Jay has stated that the first generation of critical theory is best understood as not promoting a specific philosophical agenda or a specific ideology, but as "a gadfly of other systems." Critical theory was established as a school of thought primarily by five Frankfurt School theoreticians, Herbert Marcuse, Theodor Adorno, Max Horkheimer, Walter Benjamin, and Erich Fromm, drawing on the critical methods of Karl Marx and Sigmund Freud. Modern critical theory has additionally been influenced by György Lukács and Antonio Gramsci, as well as the second generation Frankfurt School scholars, such as Jürgen Habermas. Concern for economic base and superstructure is one of the remaining Marxist philosophical concepts in much of the contemporary critical theory. While critical theorists have been frequently defined as Marxist intellectuals, their tendency to denounce some Marxist concepts and to combine Marxian analysis with other sociological and philosophical traditions has resulted in accusations of revisionism by Classical, Orthodox, and Analytical Marxists, and by Marxist-Leninist philosophers.

Cultural theory is the branch of comparative anthropology and semiotics (not to be confused with Cultural Sociology or Cultural Studies) that seeks to define the heuristic concept of culture in operational and/or scientific terms.

In the 19th century, "culture" was used by some to refer to a wide array of human activities, and by others as a synonym for "civilization." In the 20th century, anthropologists began theorizing about culture as an object of scientific analysis. Some used it to distinguish human adaptive strategies from the largely instinctive adaptive strategies of animals, including the adaptive strategies of other primates and non-human hominids, whereas others used it to refer to symbolic representations and expressions of human experience, with no direct adaptive value. Both groups understood culture as being definitive of human nature.

According to many theories that have gained wide acceptance among anthropologists, culture exhibits the way that humans interpret their biology and their environment. According to this point of view, culture becomes such an integral part of human existence that it *is* the human environment, and most cultural change can be attributed to human adaptation to historical events.

Moreover, given that culture is seen as the primary adaptive mechanism of humans and takes place much faster than human biological evolution, most cultural change can be viewed as culture adapting to itself.

Although most anthropologists try to define culture in such a way that it separates human beings from other animals, many human traits are similar to those of other animals, particularly the traits of other primates. For example, chimpanzees have big brains, but human brains are bigger. Similarly, bonobos exhibit complex sexual behaviour, but human beings exhibit much more complex sexual behaviours. As such, anthropologists often debate whether human behaviour is different from animal behaviour in degree rather than in kind; they must also find ways to distinguish cultural behavior from sociological behavior and psychological behavior.

W. Brian Arthur, economist of complexity economics, explored acceleration and amplification of the various aspects of culture change. In his book, *The Nature of Technology* (2009), Arthur attempts to articulate a theory of change that considers that existing technologies (or material culture) are combined in unique ways that lead to novel new technologies. Behind that novel combination is a purposeful effort arising in human motivation. This articulation would suggest that we are just beginning to understand what might be required for a more robust theory of culture and culture change, one that brings coherence across many disciplines and reflects an integrating elegance.

To speak briefly, critical theories are the theories about the written language (including all kinds of signs) and texts (including social texts). The emergence and application of these theories are closely related to "the language turn" in the 20th century.

Observing in a whole, literary theories in the past were based on "the modes of expression" of language, namely, on the concept that language was used to imitate, reproduce or reflect reality. That is to say, literature could reflect the truth and essence of reality through language's imitation and reproduction of reality. In other words, there was a transcendental existence that was prior to man and independent of man's consciousness outside language. What literature reflected was the truth and essence of this existence. Yet this kind of truth and essence that are imagined prior to language does not exist. Before the imitation and reproduction of language take place, this kind of truth and essence cannot automatically and directly appear before man because any truth or essence cannot be tenable without the expression of language. In the final analysis, the so-called objective truth can only be a subjective hypothesis because man's thinking can not go without language and man enters "the prison-house of language"—a language that exists prior to him once he was born. This language is a relation web of a fixed meaning that determines man's position of existence, his relation to nature, society, history, the other, himself, and the ways by which he acts and associates with the others. Therefore, man does not freely control language but is controlled by language. Language is not an instrument that is dead and handy to be used.

In the light of this view of language, Contemporary Western Critical Theories, especially the theories of Post-structuralism, have generally abandoned the modes of expression of language. Language is no longer the imitation of the outside reality and does not reflect the truth and essence any more. The so-called truth is only an unreal image constructed by language. The so-called meaning can only be produced in the language itself. Meaning is produced in the process that language is used and is the outcome of the permutations and combinations of language signs. Thus, reading and interpretation do no longer "find" truth and meaning but "invent and create" truth and meaning. Therefore, all texts do not have absolute meanings any more and have lost the center of unity. Interpretation has become a free personal activity.

Why did such "a language turn" emerge in the 20th century? This should be examined through the development of the human society. As it has entered the postmodern times or the computer era from the modern times, the whole society has changed tremendously. The computerized electronic structure, the huge commercial web, and the great invisible systems have given rise to the fearful prospect of new totalitarianism. The few people in the dominant position will make a unified, all-embracing, extra-interplanetary organizational structure designed for automation. People will not actively play their roles as autonomous persons but will be turned into passive and aimless creatures controlled by machines. Their proper roles will either be devoured by machines or rigorously limited and controlled because the interests of the individuals and collective organizations have been lost. In such a situation, they as individuals do not know where to go. They are vacillating and hesitating, confused and irresolute in giving opinions, and dispersed and inconsistent in actions. They fear and doubt but cannot focus on the object that they fear and doubt. It is just this terrible prospect that causes the rising of the critical theories that are grounded on the philosophy of skepticism, especially of the theories of Post-structuralism that reached its peak in the 1970s and the 1980s. Meanwhile, the theories on the basis of the ideas of humanism, such as Reception Aesthetics and Reader-Response Criticism, have been admitted and developed in this period, which stress the role of the individual consciousness and resist the monopoly and control of the great systems.

Another very important aspect of the development of Contemporary Critical Theories is "the cultural turn." Along with the development of globalization and the appearance of the commercialization of knowledge, it is especially the development and the running ways of transnational corporations that have already made the economic power begin to endanger the governments of states, at least having caused that a part of the decision about investment has gone beyond the scope of states' control.

Besides, along with the development of the postmodern society or the computer society, the nature of knowledge has changed. The supply and use of knowledge have become a relation between production and consumption. Knowledge has also become commercialized. Thus, the productive force of knowledge has not only constituted a key for a country's development but also at the same time become an important factor of the rival for the world power. Some day the countries in the world will have struggles to scramble for knowledge and control information as they had wars to control territories and plunder raw materials or cheap labor force in the past. Thus, on the one hand, knowledge has opened new areas for commerce, and on the other hand, it has brought about new challenges for political strategies. Consequently, in the West the tendency of knowledge to be politicalized has appeared, the governments and all kinds of institutions are competing in reinforcing the control of culture with the result that a wave of antimonopoly, antiauthority and anti-control has been surging high and with this Cultural Studies has been aroused and the theories of ideological studies that is carried out by countries, nationalities, races, sexes, classes, etc. have appeared.

Simply speaking, these theories are concerned with the social practices of human beings, the production and reproduction of human experiences, and the constitution of the human subject. Today, like the present situation of its development, Cultural Studies is a field in which all branches of learning are mixed and is hard to define like the theories themselves. It can be said that Cultural Studies and theories are not mutually exclusive: theories are the theories of culture and Cultural Studies is the practice of theories; or Cultural Studies is the practice of culture and theories are the theories about cultural practice. Therefore, critical theories must be considered in this sense and must not be limited to the theories about the written language or texts.

The Characteristics of Contemporary Western Critical Theories

The present-day theories have two most important characteristics: 1) they are heterogeneous, that is, they do not seek homoousia; 2) they unprecedentedly criticize the basis and hypotheses of traditional criticism. Jonathan Culler, American famous critic, has summed up four characteristics of the contemporary Western critical theories: 1) they go beyond the braches of learning—the effect of language lies outside its original branches of learning; 2) they are analytical and speculative—they seek to find out the connotations of many things such as sexes, language, meaning, works, the subject, etc.; 3) they take a critical attitude towards common sense—they criticize the concepts that are naturally accepted; 4) they are introspective—they investigate thoughts and explore the categories in which people make things produce meaning, which include not only literary practice but also the practice of other discourses.①

Literary study is always a branch of learning with plural meaning. It constitutes all kinds of traditional practices, such as histories of literatures, literary biographies, moral-aesthetic criticism, new criticism, etc. They co-existed in a quite stable state of disequilibrium until the 1960s and shared the same or similar understanding of writers, the nature of literary works, and the aims of criticism. Critics might have controversies over whether a work could be accepted as one of classics but they had no doubt about the existence of the so-called "literature" itself, no doubt about the opinion that the author determines the meaning of a work, and no doubt about the view that criticism attaches itself to the literary object that it studies either. All these have been sternly queried and reevaluated by the present-day theoretical discourses.

The present-day critical theories think that they have already become an independent branch of learning and the day-to-day work that is indispensable to literary study. They refuse to accept the border position to depend on literature and do not acknowledge that they are an outside concern that is closer to philosophy for literature. They put themselves in the core of the critical cause and insist that all critical actions cannot overstep theories. As many theorists have pointed out, the traditional form of criticism that is used to study literature and the response to a famous literary work cannot work without theories and cannot be a purely academic endeavor. All forms of criticism are grounded on certain theories or a mixture of theories whether they are aware of this or not. The theoretical works have already shown that in literary study those ways that are regarded as "natural" and "common sense" rely actually on a set of theoretical instructions. For the part of critics, they have already melted these instructions in their blood and carried out them in their actions and so they need not prove this again in their own practice.

After they have transformed themselves into the routine work of literary study, theories have caused a series of heated disputes. Some critics consider that theories are deeply contained in the daily work of literary study and in the analysis of some concrete works; the others think that theories should not direct straight at the object of literary study but should operate in the abstract and abstruse fields. Thus, they separate themselves from the traditional ways such as close reading and direct study of works. Most theories are abstract, do not directly provide a method to discuss a literary text but possess a great significance to the ways of literary study. This significance cannot be abolished because theories are short of direct practical value. Criticism as a branch of learning is fundamentally based on its direct relation to the object of study, which is

① Jonathan Culler, *Literary Theory*, Cambridge, Mass.: Harvard University Press, 1997, p. 15.

determined by history and is not inevitable or natural. A part of attack upon orthodox criticism involves the determination of the natural ways of literary study. If literary theories sneer at tradition, they attack it and make it seem to be single but not plural. That is because the object of their attack is not the variety that constitutes those traditional critical practices but the basis and a whole set of hypotheses of traditional criticism. Traditional criticism stubbornly insists that the basis or the set of hypotheses can only be "natural" and "perceptible."

The basis of traditional criticism is a determinacy of epistemology and ontology, thinking that the relation between author, text and reader is determinate. Every form of criticism lays special emphasis on a different aspect. For example, the criticism on a biography stresses the author; the criticism on history or sociology, the background; New Criticism, the text itself; moral-aesthetic criticism, the relation between the text and reality, etc. They all, however, accept the literary theory of mimesis in the broad sense. That is to say, literature always reflects and provides in this way or that way the so-called "truth" about life and the living situation of human beings. The task of literature is to depict life and describe experiences and feelings in a potential way. The work of criticism is to reveal the true value and the meaning of this description. Here is a paradox: this description is contained in literature but needs to be revealed by critical activity.

The theory of mimesis regards language as a transparent medium through which reality can be reproduced in an aesthetic way and go beyond the expression of the written language. This view of language is again related to a universal world outlook: man is the center of the world and cognition is the product of experiences. Experiences are prior to language that expresses them and language is only the instrument used to express them. According to this opinion, literature is the product of a collective of outstanding individuals who can represent the universal and eternal truths by using language. In other words, literature is the action of a few excellent people.

What the present-day theories query and criticize is just this set of hypotheses and in their critical practice the present-day theories have formed multiple different theoretical viewpoints. Owing to their criticism, traditional common understanding around literary study and the ideology that supports it have now already disintegrated. For instance, Feminism has introduced culture and politics into literary study, Reader-response Theory has shifted its study center from the relation between author and text to the relation between text and reader, new Marxism lays emphasis on the proposition that culture should intervene and interfere society, Post-structuralism subverts the traditional metaphysical cognition, Post-colonial Theory opposes cultural hegemony, postmodernism pushes forward diversity or pluralism, etc. The current cultural studies does more to recognize from many aspects the role and function of culture, especially the role and function of culture in the world today: in a world in which all kinds of social groups are mixed and in a world that is constructed by state powers, media industry, and transnational corporations, how does cultural production operate? How is the cultural identity of individuals and groups constituted? How are people influenced and controlled by cultural power and to what extent are they dominated by cultural forms? To what extent or in what ways can cultural forms be used for other purposes? To what extent can people become the subject that is responsible for their own actions? Again to what extent will people's choice be limited by the power beyond their control? Obviously, the answers to these questions go far beyond the limits of traditional criticism but will undoubtedly give great impetus to the development of the whole literary study.

As we have said, the new theories are produced and developed on a social basis. For nearly half a century, along with the development and the use of high and new science and technology and globalization coming with it, an unprecedented change has taken place in the whole structure of human society and international relations, along with which a tremendous change has also taken place in ideology, moral concepts, and the thinking manner of people. When they face the new situation, the problems that how people will understand society and how they will deal with the society that constantly changes become the important tasks of ideological circles and intellectual circles. Thus, the intellectuals who have keen insight and consciousness of responsibility take a rethinking and critical attitude towards tradition, put forward new ideas and theoretical elaborations from different aspects, and have formed a prosperous situation in which diverse theories co-exist at the same time and influence each other.

In this course, "Essentials of Contemporary Western Critical Theories," we shall study and discuss the theories of the following schools: Russian Formalism, Anglo-American New Criticism, Marxist Criticism, Psychological and Psychoanalytic Criticism, Myth and Archetypal Criticism, Structuralism, Reception Aesthetics and Reader-response Theory, Post-structuralism, Postmodernism, Feminist Criticism, New Historicism, Post-colonial Studies, Gender Studies, Cultural Studies, Postmodern Ecological Literary Criticism, Ecological Post-modernism, Postmodern Ethical Literary Criticism and Post-humanism.

Volume 1
上卷

陈世丹　史岩林　张东芹　著

Chapter One

Russian Formalism

Almost all of the important critics and thinkers have placed focus on the formal aspects of art and literature. Among them, we may mention several names, such as Aristotle, ancient and medieval rhetoricians, Kant, many of the Romantics, and writers in the 19th-century movements of symbolism and aestheticism. This climax came with the birth of the new literatures and critical theories at the early 20th century, beginning with the Formalist movement in Russia and with European modernism, exerting subsequently a major influence on the New Criticism in England and America and later schools such as the neo-Aristotelians. Terry Eagleton, English famous Marxist critic, pointed out that contemporary Western critical theories started from Russian formalism. Along with movements in futurism and symbolism, the Russian Formalists were a group of writers who flourished in Russia from the 1910s to the 1930s. Though lasting for a very short period of time of about 15 years, Russian Formalism has left a far-reaching influence. Its traces could be found in the Prague School, Anglo-American New Criticism, and French Structuralism.

A. Two Different Groups and the Main Russian Formalists

It is generally believed that Formalism started in 1914 when Victor Shklovsky published "The Resurrection of the Word", and ended with his essay "Monument to a Scholarly Error" in 1930. Organizationally the formalists centered around two different though interrelated groups.

One group, the "Moscow Linguistic Circle," was founded in 1915 by linguists like Roman Jakobson, which based literary study on linguistics by insisting on the differentiation between poetic and practical language; Other members of the group also included Osip Brik and Boris Tomashevsky. The other group, the "Society for the Study of Poetic Language," was founded in 1916 in St. Petersburg, headed by Viktor Shklovsky, the main members of which were Boris Eichenbaum, Yuri Tynyanov and others, and whose interest was in the general principles governing literature and distinguishing it from other forms of verb expression. Besides them, other important critics associated with these movements should also be mentioned, e.g. Leo Jakubinsky and the folklorist Vladimir Propp.

Having studied at the University of St. Petersburg in Russia, denounced by Leon Trotsky for his formalist views, Shklovsky became a founding member of the Society for the Study of Poetic Language. His essay "Art as Techniques", a primary document of the early Formalists, is often regarded as the manifesto of Russian Formalism. The article does its utmost to oppose the then quite current aesthetic theories maintaining that the nature of art is thinking in images and that to study a work one must start with images. Shklovsky considered that the main traits of poetry are not images but the techniques which are used to process and arrange words. Poetic images have the same function with other techniques such as comparison, repetition, symmetry, and hyperbole, all of which are used to heighten people's direct experiences with poetry and deepen the impression on the reader. The purpose of using these techniques is to remove the automatic ways of experiences to which people are already used, prolong and reinforce the new ways of experiences, and acquire the effects of defamiliarization. His formalism can possibly accommodate cultural change and the relative status of radical innovation. But it is unclear to what extent his view of art as transforming the perception of an object may have epistemological implications. For example, if art represents the stone as stony, this surely implies that the quality of stoniness is somehow an objective attribute which has faded from recognition owing to automatism. But, to rediscover an attribute which convention has ignored is not necessarily to offer a new perception; nor, for that matter, could such a recovery be formalistically divorced from the meaning of the object.

Boris Eichenbaum was one of the leaders of the Society for the Study of Poetic Language. It is in "The Theory of the 'Formal Method'" that Eichenbaum expounds the evolution of the central principles of the formalist method. Eichenbaum states that the ideology behind formalism was positivism, an attempt to emulate the models and methods of what is perceived as "science," an attempt to focus on immediately given empirical data rather than on general schemes or theories for uniting and understanding such isolated information. In the context of early 20th-century Russia, Eichenbaum evidently sees this strategy as revolutionary, as attempting to free art from serving ideological and political ends.

Jakobson also made contribution to the founding of the Moscow Linguistic Circle and was involved in yet another Russian Formalist group, the Society for the Study of Poetic Language. The Formalists were in some ways regarded as important precursors of Structuralism: in 1926 Jakobson founded the Prague Linguistic Circle, which engaged critically with the work of Saussure. And, fleeing from Nazi occupation, he moved to America in 1941 where he became acquainted with Claude Lévi-Strauss; in 1943 he co-founded the Linguistic Circle of New York. His ideas proved to be of greatest impact first in France and then in America. His work occupies a central and seminal place in the development of formalism and Structuralism. In his paper "Linguistics and Poetics" (1958) Jakobson argues that, since poetics concerns the artistic features of a "verbal message," and linguistics is the "global science of verbal structure," poetics is an integral part of linguistics. Jakobson's essay "Two Aspects of Language and Two Types of Aphasic Disturbances" (1956) suggests that language has a bipolar structure, oscillating between the poles of metaphor and metonymy.

B. The Object of Literary Study of Formalists

The name Formalism implied that in the hands of those Formalists the object of literary study was changed from the contents represented by a literary work (such as the social reality, the author's life, and the main ideas of the work) to the literary form itself. The object of its criticism was the traditional methods of literary criticism that was then current in the critical circles: the criticism on biography type that interpreted the text according to the author's life; the sociological criticism that completely summed up the work as the reflection of the social trend of thought; and the philosophical criticism that the critic borrowed literature to expound his own philosophical ideas. Traditional literary criticism explored mainly what contents that literature represents. Therefore, it investigated the author's life, the social events that were related to the work and the main ideas that the work was pregnant with so that it put the organizational forms of literature and the reason why the literary work becomes literature in the secondary place.

Russian Formalists shifted the heart of criticism to the forms and structures of texts, trying to accurately describe the features and functions of the narrative techniques of the work from scientific angles, because in their opinion the object of literary study was *literariness*. Jakobson thought that "the scientific subject of literature is not literature but literariness, namely, the things that make a work be called a literary work." The discussion on literariness became the core of the theories of Russian Formalism. Consequently, the theory of mimesis in traditional literary criticism and the function of enlightening by education propagated by it were abandoned and the inherent laws of literature were stressed. According to Shklovsky, "art is always independent of life and it never reflects the color of the flag flying in the sky over a castle."

Influenced by Futurism and futurist poetry, and reacting against Symbolism's mysterious poetics (though not against its emphasis on form), Russian Formalists sought to place the study of literature on a scientific basis; their investigation concentrated on the language and the formal devices of the literary work. Russian Formalism rejected entirely the idea of the text as reflecting an essential unity which is ultimately one of moral or humanistic significance. The central focus of their analysis was not so much literature *per se*, but literariness, that which makes a given text "literary." In this sense they sought to uncover the system of literary discourse, the systematic arrangement of language which makes literature possible. Their interest in literary texts tended to center on the functioning of literary devices rather than on content; literariness was an effect of form. They thought that literariness lies in the special use of ordinary language. Literary language deviates from and distorts ordinary language. The latter is mainly used for communication while the former has no such practical function. Defamiliarization, a device put forward by Shklovsky, is manifestation of the special use of ordinary language. In his opinion, people are used to many familiar things in life and do not perceive their special nature at all; habits make people's experiences with these things (including speech actions) become automatic. The task of art is to restore people's experiences with the true features of things and make people look at the familiar things in a different light and thus have a kind of strange feelings. This is the effect that the device of defamiliarization produces.

Narrative theories were the fields that Formalists mainly explored. Their greatest interest was to find out the techniques by which a story is constructed and study the method to link all the events in a story. They strictly differentiated "story" from "plot." Aristotle defined "plot" as "the organizational arrangement of events." In other words, plot is the artistic permutation of all the events that constitute a story. For Russian Formalists, story is a series of events that are set out according to the time sequence of their happening and the law of causality while plot throws the time sequence of events' happening and the law of causality into confusion. Strictly speaking, only plot has literariness while story is merely a set of raw materials waiting to be processed and rearranged by the author.

C. Three Modes of Study of Russian Formalism

There are three modes of study of Russian Formalism and they represent the three periods of the development.

The mechanist mode of study with Shklovsky as its representative gets this name because it is used to explaining artistic phenomena with machinery as metaphor. Shklovsky regarded literary criticism as the work of overhauling of a technical worker and a literary text as the sum of all techniques. Mechanistic formalism devotes itself to the study of the origin of a literary work, trying to explain how a literary work is derived from non-literary phenomena and illustrated the basic techniques and the dominant laws by which a literary subject but not a concrete work is produced. Because mechanistic formalism separates itself from social and historical facts when it explains artistic facts, its practitioners often ignore the social and cultural situation in which a work is produced.

The organic mode of study no longer regards a literary work as the sum of all techniques but considers it a unity constituted with all functional elements. The author of a work uses some techniques because they give play to functions inside the work. This literary theory of organism regards a literary work as a functional system, in which every element occupies a specific place according to its own function. For example, a rhyme regarded as a repeated syllable performs the organizational function in a metrical poem. In the aspect of the relation between everyday life and literature, unlike mechanistic formalism that draws a hard and last line between the two, organic formalism admits that the inside organization of a literary work is under the influence of nonliterary elements. However, when compared with the inherent law of literature, these influences are accidental and secondary.

The systematic mode of study represented by Tynyanov is influenced by the linguistic theories of Saussure who points out that the speech action is the embodiment of the inherent system of the language that people speak and this inherent system is called langue. Similarly, to Tynyanov, literariness of all literary phenomena is determined by literary subjects, schools and styles. Literary work and literary system cannot be separated from each other; once straying from this system, a literary work will lose its literariness. In the same way, Tynyanov regarded the whole culture as a complicated "system of systems" and literature and science as subsystems. Inside the great system, non-literary phenomena and literature interact on each other. Though compared with the two preceding modes, systematic formalism lowers the position of literary self-discipline and it insists that what determines the development of literature is still the inside situation of literary system while non-literary background only plays a secondary role.

D. The End of Russian Formalism

Russian Formalism reached its peak at the end of the 1920s. From the middle of the 1920s, it began to suffer from the powerful challenge and criticism of Marxist literary criticism. *Literature and Revolution* by Leon Trotsky and *The Formal Method in Literary Scholarship* by Mikhail Bakhtin were then the critical works with the deepest insight. Along with the change of political situation, a change took place in the literary and artistic policies of the Soviet Union, the period of free exploration in the artistic field ended and socialist realism gradually occupied the dominant position in the literary and artistic circles. In 1930, Shklovsky published an article, declaring the disintegration of the school of formalist theories. Hereafter, the main members remaining in the country turned into other fields of study and creation while Jakobson and other members emigrated to foreign countries, helping establish the Prague School. After Nazi occupied Czechoslovakia, Jakobson and some members of the Prague School, for example René Wellek among them, migrated to the United States and they played an important role in promoting the formation and development of the Anglo-American New Criticism.

Since the Formalists' analyses seem to be "practical" rather than theoretical, they stress to understand the general nature of literature and literary devices, as well as the historical evolution of literary techniques. Though Russian Formalism as a school was eclipsed with the new regime and the official Soviet aesthetic of socialist realism, its influence was transmitted through figures such as Jakobson and Tzvetan Todorov to their own structuralist analyses and those of writers such as Roland Barthes and Gerard Genette. Even Hans Robert Jauss has made good use of Shklovsky's notion of defamiliarization in his reception theory. Formalism begat Structuralism, which in turn begat Post-structuralism. When Structuralism had its brief heyday in Anglo-American literary studies, during the 1970s, familiarity with Russian Formalism seemed like the required preliminary to immersion in Structuralism—though only the preliminary. Structuralism (a contemporary movement of thought with French sources) was what critics of the time were doing; Formalism (a bygone Russian movement) was a precursor. Subsequently, when Structuralism gave way to the many varieties of Post-structuralism as the primary focus in literary theory, Formalism gave way to Structuralism as the main topic of the introductory lecture in a theory survey.

Further Reading

Any, Carol. Boris Eikhenbaum in OPOIAZ: Testing the Limits of the Work-Centered Poetics. *Slavic Review* 49: 3 (1990): 409–426.

Brown, Edward J. The Formalist Contribution. *The Russian Review* 33: 3 (1974): 243–258.

Erlich, Victor. Russian Formalism: In Perspective. *The Journal of Aesthetics and Art Criticism* 13: 2 (1954): 215–225.

Erlich, Victor. Russian Formalism. *Journal of the History of Ideas* 34: 4 (1973): 627–638.

Garson, Judith. Literary History: Russian Formalist Views, 1916–1928. *Journal of the History of Ideas* 31: 3 (1970): 399–412.

Jakobson, Roman. A Postscript to the Discussion on Grammar of Poetry. *Diacritics* 10: 1 (1980): 21–35.

Leitch, Vincent B. *The Norton Anthology of Literary Theory and Criticism.* New York: W. W. Norton & Company, 2001: 1058–1087.

Mandelker, Amy. Russian Formalism and the Objective Analysis of Sound in Poetry. *The Slavic and East European Journal* 27: 3 (1983): 327–338.

Rydel, Christine A. Formalism (Russian Formalists) // *Encyclopedia of the Novel.* Paul Schellinger et al. Vol. 1. Chicago & London: Fitzroy Dearborn Publishers, 1998.

Steiner, Peter. Russian Formalism // *The Cambridge History of Literary Criticism.* Raman Selden. Vol. 8. Cambridge: Cambridge University Press, 1995.

Steiner, Peter. Russian Formalism // *A Metapoetics.* Ithaca: Cornell University Press, 1984.

Warner, Nicholas O. In Search of Literary Science the Russian Formalist Tradition. *Pacific Coast Philology* 17 (1982): 69–81.

Lemon, Lee T. & Marion J. Reis. Russian Formalist Criticism // *Four Essays.* Lincoln, NE: University of Nebraska Press, 1965.

Shklovsky, Viktor. *Theory of Prose.* Trans. Benjamin Sher. Elmwood Park, IL: Dalkey Archive, 1990.

Trotsky, Leon. *Literature and Revolution.* Chicago, IL: Haymarket, 2005.

Wellek, René & Austin Warren. *Theory of Literature.* 3rd. ed. San Diego, CA: Harcourt Brace Jovanovich, 1977.

Rice, Philip & Patricia Waugh. *Modern Literary Theory.* New York: Oxford University Press, 2002.

Cuddon, J. A. *A Dictionary of Literary Terms and Literary Theory.* 5th ed. Revised by M. A. R.

Harib. Malden MA, USA / Oxford, UK: Wiley-Blackwell, 2013.

Bressler, Charles E. *Literary Criticism: An Introduction to Theory and Practice.* 3rd ed. Beijing: Higher Education Press, 2003.

Zhu, Gang. *Twentieth Century Western Critical Theories.* Shanghai: Shanghai Foreign Language Education Press, 2008.

Zhang, Zhongzai, Wang Fengzhen and Zhao Guoxin. *Selected Readings in 20th Century Western Critical Theory*. Beijing: Foreign Language Teaching and Research Press, 2002.

Bibliography

Cuddon, J. A. *A Dictionary of Literary Terms and Literary Theory*. 5th ed. Malden: Wiley-Blackwell, 2013.

Rice, Philip & Patricia Waugh. *Modern Literary Theory*. New York: Oxford University Press, 2002.

Bressler, Charles. *Literary Criticism: An Introduction to Theory and Practice*. Beijing: Higher Education Press, 2004.

Richter, David H. *A Companion to Literary Theory*. Hoboken: Wiley Blackwell, 2018.

Habib, Rafey. *A History of Literary Criticism: From Plato to the Present.* Oxford: Blackwell Publishing, 2005.

泰勒，温奎斯特. 后现代主义百科全书. 章燕，李自修，等译. 刘象愚，校. 长春：吉林人民出版社，2007.

王治河. 后现代主义辞典. 北京：中央编译出版社，2004.

张中载，王逢振，赵国新. 二十世纪西方文论选读. 北京：外语教学与研究出版社，2002.

朱刚. 二十世纪西方文艺批评理论. 上海：上海外语教育出版社，2001.

Selected Readings

Victor Shklovsky: “Art as Technique”

Boris Eichenbaum: “The Theory of the ‘Formal Method’”

Chapter Two

Anglo-American New Criticism

The Anglo-American New Criticism is a "movement" in literary criticism which developed in the 1920s (for the most part among Americans). In contrast to Russian Formalism which aspired to be a "science" of literature, the Anglo-American New Criticism began by explicitly opposing itself to the scientism of a utilitarian age and arguing that as science reduces the world to types and forms, art must reinvest it with body, the concrete particular, the plenitudinous experience. Although the Anglo-American New Criticism also focuses on the formal properties of the literary text, therefore, it parts company with the methods of Russian Formalism in its adherence to an organized and humanist conception of the function of the literary work ultimately derived from Romantic aesthetics. The poem is an object, a formal autonomous entity which, in its unique existence as a for-itself, can restore the world to us. Accordingly, Cleanth Brooks in 1947 attacked the "heresy of paraphrase" as that critical practice which simply restates the poem in the terms of something else and thus destroys and negates its formal uniqueness. The Anglo-American New Criticism calls for a critical practice which could respect the autonomy of the work of art and offer a formal explication which is more than an act of rhetorical transposition.

A. The Development of New Criticism

The Anglo-American New Criticism was popular in England and America in the 20th century, occupying a dominant position in literary study. The term "The New Criticism" was derived from the title of the lecture delivered by Joel Spingarn in 1910. Spingarn was an American educator and literary critic, and his criticism and aesthetical thought was deeply influenced by Croce's expressionist theory of art. He advocated a creative and imaginative criticism which gave primacy to the aesthetic qualities of literature over historical, psychological, and moral considerations. Spingarn, however, was not directly related to the New Criticism that developed in subsequent decades. However, it was not until 1941 that John Crowe Ransom published a book called *The New Criticism*. In it he criticized the critics I. A. Richards, William Empson, T. S. Eliot and Yvor Winters, and made a plea for what he called the "ontological critic."①

T. S. Eliot is a leading figure in English-language Modernist poetry and also a forerunner of the Anglo-American New Criticism. He exercised a strong influence on Anglo-American culture from the 1920s until late in the century. His essay, "Tradition and the Individual Talent" first published in *The Egoist* (1919), formulates the influential conception of the relationship between the poet and preceding literary traditions. The concept is a direct attack on impressionistic criticism. He points out that literary texts are understood for their own right in the "literary" evolution and the writer is to be depersonalized.

Richards' *Principles of Literary Criticism* (1924) advanced literary critical notions such as irony, tension, and balance, as well as distinguishing between poetic and other uses of language. His *Practical Criticism* (1929), based on student analyses of poetry, emphasized the importance of "objective" and balanced close reading which was sensitive to the figurative language of literature. Richards' student William Empson produced an influential work, *Seven Types of Ambiguity* (1930), which was held up as a model of New Critical close reading. Across the Atlantic, New Critical practices were also being pioneered by American critics, known as the Fugitives and the Southern Agrarians, who promoted the values of the Old South in reaction against the alleged dehumanization of science and technology in the industrial North. Notable among these pioneers were John Crowe Ransom and Allen Tate, who developed some of the ideas of Eliot and Richards. Ransom edited the poetry magazine the *Fugitive* from 1922 to 1925 with a group of writers including Tate, Robert Penn Warren, and Donald Davidson. Other Journals included the *Southern Review*, edited by Penn Warren and Cleanth Brooks (1935–1942), the *Kenyon Review*, run by Ransom (1938–1959), and the still extant *Sewanee Review*, edited by Tate and others.

Ransom published a series of essays entitled *The New Criticism* (1941) and an influential essay, "Criticism, Inc.," published in *The World's Body* (1938). This essay concisely expounds the core content of New Critical principles underlying the practice of most "New Critics," whose views often differed in other respects. He emphasizes that the focus of criticism must

① J. A. Cuddon, *A Dictionary of Literary Terms and Literary Theory*, Malden: Wiley-Blackwell, 2013, p. 468.

be shifted from historical scholarship to aesthetic appreciation and understanding. Ransom describes both the conservative New Humanism and left-wing criticism as focusing on morality rather than aesthetics. He believes that literature and literary criticism should enjoy autonomy both ontologically and institutionally. His arguments have often been abbreviated into a characterization of New Criticism as focusing on "the text itself" or "The words on the page."①

Some of the core documents of New Criticism were written by relatively late followers: W. K. Wimsatt and Monroe Beardsley's essays "The Intentional Fallacy" (1946) and "The Affective Fallacy" (1949); Austin Warren's *The Theory of Literature* (1949); W. K. Wimsatt's *The Verbal Icon* (1954); and Murray Krieger's *The New Apologists for Poetry* (1956).

Roughly speaking, the New Criticism is divided into three periods:

The first period, the initiative period (1910–1930), was in the 1920s when Thomas Stearns Eliot, Ivor Armstrong Richards and William Empson in England and John Crowe Ransom and Allen Tate in America started to put forward some basic viewpoints of the New Criticism and put them into practice.

The 1930s and the 1940s formed the second period, the formative period (1930–1945), in which the people who agreed with and supported the New Criticism, a kind of formalism, increased in a large number, the viewpoints of the New Criticism rapidly expanded, directly influencing literary magazines, teaching and curriculum in colleges and universities. The main representatives were Richard P. Blackmur, Cleanth Brooks, René Wellek, and William K. Wimsatt besides the five mentioned above.

The third period, the dominant period (1945–1957), lasted from the end of the 1940s to the late 1950s. In this period, the New Criticism occupied a mainstream position. It formed an institutionalized mode of criticism but lost its revolutionary flavor; the works of critics mostly elaborated the principles of the New Criticism but lacked originality. At the end of the 1950s, the New Criticism lost its vitality; though it was still applied in college teaching, many people considered it already outmoded and began to criticize and transcend it with new theoretical concepts.

B. Five Characteristics of the New Criticism

Though the New Criticism shares many similarities with Russian Formalism, the main

① Rafey Habib, *A History of Literary Criticism: From Plato to the Present*, Oxford: Blackwell Publishing, 2005, p. 622.

purpose of both is to inquire where the unique literariness is, both deny the "weak" spirit in the late romantic poetics and invariably maintain empirical mode of reading. However, the Formalists' analyses were far more theoretical, seeking to understand the general nature of literature and literary devices, as well as the historical evolution of literary techniques; the New Critics were more concerned with the practice (rather than the theory) of close reading of individual texts. The New Criticism, however, is different from Russian Formalism in many places and has its own specific properties. Cleanth Brooks summarized the characteristics of the New Criticism as the following five points: 1) it separates literary criticism from the study of origin, making criticism lose contact with the social background, the history of thought, the political and social effects, seeking a pure literary criticism without considering "outside" factors and devoting its attention only to the literary object itself; 2) it concentrates on probing into the structure of a work, ignoring the author's thought or the reader's response; 3) it maintains a literary theory of "organic unity," disagrees with the concept of dichotomy to differentiate form from content, stresses inquiring into the relation between the words in a work and the context of the whole work, thinking that every word has its own effect on the specific context, and produces meaning with its position in the context; 4) it emphasizes the close reading of a single work, paying special attention to the slight differences between words, rhetoric modes, and the tiny differences between meanings, trying to concretely explain the unity of the context and the meaning of a work; 5) it differentiates literature from religion and morality—this is mainly because many supporters of the New Criticism have their definite concepts of religion and do not want to abandon it and do not want to replace morality or literature with it.

C. The Basis of the New Criticism

The basis of the New Criticism is Eliot's "depersonalization of art" and Richards' "immanent necessity." Therefore, it mainly pays close attention to "the poetry as the structure of poetry." The so-called structure refers to the organizational arrangement of the meaning in a text. The features of structure in fine literary works are different from that in ordinary language. The New Criticism thinks that the main feature of poetry is "unity"; it is not the unity in logic but the unity that makes contradictory meanings harmonious. As Wimsatt pointed out, poetry has objective specific properties because it has a kind of completeness of meaning that is established by the forms differentiated within and the harmonization of different parts. Thus, completeness is linked with synthesis and complicacy. That is to say, the meaning of a text is the product of the interaction of its parts upon each other. Therefore, to the New Criticism, synthesis and complicacy and unity together constitute the key elements of the analysis of a literary work.

D. The Concept of "Meaning" in the New Criticism

In the New Criticism, the concept of "meaning" is extremely important. It is in the crossing point of many basic opinions and it exerts important effect on the formation of reading habit. The New Criticism thinks that the value of a work does not lie in its content but in its structure. Searching for contents in a poem, summarizing or interpreting a text all violate the principles of the New Criticism because to do like this will make "meanings" become viewpoints or statements, then forms lose contents, and literature conflict with philosophy and politics. If we equate "meaning" with interpretation, we will belittle the value of "meaning" because interpretation does not constitute the core of the meaning that forms the quintessence of a poem. As the New Criticism sees it, "meaning" is one of the aspects of structure. Brooks thinks that the so-called structure is the structure of the [text's] meaning, the critic, and the interpretation; the principle of unity that makes the structure pregnant with meaning is the principle that balances and harmonizes implication, attitude and meaning. Therefore, the task of reading is to examine and evaluate the structure synthetically composed of the elements including linguistics, rhetoric, semantics, philosophy, psychology, etc. Thus, structure becomes the most important concept of criticism. To the New Criticism, meaning is a subordinate category of structure as well as an element that cannot be cut apart from structure; the literary structure with unity will neither be involved in generating and acceptance nor considered an element that can be interpreted and a viewpoint that can be inferred; the statement of meaning plays at most a role of a framework.

E. The Reading of the New Criticism

According to the views of the New Criticism, only until one finds out unity, balance and harmony in structure is reading completed. In other words, both processing and arranging all the powers in the text, for example, analyzing tension, conflict and divergence, are to realize the harmony in this structure. Brooks likes the term "irony" best because it is a most effective instrument of interpretation and it can realize the unity of the different elements of a text. Therefore, the New Criticism is ultimately a theory and a practice of reading; it emphasizes the united structure formed with tension and ambiguity and thinks that this structure constitutes the essence of literature as well as the purpose of analysis in criticism (or reading).

Obviously, to realize the reading manner of the New Criticism and find out ambiguity, paradox, metaphor, irony, symbolism, and the tension and the united structure that are formed with the preceding elements, a critic or a reader must closely read a work—that is the close reading of the New Criticism that people often talk about. The New Critics take more interest in "close reading" and detailed textual analysis than the mind and personality of the writer, sources, the history of ideas and political and social implications. Vincent Leitch summarized "the close reading" as the following: when carrying out close reading, the New Criticism generally does: 1) picking out a short text which is usually a transcendental or a modern poem; 2) eliminating the "generating" mode of criticism; 3) avoiding the exploration of the theory of "reception"; 4) supposing that a text is an independent, autonomous, and non-historical object which lies in space; 5) presupposing that a text is complicated and synthetic as well as effective and united; 6) doing multiple and looking-back reading; 7) supposing that every text is a drama that is constituted by conflicting powers; 8) constantly concentrating on a text and the multiple and mutual relation between semantics and rhetoric in the text; 9) insisting the power of literary language that is basically metaphorical and therefore also marvelous; 10) refraining from interpretation and summary, making clear that this statement of interpretation is not equal to the meaning of a work; 11) seeking a synthetic structure that is entirely balanced or united and is composed of harmonious elements of the text; 12) placing disunity and contradiction and conflict in the secondary position; 13) regarding paradox, ambiguity and irony as the control of disunity and the guarantee of the united structure; 14) regarding the (inherent) meaning only as an element of structure; 15) paying attention to the structure of a text and the aspect of experiences in the process of reading; 16) trying to become an ideal reader and creating the only and true reading—a reading that classifies many types of reading. In accordance with Leitch's summary, the New Criticism's close reading is apparently different from other critical interpretations and reading practices. To the New Criticism, "reading" needs interpretation as well as evaluation while the process of close reading itself contains the standards for criticism and judgment.

F. The End of the New Criticism

The New Criticism seeks the organic unity of structure, which makes its understanding of meaning greatly limited; it seeks professional criticism (centralizing in universities where scholars constitute the specialty of criticism and make critical activities divorced from the conventional book review), which makes its scope also limited. Therefore, it can neither provide a truly scientific criticism nor supply a precise interpretative criticism. Consequently, at the end of the 1950s, the New Criticism began to decline; along with the appearance of other new theories in the 1960s it almost entirely lost its vitality.

Further Reading

Brooks, Cleanth. Criticism and Literary History: Marvell's Horatian Ode. *Sewanee Review* 55 (1947): 199–222.

Carton, Evan & Gerald Graff. *The Cambridge History of American Literature* (*volume* 8): *Poetry and Criticism* (1940–1995). Ed. Sacvan Bercovitch. New York: Cambridge University Press, 1996, pp. 261–471.

Duvall, John N. Eliot's Modernism and Brook's New Criticism: Poetic and Religious Thinking. *The Mississippi Quarterly*: 46 (1992): 23–38.

Graff, Gerald. *Professing Literature*. Chicago & London: The University of Chicago Press, 1987.

Russo, John Paul. The Tranquilized Poem: The Crisis of New Criticism in the 1950s. *Texas Studies in Literature and Language* 30 (1988): 198–227.

Wellek, René. A History of Modern Criticism, 1750–1950 // *Volume 6*: *American Criticism*, 1900–1950. New Haven: Yale University Press, 1988.

Bibliography

Cuddon, J. A. *A Dictionary of Literary Terms and Literary Theory*. 5th ed. Malden: Wiley-Blackwell, 2013.

Rice, Philip & Patricia Waugh. *Modern Literary Theory*. New York: Oxford University Press, 2002.

Bressler, Charles. *Literary Criticism: An Introduction to Theory and Practice*. Beijing: Higher Education Press, 2004.

Habib, Rafey. *A History of Literary Criticism: From Plato to the Present.* Oxford: Blackwell Publishing, 2005.

泰勒，温奎斯特. 后现代主义百科全书. 章燕，李自修，等译. 刘象愚，校. 长春：吉林人民出版社，2007.

王治河. 后现代主义辞典. 北京：中央编译出版社，2004.

张中载，王逢振，赵国新. 二十世纪西方文论选读. 北京：外语教学与研究出版社，2002.
朱刚. 二十世纪西方文艺批评理论. 上海：上海外语教育出版社，2001.

Selected Readings

W. K. Wimsatt, Jr. and Monroe Beardsley: "The Intentional Fallacy"
I. A. Richards: *Practical Criticism*

Chapter Three

Marxist Criticism

Marxist Criticism is the most vital theoretical school with the widest field of vision in the 20th century. Marxism is a theory that takes history and society as the main objects of its attention and attempts to understand the relations between the literary text and social world, recognizing that literature is a process and that the social world involves contexts of production and those of reception. Marxists regard literature as both production and reflection of and on culture and society, and the political aim of Marxist Criticism is to understand the social and political world in order to change it. Marx never formulated a complete theory or aesthetic theory, so much of the subsequent debate in Marxist Criticism has been over the question: How literature might be seen and understood in Marxist terms? Its stand of political criticism permeates to the different extents through all the theories and critical practices that have radical colors of culture and politics. In the new theories such as Post-colonialism (or Postcolonialism), New Historical Culture and Cultural Studies that have risen abruptly in the late 10 or 20 years, the shadow of Marxist Criticism can still be caught. Making a general survey of the picture of the theories in the whole 20th century, we can find that Marxist Criticism usually appears with the identity of a dialogist with other theories; it can often fill in the gaps and supply omissions of some over-biased and over-narrow-minded theoretical propositions. A critic ever thus summarized, when Reader-response Criticism supposes a universal reader, Marxism starts with classes to describe the differences between readers; when Formalism throws itself wholeheartedly into approaching the styles of literature itself, Marxist Criticism questions the ideological connotations behind the strategies in different forms; when Psychoanalytic Criticism wants to find out the personal psychological meaning in a work, Marxist Criticism examines the relation between social power and the deep psychological structure of the whole; when deconstructionist critics are concerned with the rhetoric operations that ruin central ideas or meaning, Marxism makes use of this strategy to point out that some special dominant ideology or thinking mode lurks in a work and thinks that this work encourages this kind of ideology or thinking mode. The intervention of Marxist theories will undoubtedly add the sense of being thick and heavy to literary criticism. In the process of having dialogues, the present-day Marxist Criticism also absorbs nutrient from other theories to enrich itself and thus becomes more exquisite and perfect. None of the theories such as phenomenology, hermeneutics, semiotics, and structuralist psychoanalysis is not used by Marxist Criticism. The present-day Marxist Criticism has already gone beyond the traditional limitations and seems to have become the synthesis of all critical methods.

A. Early Marxist Criticism

Marxist Criticism emerged in the late 19th century and was derived from the political and economic works by Marx and Engels. They were primarily concerned with economic, political and philosophical issues and worked out explanations of the capitalist theory and mode of production. Marx and Engels did not put forward any systematic literary and aesthetic theories and their comments on literature and art are often fragmented. As a series of responses to concrete political exigencies, Marxist aesthetics achieve a dynamic and expansive coherence through both a general overlap of political motivation and the persistent reworking of a core of predispositions about literature and art deriving from Marx and Engels themselves. These predispositions include: 1) Literature can only be understood in the fullness of its relations with ideology, class, and economic substructure; 2) The view that the so-called “objective” world is actually a progressive construction out of collective human subjectivity. What passes as “truth” then, is not eternal but institutionally created; 3) The understanding of art itself as a commodity, sharing with other commodities an entry into material aspects of production; 4) A focus on the connections between class struggle as the inner dynamic of history and literature as the ideologically refracted site of such struggle; 5) An insistence that language is not a self-enclosed system of relations but must be understood as social practice, as deeply rooted in material conditions as any other practice.① Marx’s expositions on the ever-lasting charm of ancient Greek art and Engels’ letters on literature are the documents that the later Marxist critics often quote as evidence. Their expositions on

① Rafey Habib, *A History of Literary Criticism: From Plato to the Present*, Oxford: Blackwell Publishing, 2005, p. 535.

the relation between economic basis and superstructure and on ideology become the ever-new topics in Marxist Criticism. Early Marxist Criticism rigidly adhered to the formula that economic basis determines superstructure, regarded a literary work as the reflection of reality, and thought that this is directly determined by the social economic power. This type of criticism is usually regarded as vulgar Marxist economic determinism. During the period from 1870 to the World War Ⅰ, most Marxists held the views of economic determinism, which had something to do with the economic struggles of the working class while the Western Marxists in the 20th century paid more attention to superstructure's function of change for economic basis. The 1920s and the 1930s were the time when vulgar Marxist Criticism was popular. The early Marxist social critics thought that there is a directly corresponding relation between art and social economy, that the task of art is to reflect social life with vivid language and images, and that the development and decline of art and the prosperity and wane of social economy echo each other at a distance. They probed into the origin of literature from the angles of economy and supported the formula that economic basis determines superstructure and specific social system determines specific literature.

B. Influential Viewpoints of Marxist Criticism

The situation mentioned above has been broken by the 20th century Western Marxist Criticism when it has turned Marxist Criticism into a cultural critique from the philosophical perspective.

1. Georg Lucács

Georg Lucács, the Hungarian literary historian and critic, forerunner of Western Marxism, developed the critical theory of "reflection." He thought of literary works as reflections of a kind of system that was gradually unfolding. According to him, the literary works, especially the novel, ought to reveal underlying patterns in the social order and provide a sense of the wholeness of existence with all its inherent contradictions, tensions and conflicts. In his *The Historical Novel* (1937) and *Studies in European Realism* (1950), the Hungarian critic Georg Lucács, forerunner of Western Marxism denied the simple relation of determination between economic basis and superstructure though he thought that literature is the reflection of social economic reality. He thought that a great literary work not only reproduces the then leading ideology but also contains the criticism of the leading ideology. At the same time when he held realism in great esteem, Lucács did his most to play down the achievements and potential of modernism. For Lucács, modernism is a formal reflection of bourgeois modernity in all its alienation, abstraction, solipsism, fragmentation, and what he referred to as the "attenuation of actuality." Incapable of grasping the totality, bourgeois art had diverged into a materialist naturalism, on the one hand, and a subjectivist expressionism, on the other hand, with no possibility between the two. Modernism represents a fetishized immediacy and a denial of history that simply reflects chaos and anomie of the modern world, its decadence and loss of sense of progress, without attempting critique or analysis. He thought that modernist writers' partiality for the techniques such as montage, inner monologue and stream-of-consciousness is the result of invariably stressing subjective impression only and therefore what appears in modernist works was not the objective reflection but the feeling of anxiety for the modern world. On the other hand, in Lucács' opinion, realism is able to reveal subjective personalities, full "characters" engaged in practices mediated by the larger forces of the historical process in a literary mode. Lucács thought that realistic art is great because it can present a social "totality" in which the manifest contradictions between subjective experience and objective historical forces are reconciled within the formal structures of the work. Although the debt to a Coleridgean organicism is evident in this claim for "reconciliation," for Lucács, such art could function both as a critique of industrial capitalism and as a utopian vision of a better world.

2. Bertolt Brecht

Lucács' bias against modernism caused the sharp criticism from his contemporary critics such as Bertolt Brecht, Theodor Adorno, Walter Benjamin and others. In his drama, Brecht, German dramatist and critic, rejected Lucács' reading of realism and modernism, arguing for the socialist appropriation of modernist forms and the capacity of a defamiliarizing art to expose the contradictions and ideologies of capitalism. For Brecht, a modernist art, self-reflexive, exposing its own mediating structures, would resist the kind of identification which he saw as part of the ideological naturalization of the world under capitalism. In Brecht's opinion, realism represented a passive reflection of bourgeois ideology; modernism an active attempt to expose the processes of naturalization. The debate between the two set the agenda for much of the Marxist Criticism which developed in the next few decades. Brecht introduced and used modernist experimental techniques such as montage, news report and alienation effect. He thought that Lucács respected only one concrete literary form (for example, the novels by H. Balzac and L. Tolstoy), regarded it as the only true mode of realism and therefore it was hard for him to avoid the danger to fall into formalism. On the contrary, he maintained that a writer should use all the available forms and techniques to describe reality. In his opinion, there were not any eternal aesthetic principles nor forms and modes that could have ever-lasting vitality. Even his own boldly innovated alienation effect would lose its shocking effect, became unoriginal and have nothing good to talk about once it was followed and used too much. The alienation effect he advocated was to make an actor or actress seem to be an acquaintance as well as a stranger and thus to arouse the audience to critically think about the social reality reflected in the drama.

3. Frankfurt School of Marxism

In the whole course of Western Marxist Criticism, the aesthetic ideas of the Frankfurt School of Marxism occupied a pivotal position. The main representatives of the school were Max Hirkheimer, Theodor Adorno, Herbert Marcuse and others. They criticized mass culture by thinking that it corroded and corrupted people's minds, tricked people into giving tacit consent to the unreasonable social reality, built an affirmative cultural atmosphere in the whole society, and thus made people voluntarily give up their fighting will. In order to change this situation, they did their best to give publicity to modernist high culture and resist the corrosive influence of mass culture to realize the purpose of criticizing reality. Adorno, a leading member of the Frankfurt School, associated with the Institute for Social Research, whose energies were largely engaged in developing a critique of Western philosophy and providing analytic studies of contemporary cultures. Adorno regarded the culture industry as a potent force for holding the masses in a state of submissive ignorance and believed that only an avant-garde art that utterly repudiated realism might articulate any kind of oppositional position. For Adorno, art is not a reflection of society but capable, because of its formal autonomy, of revealing the underlying structures of the real which are veiled by empiricist epistemology and by realism as the vehicle of its aesthetic expression. Art is a form of knowledge, but only avant-garde art is capable of penetrating through the veils of ideology and achieving epistemological authenticity. Adorno established a set of negative modes of cognition. He criticized Lucács' opinion on reality, considering that it had the tendency towards dogmatism. He thought that art has no direct relation to reality and there is a section of distance between them; that it is just this section of distance that gives a work of art a favorable position and adds power of criticizing reality to it. Mass culture wallows in the mire with the economic system that supports and creates it. But on the contrary, a self-disciplined modernist work standing outside commercial atmosphere could deny the related reality. In his opinion, art is a negative recognition of the realistic world. The so-called negative recognition refers to the recognition that ruins and denies the real social situation in which there is nothing but materials. To prevent the cultural industry from negating the criticism of the existing social order which is written with clear and plain language, Adorno encouraged the hard-to-understand literary experiments to maintain the distance between a work and reality and guard against the absorption and assimilation of the mass cultural industry.

4. Walter Benjamin

Having gained a great inspiration from Marx's theory on productive forces and production relations, the German essayist Walter Benjamin, contemporary with Brecht, devoted himself to inquiring into the situation of the social production of literature. Like Brecht, he also regarded art as a form of social practice that coexists with other forms of social and economic productions. To him, a writer is mainly a producer who roots himself in a historical period and processes and arranges the material now available, not a creator who undertakes writing by his natural gift. In his essay, "A Writer as a Producer," he actively advocated to make use of the current cultural forms that are still in the ascendant such as movies, radios, photographs and phonographs to change the old modes of art production, establish the cooperative relation between writer, reader and audience, give full play to the revolutionary potential of the new powers of art. Unlike most of his contemporary Western Marxist critics who vilified mass culture, Benjamin found the potential of revolutionary change from these artistic forms that appeared lately.

5. Structuralist Marxism

The 1960s was a prosperous period of Marxist theories after the World War Ⅱ. At the same time, the European thoughts were dominated by structuralist thoughts. In this kind of situation that the different thoughts converged, Structuralist Marxism with Lucien Goldmann, Louis Althusser, Pierre Macherey as the lineup appeared. Roughly speaking, Structuralism and Marxism share roughly the same thought orientation: both think that the recognition of individuals could not break away from its social existence but must put itself in the complicated social relation.

The Romanian critic **Lucien Goldmann** had developed a structuralist method of embryology to search for the historical source of the collective spiritual structure of the social group to which a writer belongs. This is a literary sociology. What it studies is the relation between the collective spiritual structure (the collective world outlook) and the social historical situation in which it is produced. Goldmann thought that the world outlook of a social group is the spiritual structure of this social group and it belongs to the phenomena of collective consciousness. The structure of a literary work is the same with the spiritual structure of the social group to which the writer belongs because the writer's stand is controlled intentionally or unintentionally by the world outlook of the social group in which he is; the world outlook of the social group internalizes his stand, which makes his work express a spiritual substance that is identical with the world outlook of the social group. In this sense, a literary work is the product of the world outlook of the social group and the achievements and vitality of literature depend on the extent that they keep identical with the world outlook of the social group. The more capable it is to express the complete and identical "world outlook" of the social class, the more vital a work is.

Louis Althusser, French critic, was the most popular of the Marxist philosophers. In his book *Lenin and Philosophy and Other Essays* (1971), he attempted to show (with the help of Jacques Lacan's psychoanalytic theory) how ideology works in society. To him, ideology is not conscious beliefs, values, attitude orientations and the like, nor a false consciousness that hinders people to correctly and closely look at the true social situation and covers the real conflict between the ruling class and the working class. Ideology is the reappearance of the imaginary relation between individuals and their true existing situation. In his opinion, we are all the "subjects" within the ideological atmosphere and cannot escape the influence and infiltration of ideology. Ideology addresses inquiries to the subjects with the aid of religion, education, law and other state apparatuses and makes us willingly and gladly accept our social positions in the social structure. On the one hand, ideology contributes to our understanding of the world but, on the other hand, it covers the true relation between the real world and us. Thus, it creates a situation that the ruled class takes the ideological system of the ruling class for granted and as a matter of fact safeguards the interests of the ruling class. In the relation between literature and ideology, unlike those vulgar Marxist critics who thought that literature is completely an expression of the consciousness of the ruling class, he held that art lies between ideology and scientific understanding.

Pierre Macherey, a follower of Althusser, had further developed Althusserian theory of ideology. In his most important work, *A Theory of Literary Production* (1966), he pointed out that literary writing is not a creation but a process of production. Just like productive labor, a writer's task is to process the preexisting materials such as literary genres, conventions, language and ideology into a finished product. In the writing process of a text, anything entering the text is liable to change as a raw material of an industrial product will change after it is technically processed; ideology will be the same when entering a text. While writing, a writer will be unconsciously limited by the difference between the ideological discourses and will write a work with differences and contradictions in meaning. To Macherey, a critic's task is to analyze and explain the reasons for these differences and contradictions by racking his brains.

6. Raymond Williams

In his "Cultural Materialism," Raymond Williams, English critic, contributed to the study of British culture with his reinterpretation of some key Marxian concepts. Take the concept of basis as an example. The traditional understanding took economic basis as an autonomous and self-sufficient entity, mechanically corresponding to superstructure. Hence was the economism of the vulgar Marxism. Williams argued that Marx himself underwent a gradual change in his understanding of the determinism of economic basis. While the early Marx preferred a "scientific" determinism, relying on the external force as sole determinant, the later Marx seemed to be more aware of the subjective determinants. Williams proposed the idea of "historical objective determinism," namely, the economic basis functions via society at large and the will of man living in society. In other words, every layer of society participates in the determination process, hence the Althusserian concept of over-determination. Williams made it clear that there are at least three forms of Marxism: the writings of Karl Marx, the systems developed by later Marxists out of these writings, and Marxisms popular at given historical moments.

7. Terry Eagleton

The principal theorist of Marxist Criticism in Britain is Terry Eagleton, who had developed various views of Althusser and Macherey and suggested that a basic problem is to make clear what is the relation between an ideology (e. g. Marxism) and literature. His earlier writing examined in some depth certain Marxist categories of literary-cultural analysis, his later, more popularizing work has argued persuasively the need for theory. Eagleton has revaluated the tradition of English literary criticism, redefined the function of the critic, and reappraised a specific writer from a historical materialistic perspective. These are the essential aspects of the general task of Marxist critics. However, in Eagleton's works, what is more outstanding is his firm critical contact and historical background to other modern critical trends. In his view expressed in his *Criticism and Ideology* (1976), texts do not reflect reality but act on an ideology and give rise to a kind of effect that seems to be real. By ideology, he did not necessarily mean political or Marxist ideology but all systems and theories of representation that help to make up a picture of a person's experience. He examined both ideologies "outside" the text and the ideologies in the text. The ideology that he understood refers to the reproductive systems including aesthetics, religion, judicature, etc. It is just with these reproductive systems that people understand and recognize the real life. To him, ideology is the process of real life while the meaning and ideas produced by a literary work are the results of reprocesses of the ideological process. Therefore, he opposed Althusserian view that literature can keep a distance from ideology. He stressed that literature is not purely a reflection of ideology but a specified ideology; the task of literary criticism is to examine the law of literature as the discourse of an ideology. Since the end of the 1970s and the beginning of the 1980s, he consciously shook off some influences from Althusser and turned to the revolutionary ideas of Brecht and Benjamin. As for the theories of deconstruction that appeared later, on the one hand he thought that these theories contribute to the disintegration of all the forms of recognition that are taken for granted and on the other hand he criticized their nihilistic tendency towards denying objectivity and material interests, especially the class interests. He put forward the idea that Marxist literary criticism should start from politics rather than probe into any empty philosophy; the task of critics is to necessarily break with the existing literary concepts and reveal their ideological roles to create the subjectivity of readers.

8. Fredric Jameson and His Dialectical Criticism

Fredric Jameson is the leading Marxist critic in America. His *Marxism and Form* (1971) and *The Prison-House of Language* (1972) established his position in the critical circles. In *Marxism and Form* after inquiring into the aesthetic ideas of Adorno, Benjamin, Marcuse, Lucács and others, he advanced the ideas of Dialectical Criticism. According to the current explanation, Dialectical Criticism belongs to the tradition of Hegelian Marxism, and it pays close attention to some major propositions of Hegelian philosophy, such as the relation between the whole and the part, the antithesis between the concrete and the abstract, the concepts of the wholeness, the dialectical relation between phenomena and essence, the interactive relation between the subject and the object, etc. In accordance with the dialectical ideas, the object is not constant and unchangeable. It is mutually related with the larger whole and at the same time closely related with the thinking subject as a component part of the historical environment. This criticism does never analyze a literary work in isolation but sees it as a part of a large structure (a literary circulation or movement) or the historical environment. When he analyzes a work, a dialectical critic will realize that the analytical categories (styles, characters, images), which he relies on, are finally regarded as a part of the historical environment, in which he is, and moulded by the historical environment. A main task of Dialectical Criticism is to reveal the intricate relation between the internal form of a work and the social reality by seeing through the surface of the text. While receiving Hegelian tradition, Jameson absorbed and synthesized the theories of Structuralism, Post-structuralism, psychoanalysis and the theories of Althusserian ideology. In his representative work *The Political Unconsciousness* (1981), Jameson attempts to integrate this dialectical thinking with insights from Structuralism and Freud, using the Freudian notion of repression to analyze the function of ideology, the status of literary texts, and the epistemological function of literary form.[①] He pointed out that literary works should be understood as symbolic acts that provide imaginary and ideological solutions to the social and political contradictions that cannot be solved. All ideologies have the function to suppress resistance and this suppression usually permeates through the deep unconsciousness, and therefore it is a political unconsciousness. In subsequent work such as *Postmodernism, or, The Cultural Logic of Late Capitalism* (1991), Jameson performed the valuable task of extending Marx's insights into the central role of postmodernism in determining the form of our artistic and intellectual experience.

Further Reading

Anderson, Perry. *Considerations on Western Marxism*. London: New Left Books, 1976.

Duiker, W & Spielvogel, J. *The Essential World History*. Vol, II: since 1500. 3rd ed. Belmont: Thomson Higher Education, 2008.

Eagleton, T. *Marxism and Literary Criticism*. Berkeley: University of California Press, 1976.

Fetscher, Iring. *Marx and Marxism*. New York: Herder and Herder, 1971.

Grahl, Bart & Paul Piccone. *Towards a New Marxism*. St. Louis: Telos Press, 1973.

Hobsbawm, E. J. *The Age of Capital*. New York: Charles Scribner's Sons, 1975.

Howard, Dick & Karl E. Klare. *The Unknown Dimension: European Marxism since Lenin*. New York: Basic Books, 1972.

Jay, Martin. *Marxism and Totality: The Adventures of a Concept from Lukacs to Habermas*. Berkeley: University of California Press, 1984.

Korsch, Karl. *Marxism and Philosophy*. New York: Monthly Review Press, 1970.

Lukacs, Georg. *History and Class Consciousness: Studies in Marxist Dialectics*. London: Merlin, 1971.

McInnes, Neil. *The Western Marxists*. New York: Library Press, 1972.

McIntosh, I. *Classical Sociological Theory: A Reader*. Edinburgh: Edinburgh University Press, 1997.

Mclellan, D. *The Thought of Karl Marx*. London: Macmillan Press, 1971.

Merleau-Ponty, Maurice. *Adventures of the Dialectic*. Evanston, IL: Northwestern University Press, 1973.

① Rafey Habib, *A History of Literary Criticism: From Plato to the Present*, Oxford: Blackwell Publishing, 2005, p. 543.

Van der Linden, Marcel. *Western Marxism and the Soviet Union*. Leiden: Brill, 2007.
Williams, Raymond. *Marxism and Literature*. Oxford: Oxford University Press, 1978.

Bibliography

Cuddon, J. A. *A Dictionary of Literary Terms and Literary Theory*. 5th ed. Malden: Wiley-Blackwell, 2013.

Rice, Philip & Patricia Waugh. *Modern Literary Theory*. New York: Oxford University Press, 2002.

Bressler, Charles. *Literary Criticism: An Introduction to Theory and Practice*. Beijing: Higher Education Press, 2004.

Habib, Rafey. *A History of Literary Criticism: From Plato to the Present*. Oxford: Blackwell Publishing, 2005.

泰勒，温奎斯特. 后现代主义百科全书. 章燕，李自修，等译. 刘象愚，校. 长春：吉林人民出版社，2007.

王治河. 后现代主义辞典. 北京：中央编译出版社，2004.

张中载，王逢振，赵国新. 二十世纪西方文论选读. 北京：外语教学与研究出版社，2002.

朱刚. 二十世纪西方文艺批评理论. 上海：上海外语教育出版社，2001.

Selected Readings

Louis Althusser: “Ideology and Ideological State Apparatuses”
Terry Eagleton: “Ideology and Literary Form”
Fredric Jameson: “Third-World Literature in the Era of Multinational Capitalism”

Chapter Four

Psychological and Psychoanalytic Criticism

Psychological criticism emerged in the 20th century which seeks to explain the significance of literary texts in terms of psychological development and conflict. The theories and writings of Sigmund Freud (1856–1939) provide its foundations. Critics, rhetoricians, and philosophers since Aristotle have examined the psychological dimensions of literature, ranging from an author's motivation and intentions to the effect of texts and performances on an audience. The application of psychoanalytic principles to the study of literature, however, is a relatively recent phenomenon, initiated primarily by Freud.

Psychological criticism emerged in the 20th century which seeks to explain the significance of literary texts in terms of psychological development and conflict. The theories and writings of Sigmund Freud provide its foundations. Psychological criticism deals with a work of literature primarily as an expression of the state of mind in the fictional form and the structure of personality of the individual author. Even in the ancient times there was the method to discuss literature and art from the angle of psychology. Plato considered that poetry makes people's mind weak and degenerate and that the ability of writing poetry belongs to the spiritual obsession and craziness; Aristotle put forward the doctrine of heart purification; Coleridge gave a discussion of imagination, which can prove that the history of psychological criticism has a distant source and long stream. Traditional psychoanalytic criticism in the true sense began from the publication of the book *Dream Interpretation* (1900) at the beginning of the 20th century. Among the prevalent critical patterns in the contemporary era, the psychoanalytic criticism is one that appeared earlier and has a far-reaching influence. It applies Sigmund Freud's study of psychoanalysis and other theories of psychology into literary criticism.

A. Four Stages of Psychoanalytic Criticism

Tracing back its over-one-hundred-year course of development and examining the unconscious objects of its study, we can see that in the different stages of its development the points that psychoanalytic criticism laid special emphasis on were also different. The traditional psychoanalytic criticism (the *id* psychological criticism) represented by Freud himself mainly studied the unconscious psychology of the author himself (or the characters in a work) and a literary work is analyzed as the psychological sign of its author. The self-psychoanalytic criticism in the post-Freudian era began to analyze the reader's psychological response to the text, giving prominence to the interacting relation between the reader and the text. In the archetypal psychoanalytic criticism of Carl Gustav Jung, a literary work is not a place to embody the psychological sign of its author nor a channel to satisfy the concealed fantasy in the reader's personal unconsciousness but a reproduction of the collective unconscious. Jacques Lacan and others, relating the traditional psychoanalytic criticism to the structuralist linguistics, re-explained and reformed many concepts in the traditional psychoanalytic criticism. The unconscious, for instance, is considered the product of language and has the same structure as that of language.

B. Representative Critics and Their Theories

1. Sigmund Freud

Freud divided personal psychology into three parts: the conscious, the preconscious and the unconscious. The conscious is the system of mental perception and man's rational, logical and purposeful sensations and organization for the outside world. The preconscious means the personal experiences that are now not in one's consciousness but can be recalled by focusing one's attention on it or under the circumstances without bother. The preconscious lies between the conscious and the unconscious, playing the role to admonish and mediate, and preventing the instinctive desire of the unconscious from entering the conscious area. The unconscious consists of all the desires and images excluded from the conscious. It is the irrational content full of instinctive impulse and outside the personal consciousness. In the pattern of psychological structure that Freud put forward later, he called the unconscious and irrational part of psychology *id* and the rational and conscious part of psychology *ego*. The main task of *ego* is to control and keep *id* within bounds. *Id* acts in accordance with the so-called "pleasure principle" while *ego* with the "realistic principle." *Superego*, representing the social morality, working together with *ego*, firmly controls all the ideas and instinctive impulses in the unconscious that are not allowed by the social morality. These contents in the unconscious state often include the sexual desire and fear in the infant period, which can only appear in the form of disguise, appearing in dreams, oral slips, or in the creative activities of literature and art. To Freud, the concealed emotion, arising in the infant period, that hates the side of parents with the same sex, is the important component part of the unconscious. In a boy's unconsciousness, he takes his father as his enemy and has a sense of fear that he would be castrated by his father while wishing to combine with his mother. Freud called the emotional complex "Oedipus Complex"—that is repressed but continually present in the adult's unconscious of the male infant to possess his mother and have his rival, the father, out of the way. Freud derived the term from Sophocles' Greek tragedy *Oedipus the King*, whose protagonist unknowingly kills his father and marries his mother.

Freud thought that a dream is a false satisfaction to the repressed desires. Because they are not approved by the social morality and excluded from the level of the conscious, man's many desires often have to appear in the disguised images and in a circuitous way in the dreams. The contents of dreams are divided into manifest ones and latent ones. The former are the things in the dreams that can be recalled later while the latter refer to the concealed desires hidden behind the manifest contents. The latent contents need to take the forms of condensation and displacement in order to transform into manifest contents. "Condensation" means that many ideas and images are condensed into one kind of idea or image; "replacement" indicates that a kind of worry, desire or a character is displaced as another kind.

The traditional psychoanalytic criticism that Freud himself established regards a literary work as the appearance of the author's unconsciousness, identifies a literary text with a sign or a dream and identifies the author with a dreamer. This method of study has a theoretical premise that the end of a literary work is the end of a dream revealed by the psychoanalysis: to satisfy a kind of unspeakable desire that was formed in one's childhood and hidden in the unconscious. In his essay "Creative Writers and Daydreaming," Freud compared the creation of creative writers with daydreaming, for writers' imaginative activities are like the psychological imaginations of children who are playing games. Both have the self-entertainment nature. A creative literary work is the continuity or replacement of the games in the writer's childhood. Under the oppression of instinctive need, a writer moves from reality to fantasy, processes and reforms his daydream through creation so that it can be accepted by others and he himself can escape from the repression of instinct for the time being and obtain pleasure. At the same time, the writer's work becomes the source of the listeners' or audience's pleasure. In his work, the writer projects his emotion on the protagonist and changes himself to the leading role of his daydream and the story. Sometimes his emotion is also poured on a number of different characters. He considered that a piece of work is just like a daydream. It is the continuity or displacement of the game that we played in our childhood. Therefore, carefully examining the characters in a work can dig out the unconscious psychology of its author. According to this critical pattern, Freud wrote some articles discussing Leonardo da Vinci and Dostoevsky and analyzing Hamlet, the Macbeths, and Falstaff. In addition, the representative works of the traditional psychoanalysis also include Ernest Jones' *Study of Hamlet* (1910), Otto Rank's mythical analysis, and Mary Bonaparte's *Analysis of Edgar Allen Poe* (1933). Generally speaking, these critics employed the concepts of the early psychological criticism such as the unconscious, Oedipus Complex, and the oral cavity and anus periods experienced by children's sexual development. Some analyses do their utmost to seek symbols of phalluses, usually appear too simplified, and are often ridiculed as "vulgar Freudianism."

2. Norman Holland

The post-Freudian self-psychological criticism revised the traditional psychoanalytic criticism and developed a set of critical patterns to discuss the reader's unconscious psychology. The traditional psychological criticism stresses revealing the meaning of the text in the writer's personal psychological fantasy while the self-psychoanalytic criticism emphasizes that fantasy also lies in the unconscious of the reading public and that there is a relation of conspiracy between the reader and the writer: the element of the form of a literary work also covers the reader's fantasy and helps him temporarily relieve repression and get pleasure. Thus, a literary work becomes the projection of the reader's unconsciousness and analyzing the reader's response becomes a main task of literary criticism. Norman Holland was an important representative of the reader's response psychoanalytic criticism. In his works *The Dynamics of Literary Response* (1968) and *Five Reader's Reading* (1975), Holland, using the psychoanalytic theory, discussed the reading process and the dynamics of literary response. The earlier Holland only deviated, to a certain extent, from the orthodox Freudianism explained in "Creative Writers and Daydreaming." He considered that the pleasure that the reader gets in reading comes from that a literary work transforms the reader's unconscious desires and fears into the things that can be culturally accepted. A text becomes a place where the writer and the reader who indulge together in fantasies make conspiracy. *The Dynamics of Literary Response* provides for us a "dictionary of fantasies." He adopted Freud's theories about the stages of the development of children's sexual psychology, thinking that every stage determines the way in which fantasies get embodied in texts. Meanwhile, he accepted the views of self-psychology, considering that literary forms have functions of defending and regulating, just with which the unconscious desires are examined. He tried hard to offer a pattern to show how fantasies move upward from the unconscious level to the meaningful conscious level and give objective appraisement so as to establish a kind of receptive aesthetics. Later, Holland completely moved from paying close attention to the text to following the reader with interest, no longer regarding the text as a fixed entity that can produce the predictable effect on the reader. He further highlighted the role of the reader and put forward a transactive theory to explain the relation between the reader and the text. According to his explanation, the whole process of "transaction" is divided into four periods: 1) the reader first comes into contact with a text ("expectation"), 2) chooses the desires to bring into the text, 3) obtains the projection of the satisfied desires (the typical "fantasies"), and 4) interprets again the desires into themes ("transformations"). From the experiment of the interaction between the texts and him and the other people, he pointed out the relation between the readers' free association from the texts and their own personalities and their life experiences. Holland held that the readers, while reading, usually project their psychological experiences accumulated by himself in life into the texts and unconsciously create in the texts a world that has already existed in mind. In his opinion, the readers' different interpretations of the texts are actually the products of the fear, the defense, the need, and the desire that they project into the texts.

3. Carl Gustav Jung

The archetypal criticism, advocated by Jung, totally different from the traditional psychoanalytic criticism and the reader's response psychoanalytic criticism, does not think that a literary work is the product of the writer's own fantasy in broad daylight nor think that it is the projection of the reader's unconscious psychological experience but does think that it originates from mankind's collective unconscious and that the writer's creation is often controlled by the collective unconscious. The so-called collective unconscious is all psychological experiences accumulated and inherited down by human beings since the remote antiquity, that is, a kind of specific psychological gift formed by hereditary power. The concept of the collective unconscious is the foundation stone of Jungian theory. The content of the collective unconscious is the archetype. In his essay, "On the Relation Between Analytic Psychology and Poetry," Jung called the archetype a primitive image. This image may be a character, or a monster or a process. It constantly reappears in the history. Whenever the creative fantasy gets freely expressed, it emerges. These archetypes take place in the experiences of human ancestors and are accumulated and inherited down as the collective memory of a race. In the remote antiquity, they appeared as mythical images, gradually went into the unconscious psychology of human beings, and appeared in the same forms in the mythical legends and totems as well as in literary works and the dreams of the different nationalities in the world. Archetypal criticism digs up and constructs archetypes and explains the human psychological agreement in secret in different times mainly through analyzing the motif, the symbols, and the images of characters appearing in a literary work, which is just the reason why a literary work with archetypal images can strike a sympathetic chord in the reader's heart (in Jung's words, arouse the voice of the whole mankind). The archetypes summarized by archetypal critics mainly include: 1) all kinds of images such as water, the sun, colors, circles, snakes, numerals, old women, wise old men, and so on; 2) the archetypal motifs or modes such as creation, immortality, and different types of heroes (including the hero archetype carrying out the tasks of pursuit, the hero archetype having experienced the growth process, and the hero type having made sacrifice); 3) the archetypes of genres such as the spring mythos (narrative structures) corresponding to comedies, the summer myths to romances, the autumn mythos to tragedies, the winter mythos to ironies, which are summed up by Northrop Frye in his *Anatomy of Criticism* (1957). The books of literary criticism by Jung himself are not many, but his theory inspires an important school of literary criticism. Myth and Archetypal Criticism initiated by Frye will be introduced in next chapter.

4. Jacques Lacan

To a certain extent, Lacan's psychoanalysis is established on the basis of some important inferences of structuralist anthropology and linguistics. He introduced linguistic study into psychoanalysis. The work of the French psychoanalyst Jacques Lacan centers around his extensive re-reading of Freud in the light of insights furnished by linguistics and Structuralism. Lacan's project was not merely to apply these discourses to psychoanalysis, but rather to enable the mutual reinterpretation of all of these areas of inquiry. He effectively employed these disciplines, as well as mathematics and logic, to reformulate Freud's account of the unconscious and his own account of human subjectivity in a Saussurean terminology of the connections between signifier and signified. An important view that he held is that, like language, the unconscious has a latent structure. People's understanding of the world and the Other is determined by language which is also the premise of self-understanding and there is no subject outside language. He explained the forming process of Oedipus Complex from the angle of structuralist linguistics. Oedipus Complex is an important stage of self-forming. Lacan thought that Oedipus Complex is a process which must be experienced by a male child who begins to know himself, the world and other people and which helps him be clear about his own position in the family. Incest taboo can manifest itself only through differentiating family members from each other with the language categories like "father," "mother," etc. Lacan also explained the activity ways of the unconscious with the aid of linguistic category. He replaced Freud's "condensation" and "displacement" with "metaphor" and "metonymy." He thought that all kinds of unconscious manifestation such as oral slips, jokes, dreams, etc. are controlled by the language mechanisms like "metaphor," "metonymy," etc. In his essay, "The Mirror Stage as Formative of the Function of the 'I' as Revealed in Psychoanalytic Experience," Lacan pointed out that an infant forms his initial understanding of himself in the mirror stage that he experiences from his 6th to his 18th month. At first, the infant could not distinguish his own image from that of the adult with him in the mirror. Only having got the concept of image does he understand that the image in the mirror is not a true thing. Finally, he can differentiate his own image from that of the adult and his self consciousness is set up in this instant. Lacan's psychoanalytic theory arouses many feminist critics' interest. He emphasized that the subjectivity of sexual distinction is produced in the cultural construction (the process of expressing meaning). This means that women's subordinate position in the society is not caused by the natural difference between the two sexes but mainly the result of a discourse construction. The famous feminist critics such as Juliet Michell, Julia Kristeva, and others, all ever explained and employed Lacan's theory. By dethroning the unconscious from this unwitting disposition toward transcendence in Freud's work, by immanentizing it within the vast networks of signification into which the child is born and which in effect constitutes the child's psychology as a network of significations, by resituating the unconscious within language, by redefining it as and through language, Lacan returns us to the startling and revolutionary nature of the Freudian discovery.

C. The Influence

The influence of psychoanalysis has extended to almost all aspects of modern literary theory. Simon O. Lesser (1909–1979) furnished a psychoanalytic account of the reading process. Under the influence of Lesser, Norman Holland (1927–) used ego psychology and the concept of the literary text as fantasy to elaborate his version of reader's response criticism, studying the manner in which texts appeal to the repressed fantasies of readers. Feminist critics such as Juliet Mitchell have used Freud's ideas in their explanations of the operations of patriarchy; others, such as Kristeva, have modified his notions in undertaking their analyses of language and gender. Members of the Frankfurt School of Marxist thinkers, such as Herbert Marcuse, have adopted Freudian concepts in their analyses of mass culture and ideology. Other important theorists include Norman O. Brown (1913–2002), D. W. Winnicott, Gilles Deleuze and Félix Guattari, who have explored the ideological bases of psychoanalysis.

Further Reading

Barthes, Roland. The Death of the Author // *The Norton Anthology of Theory and Criticism*. Ed. Vincent B. Leitch. Trans. Stephen Heath. New York: W. W. Norton & Company, 2001.

Bowie, Malcolm. *Psychoanalysis and the Future of Theory*. Cambridge: B. Blackwell, 1994.

Ellmann, Maud.. *Psychoanalytic Literary Criticism*. London: Taylor & Francis Ltd, 2015.

Felman, Shoshana. *Literature and Psychoanalysis: The Question of Reading, Otherwise*. Baltimore: Johns Hopkins University Press, 1982.

Frankland, Graham. *Freud's Literary Culture*. New York: Cambridge University Press, 2000.

Freud, Sigmund. "The 'Uncanny.'" // Vincent B. Leitch. Trans. Alix Strachey. *The Norton Anthology of Theory and Criticism*. New York: W. W. Norton & Company, 2001.

Strachey, James. *Standard Edition of the Complete Psychological Works of Sigmund Freud*. 24 Volumes. London: Hogarth Press, 1953–1974.

Hertz, Neil. Freud and the Sandman // *The End of the Line: Essays on Psychoanalysis and the Sublime*. Aurora, CO: The Davies Group, Publishers, 2009.

Muller, John & William Richardson. *The Purloined Poe: Lacan, Derrida and Psychoanalytic Reading*. Baltimore, Maryland: Johns Hopkins University Press, 1988.

Rudnytsky, Peter L. & Ellen Handler Spits. *Freud and Forbidden Knowledge*. New York: New York University Press, 1994.

Smith, Joseph H. *The Literary Freud*: *Mechanisms of Defense and the Poetic Will*. New Haven: Yale University Press, 1980.

Bibliography

Cuddon, J. A. *A Dictionary of Literary Terms and Literary Theory*. 5th ed. Malden: Wiley-Blackwell, 2013.

Rice, Philip & Patricia Waugh. *Modern Literary Theory*. New York: Oxford University Press, 2002.

Bressler, Charles. *Literary Criticism: An Introduction to Theory and Practice*. Beijing: Higher Education Press, 2004.

Habib, Rafey. *A History of Literary Criticism: From Plato to the Present.* Oxford: Blackwell Publishing, 2005.

泰勒，温奎斯特. 后现代主义百科全书. 章燕，李自修，等译. 刘象愚，校. 长春：吉林人民出版社，2007.

王治河. 后现代主义辞典. 北京：中央编译出版社，2004.

张中载，王逢振，赵国新. 二十世纪西方文论选读. 北京：外语教学与研究出版社，2002.

朱刚. 二十世纪西方文艺批评理论. 上海：上海外语教育出版社，2001.

Selected Readings

Sigmund Freud: "Creative Writers and Daydreaming"

Carl Gustav Jung: "On the Relation of Analytical Psychology to Poetry"

Jacques Lacan: "Desire and the Interpretation of Desire in *Hamlet*"

Chapter Five

Myth and Archetypal Criticism

In a general sense, a myth is a story which is not "true" and which involves (as a rule) supernatural beings—or at any rate suprahuman beings. Myth is always concerned with creation and explains how something came to exist. Myth embodies feeling and concept—hence the Promethean or Herculean figure, or the idea of Diana, or the story of Orpheus and Eurydice. Many myths or quasi-myths are primitive explanations of the natural order and cosmic forces. The word "archetype" consists of "arche" (original) and "typos" (form) in Latin. The archetypal idea has always been present and diffused in human consciousness. Plato was the first philosopher to elaborate the concept of archetypal or ideal forms (Beauty, Truth, Goodness) and divine archetypes. Archetype is the symbol often used in literature but it is different from symbol. It mainly refers to an "original image," namely, the image of early human beings who used the totem worship, dreams, myths, and legends to express the original images, such as the sun symbolizing light and water symbolizing holiness and purity. In Greek mythology there are Apollo, god of the sun, and Prometheus who stole fire from the gods and gave it to man. Myth and Archetypal Criticism was in vogue from the 1940s to the mid-1960s and its practitioners included Richard Chase, Leslie Fiedler, Daniel Hoffman, and Philip Wheelwright. Drawing on the findings of anthropology and psychology regarding universal myths, rituals, and folktales, these critics were intent on restoring spiritual content to a world they saw as alienated, fragmented, and ruled by scientism, empiricism, positivism, and technology. They wished to redeem the role of myth, which might comprehend magic, imagination, dreams, intuition, and the unconscious. They viewed the creation of myth as integral to human thought, and believed that literature emerges out of a core of myth, where "myth" is understood as a collective attempt on the part of various cultures and groups to establish a meaningful context for human existence.

A. General Ideas of Myth and Archetypal Criticism

Northrop Frye, Canadian critic and theorist, explained that archetype is a type or an image that appears repeatedly. He used archetype to mean a symbol. Archetype relates a poem to other poems. Every poet uses his own unique images. However, when many poets, especially the poets a thousand years ago and as far as ten thousand miles away, used some same images without prior consultation, people would ask, why could they use the same images? For instance, from time immemorial, many nations regard the sun and mountains as the masculine images, but relate the moon and water to feminine images. In the literature in all the parts of the world, we find that fields and gardens symbolize the universality of systems. The ancient Roman poet Virgil's pastoral songs, Sidney's "Arcadia," Spenser's "The Faerie Queene," the religious hints about flocks of sheep in the *Bible*, and Shakespeare's forest comedies are all full of pastoral images.

Symbols or images, through the literary works of one generation after another, have extended to an archetypal symbol of the literary whole. It has become a mysterious sign that can be exchanged. The Cross symbolizes Christianity and the death of Jesus Christ and it is an image that has already been universally accepted among Christians.

Archetypes can be 1) images, 2) detail descriptions (such as the transition of the four seasons, birth and old age, sickness and death, etc.), 3) plots (e.g. the fight between the good and the evil, the conflict between spirit and flesh, the good fortune of Cinderella type) and 4) character types. Characters can be divided into two types: the good ones and the evil ones. Again, the good ones can be divided into two types: one type who save people's souls such as God and the clergymen; another type who are heroes and brave men who save people in dire peril.

B. Main Views of Myth and Archetypal Criticism

Archetypal criticism studies the above-mentioned four types of archetypes that repeatedly appear in literature. In his famous work *Anatomy of Criticism* (1957), Frye continued the formalist emphasis of the New Criticism but insisted even more strongly that criticism should be a scientific, objective, and systematic discipline. Moreover, Frye held that such literary criticism views literature itself as a system. For example, the mythoi of Spring, Summer, Autumn, and Winter gave rise to fundamental literary modes such as comedy, tragedy, irony, and romance.

Given the recurrence of basic symbolic motifs, literary history is a repetitive and self-contained cycle. Hence the historical element ostensibly informing Frye's formalism is effectively abrogated, literature being viewed as a timeless, static, and autonomous construct. Frye's static model, exhibiting recurrent patterns, is a feature shared by structuralist views of language and literature. Frye borrowed the word "archetype" from Jung's works. Frye often said that his theory of archetypal criticism was formed under the inspiration of Jung's theory of collective unconscious. Therefore, he called his own theory of archetypal criticism Jung's critical theory. Some critics call Jung's "analytic psychology" "archetypal psychology." The popularity of archetypal criticism can not be separated from Jung and Frye.

Jung thought that the content of the personal unconscious mainly consists of the moods with emotional coloring and it constructs one side of the individual in the psychological life. But the content of the collective unconscious is the so-called archetype. To him, the content of the collective unconscious is archetype or primitive images, that the personal psychology is established through evolution, and that it is connected with the past of the individual and the past of the race. Starting from one's birth, this consciousness imperceptibly influences his psychological activities. This ancestral experience inherited in everybody's mind is called "the racial memory," "the primitive image" or "archetype."

Jung said that archetype is the typical pattern of comprehension. Whenever we face the mode of understanding that is universally identical and happens repeatedly, we are communicating with archetype. He added that there are as many archetypes as there are typical situations in life. These experiences have been deeply engraved in our psychological structures because of constant repetitions. He held that the process of creation is to activate archetypal images from the unconscious, process and manufacture them so as to make them a complete work.

In 1934, when he discussed the archetypes in his *Archetypal Patterns in Poetry* (1934), Maud Bodkin for the first time moved his interest from myth to archetype.

In the 1980s, again appeared the theory of feminist archetypal criticism, the works of which include *The Archetypal Patterns in Women Fiction* (1981) by Annis Pratt, *Women as the Makers of Myths*: *Women's Poetry and Visual Art in the Twentieth Century* (1984) and *The Feminist Archetypal Theory*: *Jung's Cross-Disciplinary Ideas* (1985) by other feminists.

James George Frazer, Scottish anthropologist, also did outstanding contribution to archetypal study. His famous work *The Golden Bough*: *A Study in Magic and Religion* (1890–1936) gives a brilliant exposition of the problems of myths, religion, etc. It is a work that Frye often quoted.

Archetype is closely related with rituals and myths. Frye thought that literature expresses myths and rituals and that the literary narration is an act that symbolizes communication carried out repeatedly, namely, a ritual. Archetypal criticism sees the literary narration as a ritual. Religion originates from rituals and myths; all kinds of rituals and myths were the main contents and manifestations of the prehistoric human spiritual life. Rituals reflect many natural phenomena that go round and begin again in nature, such as spring, summer, autumn and winter, the sun's rising and setting, the tide's coming in and going out, the grass and trees, withering and thriving, birth and death, etc. The symbolic images are closely related to these natural phenomena: the sun symbolizes light, night symbolizes darkness, and the four seasons signify the periods of human life.

Many rituals still popular in all parts of the world originate from prehistoric human rituals. The dance of flying birds before mating inspired the dance ritual of the primitive people. The natural disasters such as earthquake, volcanic eruption, flood, drought, and storm forced the primitive people to pray to God for His blessings by using all kinds of rituals. The activities such as offering sacrifices to gods, holding wedding ceremonies, funerals, carnivals, and celebrations of harvest, etc. all originate from the rituals of the primitive people; religion also originates from the primitive ideas and rituals.

Rituals reflect man's wishes and loathing. Some people hold the idea that people would reincarnate and be born again after death. Driving out, punishing, putting to death, etc. are the rituals to express loathing.

Rituals and myths produced religion while religion and literature are outside and inside each other and supplement and complete each other.

Frye studied the *Bible* as a source of the literary structure. He thought that many literary works even employ the words used in the *Bible* as their titles, for example, Tolstoy's *Resurrection* (1900), Yeats' poems "The Second Pantecost" and "Revelations," Hemingway's *The Sun Also Rises*, etc.

From the ancient Greek tragedies to Shakespeare's plays, we can deeply feel the religious influence upon literature, and see the religiousness of literature, ritual praying, chanting incantations, and all kinds of non-religious rituals often appearing in literary works. The tragedy devoted to Dionysus, god of wine, is a ritual itself. Acting or watching tragedies could also be considered a ritual originating from ancient ritual; it is merely that modern people have no longer paid much attention to the ideas of rituals and the origin of the popular rituals has faded from modern people's memory.

Frye's definition of myth is that myth is the unity of rituals and dreams in the exchange of words... Myth explains rituals and dreams and makes the two mutually exchange. Myth is the indispensable key element of epics. Many modern writers think that in today's literary creation writers still need to borrow ancient myths and construct new myths in which they build new literary images. In Yeats' poems, Eliot's poem "The Waste Land," and Joyce's novel *Ulysses*, we can see new myths and new images. In his poem "Vala, or The Four Zoas," the English poet Blake creates a myth, expressing the alienation of human spirit and the split of personality. Yeats' "A Vision" is an essay full of the images of complicated and abstruse mysticism and symbolism, from which we can see the poet's wishes to construct his personal system of myths. Eliot's "The Waste Land" adopts the mythic archetypal pattern of the binary oppositions (death/resurrection, water/fire, etc.).

Myths and rituals are the efforts that the primitive people made to seek their own position while existing together with the heaven, the earth, and gods, and the efforts that the primitive people made to seek getting along well with the heaven, the earth and gods when they were unable to resist natural disasters. This is a kind of interpretative system to seek the meanings of the universe and themselves. Jung said that this system provides for the primitive people the prospects that far surpass their limited living scope, gives them a broad space to display their personalities, and also offers them the whole life of man as a complete man.

The primitive people used many vivid images to describe and explain all kinds of natural phenomena, manifesting their imaginative power full of poetic meaning. The change and the cycle of the four seasons bring out many myths about the four seasons and the gods of the four seasons which have not yet declined until now. Shelley's famous lines "If winter comes, / Can spring be far behind?" use the images of winter and spring in myths. We can call the symbols of the four seasons "archetypal imaginations," which regard a certain object, event, phenomenon as a thing to have universally symbolic meaning. The writer who has such an archetypal imagination uses the archetypal pattern, which can produce a kind of feeling that is strange but seems to be met before at the same time in the reader's mind. This kind of feeling that seems to be met before originates from "the racial memory" or the collective unconscious.

The archetypal study in literary works is a kind of literary anthropology because what it pays close attention to is the initial images, rituals, myths, folk legends, etc. that are related with literature and anthropology. Archetype has accumulated the wisdom and psychological energy of one generation after another. Vertically, it makes the modern people in a direct line of succession of the primitive people, our ancestors; horizontally, it makes a race or a nation relate with other races and nations. It is where the mysteries of literature and art are as well as where the value of archetypal criticism is.

Further Reading

Devika, S. Archetypal Criticism. Dr. S. Devika. Retrieved 29 March 2017.

Bremm, Doris. Archetypal Criticism. *The English Literature Companion*. Ed. Julian Wolfreys. Houndmills, Hampshire: Palgrave, 2010, pp. 270–272.

Abrams, M. H. Archetypal Criticism. *A Glossary of Literary Terms*. Fort Worth: HBJ, 1993, pp. 223–225.

Bates, Roland. *Northrop Frye*. Toronto: McClelland and Stewart, 1971.

Frye, Northrop. The Archetypes of Literature // Vincent B. Leitch. *The Norton Anthology of Theory and Criticism*. New York: Norton, 2001, pp. 1445–1457.

Knapp, Bettina L. Introduction // *A Jungian Approach to Literature*. Carbondale and Edwardsville: Southern Illinois University Press, 1984, pp. ix-xvi.

Leitch, Vincent B. Northrop Frye // Vincent B. Leitch. *The Norton Anthology of Theory and Criticism*. Ed. New York: Norton, 2001, pp. 1442–1445.

——. Carl Gustav Jung // *The Norton Anthology of Theory and Criticism*. New York: Norton, 2001, pp. 987–990.

Segal, Robert A. Introduction // *Jung on Mythology*. Princeton: Princeton University Press, 1998, pp. 3–48

Sugg, Richard P. *Jungian Literary Criticism*. Evanston, Ill.: Northwestern University Press, 1992.

Walker, Steven F. *Jung and the Jungians on Myth*. New York: Garland Publishing, 1995, pp. 3–15.

Bibliography

Cuddon, J. A. *A Dictionary of Literary Terms and Literary Theory*. 5th ed. Malden: Wiley-Blackwell, 2013.

Habib, Rafey. *A History of Literary Criticism: From Plato to the Present*. Oxford: Blackwell Publishing, 2005.

Rice, Philip & Patricia Waugh. *Modern Literary Theory*. New York: Oxford University Press, 2002.

Bressler, Charles. *Literary Criticism*: *An Introduction to Theory and Practice*. Beijing: Higher Education Press, 2004.

泰勒，温奎斯特. 后现代主义百科全书. 章燕，李自修，等译. 刘象愚，校. 长春：吉林人民出版社，2007.

王治河. 后现代主义辞典. 北京：中央编译出版社，2004.
张中载，王逢振，赵国新. 二十世纪西方文论选读. 北京：外语教学与研究出版社，2002.
朱刚. 二十世纪西方文艺批评理论. 上海：上海外语教育出版社，2001.

Selected Readings

Northrop Frye: "The Archetypes of Literature"
"Mythical Phase: Symbol as Archetype"
"Archetypal Criticism: Theory of Myths"

Chapter Six

Structuralism

Structuralism is an intellectual movement which began in France in the 1950s and its origins are connected with the work of the anthropologist Claude Lévi-Strauss (1908–2009) and the literary critic Roland Barthes (1915–1980). Structuralism was introduced into Britain mainly in the 1970s and gain great influence throughout the 1980s. Structuralism has effected a number of fields of knowledge and inquiry—especially philosophy, anthropology, history, sociology and literary criticism. It has led to a fundamental reconstruction of mankind's and womankind's position, behavior, function and attitude historically—and now. Broadly speaking, it is concerned with "language" in a most general sense: not just the language of utterance in speech and writing. It is concerned with signs and thus with signification. Structuralist theory considers all conventions and codes of communication; for example, all forms of signal (smoke, fire, traffic lights, Morse, flags, gesture), body language, clothes, artefacts, the means by which human beings convey information to each other: from a railway timetable to a thumbs-up sign; from a PR brochure to a siren. Everything, then, in the theory of Structuralism, is the product of a system of signification or code. The relationships between the elements of the code give it signification. Codes are arbitrary (all signs are arbitrary) and without them we cannot apprehend reality.

As far as literature and literary criticism are concerned, Structuralism challenges the long-standing belief that a work of literature (or any kind of literary text) reflects a given reality; a literary text is, rather, constituted of other conventions and texts. The critical theory of Structuralism was extremely popular in the middle and late 1960s and the 1970s, a kind of formalist critical theory appearing after Russian Formalism and Anglo-American New Criticism. Structuralism was imported into America from France during the 1960s and its leading exponents included Roman Jakobson, Jonathan Culler, Michael Riffaterre, Claudio Guillen, Gerald Prince, and Robert Scholes. Other American thinkers working in the field of semiotics have included C. S. Peirce, Charles Morris, and Noam Chomsky. In his renowned study *Structuralist Poetics* (1975), Jonathan Culler explained that structuralist investigations of literature would seek to identify the systems of conventions underlying literature. Robert Scholes, in *Structuralism in Literature: An Introduction* (1974), sought a scientific basis for the study of literature as an interconnected system of various texts. Other key texts of Structuralism in America included a special issue of *Yale French Studies* (1966), and volumes entitled *Structuralism* (1970) edited by Jacques Ehrmann and *The Structuralist Controversy* (1970) edited by Richard Macksey and Eugenio Donato. Also influential in America was the work of Roman Jakobson, who taught for many years at various American universities, and who worked out an influential model of communication as well as a distinction between metaphor and metonymy in the analysis of narratives.

A. Ferdinand de Saussure

Swiss linguist Ferdinand de Saussure laid solid foundations for the development of Structuralism. His insights paved a way for the subsequent success achieved by the French anthropologist Claude Lévi-Strauss, Roland Barthes, and others. In his *Course in General Linguistics* (1916), Saussure distinguished langue, the system and rules of language, from parole or speech. Saussure, opposing the research method of the historical linguistics that explores the changes of language, advocated to synchronically analyze language and digged out the latent and dominant system of language through concrete speech acts. He put forward the important difference between *parole* (speech) and *langue* (language). *Parole* stands for the words and sentences that people use in their everyday association and *langue* refers to the rule system that governs the concrete speeches. A word (a symbol) consists of two parts: the signifier and the signified. The former is the sign of the word's sound and writing and the latter is the concept that the word expresses. Like the two sides of a piece of paper, the two cannot be separated. The relation between the signifier and the signified is established by popular usage, it is arbitrary, and there is no necessarily corresponding relation between them. The production of meaning is the result of differentiating from each other between symbols, that is, the meaning of words is not produced according to reality. Language is an independent and self-sufficient system. Therefore, meaning is not determined by the subjective intention of the speaker but by the whole language system. Just as some critics point out, the important inspiration given to literary criticism by these important linguistic principles is that it denies the practice that in some traditional literary criticisms (e.g. mimesis, expressionism, pragmatism) writers and the social reality are regarded as the tangency point of interpreting literary works, and critics turn to pay close attention to the way in which a meaning is produced but not to the meaning itself. The main task of linguists is not to study the individual speeches but to study the whole system of language. Similar with this situation, literary structuralists hold that the individual works should be considered something like speeches and they are full of the laws of literary language.

B. Claude Lévi-Strauss

In addition, Saussure himself also thought that language and social behavior in any forms are similar in structure and framework. On this premise, to other branches of humane studies, the method of language study has the meaning of paradigm that can be applied into other branches of humane and social studies. Following this train of thought, Claude Lévi-Strauss introduced Saussure's linguistic theory into cultural anthropology. Lévi-Strauss and others absorbed Saussure's ideas that language is characterized by structures and applied this theory to practice in more areas. They emphasized the deep structures that underlie various phenomena and even viewed these structures as basic characteristics of the human mind. His structural analysis of the myths, the relations between relatives, and cooking techniques of the original inhabitants on the American Continent shows that, like language, these myths, relations between relatives, and cooking techniques are all systems with structures. Their individual component elements are meaningful just because they are a part of a complete system. In his analysis, a myth is resolved into elementary units (elements of myth, mythemes) like the elementary phonetic units (phonemes) of language. Just as Eagleton said that, only through a special way to combine them with each other can they produce any meaning. The principles governing this combination can be considered a kind of grammar, that is, a set of relations under the surface of narrative, which form the true meaning of myths.

Drawing on Saussure's ideas, he believed that myth was a specific form and use of language. According to Lévi-Strauss, in addition to langue and parole, myth uses a third referent which combines the properties of the first two. On the one hand, a myth refers to events that happened a long time ago; but what gives the myth an lasting value is that the specific pattern described is timeless: it explains the present and past as well as the future. He suggested that in modern societies myth has been largely replaced by politics: for example, the French Revolution is regarded as both a sequence of events in the past and as a timeless pattern detectable in the social structure of contemporary French. Hence the myth had a double structure, historical and ahistorical. Lévi-Strauss held that the structure of mythical thought addresses our inability to connect two kinds of relationship by asserting that contradictory relationships are identical inasmuch as they are both self-contradictory in a similar way. Hence the Oedipus myth is a kind of logical tool. He saw the purpose of myth as providing a logical model capable of overcoming a contradiction. An important claim of Lévi-Strauss was that his method eliminates the problematic quest for a true or earlier version of a myth. He defined the myth as consisting of all of its versions. Even Freud's account of the Oedipus myth is part of the myth. Even when variants exhibit differences, the latter can themselves be correlated. Hence there is no single true version of which all the others are but copies or distortions. Every version belongs to the myth. A myth displays a "slated" structure, which comes to the surface through repetition. Myth grows spiral-wise until the intellectual impulse behind it is exhausted. Its growth is a continuous process whereas its structure remains discontinuous. Lévi-Strauss saw his theory as generating a novel view of the progress of thought: the logic in mythical thought is as rigorous as that of modern science; the difference, or apparent improvement, lies not in the progress of man's mind but in the discovery of new areas to which it may apply.

Structuralist analysis also includes the anti-humanitarian view, since language is an institution, individual human agency is unprivileged, neither human beings nor social phenomena having essences. Therefore, Structuralism is completely different from the Romantic notion of the author as the source of meaning, and shifts emphasis away from authorial intention toward the broader and impersonal linguistic structure in which the author's text participates, and which indeed enables that text.

C. Tzvetan Todorov

The achievements of literary Structuralism are conspicuously embodied in the narrative theory of Tzvetan Todorov, A. J. Greimas, Gerad Genette, and others as well as in Roland Barthes' literary criticism. Like Russian Formalism, Structuralism deeply believes and tries hard to explore the existence of a branch of literary science, which is established on the basis of forms but not on the basis of contents. Therefore, it is similar with the Anglo-American New Criticism. But just as some critics point out, the difference between it and Russian Formalism is that the latter does not pay close attention to the deep laws and structure of literary texts; the Anglo-American New Criticism that stresses the organic consistence of the meaning of texts contrasts sharply with Structuralism that maintains the plural signification of texts. In Roland Barthes' words, criticism actively creates meaning for texts but not passively interprets the meaning of texts because a basic premise of Structuralism is to recognize humanist activities and their products, and even that mental perception and thoughts themselves are constructive but not natural.

The theory of structuralist narratology and the practice of structuralist criticism are extremely loaded down with trivial details. In the following, we will take Tzvetan Todorov's analysis of *Decameron* (1353) as an example to briefly explain the operation strategies of structuralist narratology. The starting point of Todorov's theory is that language is the master pattern of all systems of expression; narrative and language have similar structures and therefore there is a set of narrative grammar. In his narrative analysis, he mechanically applied the linguistic category to analyze stories. He divided narrative into the three levels such as semantics, syntax and vocabulary. Semantic level refers to the contents of the story, syntactic level means the ways of relation between events, and vocabulary level indicates the use of concrete words and phrases, namely, the language used to narrate stories. Among them, syntactic level is the content that Todorov mainly studied. Syntax consists of two basic units: proposition and sequence. Proposition is produced either by the combination of characters with the irreducible actions (e.g. A falls in love with B or A joins B's family) or by the combination of characters with the most essential attributes (e.g. A behaves wickedly or B is a Queen). Sequence is the assembly of all kinds of statements involved forming a complete story. One story may have many sequences but at least contains one sequence. All kinds of narrative units are seen as all kinds of parts of speech: characters are about equal to proper nouns, characters' actions verbs, and characters' attributes adjectives. Similarly, proposition and sequence respectively bring the functions of sentences and paragraphs into play. The combination of proper nouns (characters) with adjectives (attributes) or with verbs (actions) forms proposition. Thus, the whole text is just like a written sentence structure.

Narrative Units		**Language Units**
Characters	←——→	Proper nouns
Characters' actions	←——→	Verbs
Characters' attributes	←——→	Adjectives
Proposition	←——→	Sentences
Sequence	←——→	Paragraphs

Among them, all the attributes can be simplified as three sorts of adjectives: state (unstable attributes, such as happiness and unhappiness), inherent quality (comparatively stable attributes, such as the good and the evil), and condition (the most stable attributes, such as characters' sexual distinction, religious beliefs, and their social positions). All the actions can be simplified as three verbs: to modify, to transgress, and to punish. This important discovery makes Todorov see that in all the small stories of *Decameron* that he analyzes, such as fixed pattern appears again and again: changes happen constantly, all kinds of evil acts have all the time gone scott-free without getting punished. This pattern helps Todorov find that the values that *Decameron* represents and the values that the times in which the writer was pursued have an important interrelation between them. In the times in which Boccaccio lived, the new value system that was interrelated with the capitalist free enterprise institution and sang praises for personal courage and insight and creative initiative was being gradually established and it began to replace the old commercial system with a stronger controlling power.

D. Roland Barthes

Roland Barthes' semiotic criticism is an important component part of Structuralism. In his works *Mythologies* (1957), *Elements of Semiology* (1967), *The System of Fad* (1970), etc., he extensively analyzed the cultural phenomena of the contemporary social culture. In his analysis permeates such an idea: behind clothing and conversation there is a system that gives clothing or conversation meaning. That is to say, he explained these social actions as all kinds of sign systems that operate by following language patterns. To him, any social action is governed by a set of rule system. Barthes' structuralist semiotic criticism exerted very great influence upon the early English study. It is an important theoretical source of the critical practice of Cultural Studies. *Mythologies* is a much-loved structuralist classic and one of the inaugural documents of Cultural Studies. As a collection of beautifully written mini essays originally written for a literary magazine, it is a highly contingent text, self-consciously connected to the mid-1950s struggles against the government. Barthes' structuralist semiotic criticism exerted very great influence upon the early English study. It is an important theoretical source of the critical practice of Cultural Studies.

To sum up, just as Eagleton pointed out, structuralist criticism presents two basic characteristics: 1) the nature of this criticism is analysis, not appraisal; 2) it pays no attention to the surface meaning of texts but tries hard to dig up the deep structure latent in the stories. The advantages of structural criticism lie in that it has broken the mysterious concept that a poet is a genius in traditional critical theories and especially popular in romantic critical theory. Compared with the traditional criticisms, its most revolutionary nature lies in that it gives language an extremely important position: language itself is regarded not only as the object that structuralist criticism mainly pays close attention to but also the pattern to study non-language branches of learning. The tide of Structuralism has somewhat receded before the advance of more recent theoretical movements which have impugned, among other things, its lack of historicity, its use of binary oppositions, its centralizing of the notion of structure as well as its reduction of "real" referents to elements in a self-enclosed linguistic system. It may be, however, that certain concepts of Structuralism, such as binarism, need to be revisited, if only to situate our rejection of them alongside their positive potential, a potential which may well have political dimensions, as in Barthes' earlier work. The shortcomings of structuralist criticism manifest itself in that it pays too much attention to texts themselves, separates itself from the historical and social contexts that literary works rely on for emergence, and often applies mechanically linguistic pattern. Its process of proving appears trivial and complicated. The conclusion that it draws is often paradoxical, unable to agree or decide which is right. Moreover, the scientificalness and objectivity for which structuralist criticism blows its own trumpet are also open to doubt. To Post-structuralism, when it analyzes the deep structures of works, myths, and speech actions, Structuralism actually constructs these structures secretly with its subjective foresight. Therefore, it is only an action of interpretation and far from a science that takes exploring the intrinsic structure of the field that it studies as its duty. Along with the rising of Post-structuralism and deconstruction, some structuralists such as Barthes and others began to turn to Post-structuralism and thus the era of Structuralism gradually became the past.

Further Reading

Barthes, Roland. *Elements of Semiology.* London: Jonathon Cape, 1967.

Culler, Johnathan. *Structuralist Poetics*: *Structuralism*, *Linguistics and the Study of Literature*. London: Routledge & Kagan Paul, 1975.

Foucault, Michel. *The Order of Things: An Archaeology of the Human Sciences*. New York: Pantheon Books, 1970.

Genette, Gerard. *Narrative Discourse*. Oxford: Basil Blackwell, 1980.

Jakobson, Roman. *On Language.* Cambridge: Harvard University Press, 1990.

Lévi-Strauss, Claude. *Structural Anthropology*. London: Allan Lane, 1968.

——. *The Elementary Structures of Kinship*. Rev. ed. Trans. James Harle Bell, John Richard von Sturmer & Rodney Needham. Boston: Beacon Press, 1969.

Saussure, Ferdinand de. *Course in General Linguistics*. Glasgow: Fontana/Collins, 1977.

Scholes, Robert. *Structuralism in Literature, an Introduction*. New Haven & London: Yale University Press, 1986.

Sturrock, John. *Structuralism*. London: Paladin, 1986.

Bibliography

Cuddon, J. A. *A Dictionary of Literary Terms and Literary Theory*. 5th ed. Malden: Wiley-Blackwell, 2013.

Rice, Philip & Patricia Waugh. *Modern Literary Theory*. New York: Oxford University Press, 2002.

Bressler, Charles. *Literary Criticism: An Introduction to Theory and Practice*. Beijing: Higher Education Press, 2004.

Barry, Peter. *Beginning Theory: An Introduction to Literary and Cultural Theory*. Manchester: Manchester University Press, 2017.

Goulimari, Pelagia. *Literary Criticism and Theory: From Plato to Postcolonialism*. London & New York: Routledge Taylor & Francis Group, 2015.

泰勒，温奎斯特. 后现代主义百科全书. 章燕，李自修，等译. 刘象愚，校. 长春：吉林人民出版社，2007.

王治河. 后现代主义辞典. 北京：中央编译出版社，2004.

张中载，王逢振，赵国新. 二十世纪西方文论选读. 北京：外语教学与研究出版社，2002.

朱刚. 二十世纪西方文艺批评理论. 上海：上海外语教育出版社，2001.

Selected Readings

Ferdinand de Saussure: *Course in General Linguistics*

Roland Barthes: "The Structuralist Activity"

David Lodge: "Analysis and Interpretation of the Realist Text: Ernest Hemingway's 'Cat in the Rain'"

Chapter Seven

Reception Aesthetics and Reader-response Theory

Someone ever roughly divided the development history of modern literary theories into three periods: the period of the critics' specializing in authors, for instance, the theory and practice of romanticism, the 19th-century biographical criticism, historical criticism, etc.; the period of the critics' concentrating their attention on texts, for example, the Anglo-American New Criticism and Russian Formalism; and the period of the critics' devoting their mind to the study of readers, for instance, the reader-oriented theory represented by Reception Aesthetics and Reader-response Theory since the 1970s. Reception-aesthetics is a school of literary theory which is concerned with the general response to literature in terms of reception-aesthetics rather than the individual's response, and suggests that literary work should be studied in terms of the impression or impact it makes on its contemporary audience, and that literary value is judged according to how much the view of a text alters over time. "Aesthetic distance" is the term used by Hans Robert Jauss, the representative theorist of this school, to denote the difference between the contemporary view of a work of art (at the same time of its first publication) and the present-day view. But still the idea holds that the reader has a contribution to make in the process. So there is a kind of balance and cooperation between text and what it provides and what the reader contributes. However, all readers are different and therefore may be supposed to bring a different response to any text.

A. The Development of Reception Aesthetics and Reader-Response Theory

The role of the reader or audience of a literary work or performance has been recognized since classical times. Plato was acutely aware of the disturbing power of poetry to affect people at the level of their passions and morality, as well as their basic conceptions of the gods and indeed of reality itself. For him, poetry played a very important part in appealing to our lower natures, disposing us toward irrational behavior, and distracting us from the rational pursuit of truth. Aristotle, who had a more tolerant conception of poetry, made the response of the audience an integral component of his famous definition of a properly structured tragedy: such a tragedy must inspire the purgative emotions of fear and pity in the audience. Many classical and medieval writers viewed literature as a branch of rhetoric, the art of persuasive speaking or writing. As such, literature had to be highly aware of the composition and expectations of its audience. Subsequently, several Romantic theories stressed the powerful emotional impact of poetry on the reader, and various later 19th-century theories such as symbolism and impressionism stressed the reader's subjective response to literature and art. Several other kinds of theories, such as Feminism and Marxism, have long acknowledged that literature, necessarily operating within certain social structures of class and gender, is always oriented toward certain kinds of audiences, in both aesthetic and economic terms. The hermeneutic theories developed by Friedrich Schleiermacher, Martin Heidegger, and Hans-Georg Gadamer, as well as the phenomenological theories inspired by Edmund Husserl, such as that of Roman Ingarden, examined the ways in which readers engaged cognitively and historically with literary texts.

The formalists wanted to carve out the domain of literature as a scientific, autonomous realm, where the emphasis lay not on mere subjective reactions of the reader nor on the connections of the text to its broader social circumstances but on the literary work itself: they saw the study of literature as an objective activity, and they saw the literary object itself as the repository of meaning. What needed to be studied, they argued, was the "objective" verbal structure of the literary artifact, and what needed to be identified were its specifically literary qualities, as opposed to any moral, religious, or other significance it might contain.

Reader-response theory was a reaction against formalism and objectivism, but it was also a renewal of a long and diversified tradition that had acknowledged the important role of the reader or audience in the overall structure of any given literary or rhetorical situation. In their theoretical writings, Virginia Woolf, Louise Rosenblatt, and Wayne Booth recognized that the author of a literary text uses certain strategies to produce given effects in their readers or to guide their responses. A number of post-structuralist movements such as deconstruction had challenged the formalist and Anglo-American New Critical assertion of the objectivity of the text. But it was not until the 1970s that a number of critics at the Konstanz University in Germany (the Konstanz School) began to formulate a systematic reader-response or "reception" theory. Wolfgang Iser and Hans Robert Jauss were leading members among this school. The roots of the schools' aesthetics could be found not only in the hermeneutic and phenomenological traditions mentioned above but also in the earlier thought of Alexander Baumgarten, Immanuel Kant, and Friedrich von Schiller.

B. General Ideas of Reception Aesthetics and Reader-Response Theory

Actually, while making a general survey of the development situation of the Western critical theories since ancient Greece, we find that readers are not completely ignored by critics but they are merely not like the reader in Reception Aesthetics and Reader-response Theory whose role is meticulously highlighted and emphasized and whose position suddenly rises and becomes the heart of literary criticism. When they discussed literature, the classical critics such as Plato, Aristotle, Horace, Longinus and others mainly began from the influence of literature upon the audience. In the critical theories in early 20th century, the critics of the Anglo-American New Criticism advocated to pay close attention to "poetry itself" and "concrete works," opposed studying poetry by starting with psychological effect, considered that readers had a variety of interests and different responses. Yet, it was hard for them to come to an identical conclusion about the meaning of a work, and denounce this sort of criticism as "affective fallacy," but Ivor Armstrong Richards and William Empson, having the important theoretical origins of the Anglo-American New Criticism, laid stress on readers' affective response to poetry. In addition, before the rising of the reader-oriented theory, the semiotic study had already noticed the important role of the readers. For example, in his work *The Role of the Reader*, Umberto Eco thought that some texts (e.g. *Finnegans Wake* by James Joyce in 1939) are "open-type," the production of their meaning needs the reader's cooperation; but some texts (e.g. detective fictions) are "close-type," the reader's response to the works can be predicted.

C. Main Views of Reception Aesthetics and Reader-Response Theory

In many of the reader-oriented theories rising since the 1970s, Hans Robert Jauss' theory of reception aesthetics and Wolfgang Iser's theory of reader-response, both of the two theorists working at Konstanz University in Germany, are the most original and most influential. Generally, the conventional practice of literary interpretation was to try hard to reveal the meaning deeply hidden in the text; the reader-oriented theory thinks that the meaning of the text is by no means produced by itself but the result of the mutual exchange between the text and the reader. In Iser's words, in the text there are always many gaps waiting for the reader who, while reading, arouses his imaginative power to fill up. This is quite like looking at an incomplete long picture of mountains and waters. In order to have a full view of it, the audience only has to rack his usual appreciation experience to conceive the rest. Again, Iser thought that the construction of the aesthetic object could be completed only by the reader's understanding, that is to say, the complete meaning of the text is the result of the reader's expectation. Thus, the object of literary study is changed from the text, to which Formalism paid close attention, to the reader's reading action. Though there were too many schools inside the reader-oriented theory and they held different opinions about the problem of reading process, they unanimously thought that the reader's role in the process of understanding must not be ignored, that the reader does not passively accept the meaning that the text presents but actively participates in the construction of the text's meaning.

Jauss' reception aesthetics attempts to mediate the opposition between Marxist Criticism and Formalist criticism. To him, Marxist Criticism really pays attention to history but only involves history in the aspects of social production and reproduction; Formalism which is adept in text analysis, ignores history; they have a common shortcoming, that is, they both ignore the reader (the public) in the important triangle relation: the writer—the work—the public. It is just the dimension of the reader that reception aesthetics puts forth effort to introduce into critical practice. Jauss borrows the concept of "paradigm" from the scientific philosophy to explain the phenomenon that the readers in the same era have similar ideas about literature. According to the views of scientific philosopher Thomas S. Kuhn, the scientific work of the scientists in every historical period follows the "paradigm" which is constituted by the given scientific concepts and understanding. Once crisis appears in this paradigm which fails to explain a number of problems that have appeared recently, a new paradigm will emerge as the times demands. Jauss held that there is a similar phenomenon in literature that the reader's reading and the writer's writing in a specific period are kept within bounds of literary conventions and ideas which are held by the people in this period. These ideas include not only the ideas about literature itself (e.g. genre, style, form, etc.) but also the ideas about the contexts in which literature is produced. On this basis the reader's "vision of expectations" is formed, which makes the reader read the work with a certain preconceived idea. The reader of every literary work does his reading under the leading "vision of expectations" in this period. When a work tallies with the reader's "vision of expectations," it is easier for it to be understood by the contemporaries; if the reader's vision of expectations is not identical with the work, in order to completely understand it, the reader has to adjust or break the old vision of expectations, thus forming a new vision of expectations.

Jauss' reception aesthetics is inspired and deeply influenced by the hermeneutic ideas of Martin Heidegger and Hans-Georg Gadamer. Heidegger thought that the purely objective understanding that exceeds history and times does not exist and it is inevitable to understand the things in the world with preconceptions because these things are all projections of our ideas so that comprehending and understanding them must be influenced by the established ideas. Our thinking is always controlled by the historical circumstances which we are in and therefore it is always historical though this history is not social and external but personal and internal. These ideas of Heidegger was carried out into literary theories by Gadamer who considered that the meaning of a literary work is not limited to the writer's intention, but constantly extended and enriched by the later reading and controlled by the historical circumstances which the reader is in. He sedulously stressed the historical circumstances' shaping role to the reader's understanding: as the historical existence, whatever we do is engraved with the times' mark; subject and object are equally matched, we are unable to examine the past with completely righteous and objective eyes, and the object that we study is unable to get rid of our subjectivity; our understanding of the literature in the past can only start from the limited immediate present perspective. Taking this idea of Gadamer, Jauss thought that literary texts exist in the process of constant dialogues between the past and the immediate present and the interpreter's stand at the immediate present influences his understanding and reception of the literature in the past which are done on the cultural vision at the immediate present. Therefore, Jauss put forward the concept of "the fusion of visions," combining the past with the immediate present. If the "vision of expectations" can only explain the understanding and reception of a literary work and cannot amply state the work's ultimate meaning and value, "the fusion of vision" just can solve this difficult problem. To Jauss, the meaning and value of a text is finally produced in the reception history of a text.

Starting with the microscopic angle of the reception history of literature, Jauss has developed the reception aesthetics that examines the historicity of literary changes, while Iser, who also belongs to the Konstanz University and who opens another path and begins with the microscopic analysis of textual structure, has presented the reader-response theory that specifically studies the reading activities. Jauss often pays close attention to the essential problem of society and history in general sense and his reception aesthetics has a strong coloring of literary sociology. What Iser was mainly concerned about is the individual text and the relation between it and the reader; though his reader-response theory considers the factors of society and history, these factors are subordinate in nature and they mainly relate with the meticulous discussion of texts.

To sum up, what Iser's reader-response theory mainly discusses is the reading process and it does not examine the reception situation of literary works in different historical periods. The close reading of the Anglo-American New Criticism aims at interpreting a text and summarizing its meaning. However, Iser maintains that any interpretation can only be a possible fulfillment of a literary text and the meaning of a text is the product of the interaction between the reader and the text and not the essential attribute hidden inside the text. The main task of criticism is to reveal all kinds of norms and laws that govern the reader's ideas and understanding while he is reading. Roman Ingarden, Polish literary theorist, held that a literary work is a "structure of diagram type" or a whole set of "outline" waiting for the reader to carry out concretely. Having absorbed Ingarden's views, Iser further thought that the reader's process of concretization is not to reveal the unity of the text but to reveal the gaps and all kinds of uncertain factors in the text. To him, reading is a dynamic process; along with the development of reading the gaps and the uncertain factors constantly challenge and question the norms and laws in the reader's mind and force the reader to revise and change those preconceptions and produce a kind of critical re-understanding of the comprehending norms and laws that he himself is accustomed to, thus forming new comprehending norms and laws. An excellent work often negates the comprehending norms and laws that the writer usually holds and breaks the reader's habitual expectations.

Iser was mainly influenced by Husserl's phenomenological ideas and especially inspired by the ideas of the phenomenological aesthetics of Ingarden, Husserl's student. Husserl put forward a complete set of extremely subjective theory of understanding, stressing the constructive character of man's consciousness. He thought that our understanding of the world is not to passively receive the existence of things just as a mirror reflects objects but actively conceive the world according to our own intention, for all objects are naturally intentional. In his work *The Act of Reading*, Iser examines what happens during the reading process, and how it is basic to the development of a theory of aesthetic response, setting in motion a chain of events that depends both on the text and the exercise of certain human faculties. Iser, having taken Ingarden's view that a literary work is a "structure of diagram type" full of gaps and uncertain factors needing the reader's imagination and processing to fill up, further presented the term "the appeal structure of the text" and its concept, attempting to explain that the uncertain factors and gaps themselves in a text are the text's true structural mechanism to call the reader to read. He pointed out that, in the process of reading, the reader's reading expectation is fully aroused to fill up those gaps and complete the process of concretization. As the reader goes deep into reading, his inherent vision of expectations constantly changes and new visions of expectations are unceasingly formed, which are the results produced by the role of "the appeal structure of the text." In addition, Iser also presented the term "the implied reader" which means that reading is secretly contained in the construction of a text. The implied reader is not a specific reader or some readers who actually reads or read the text but an idealized reader who completely tallies with the expectations of reading in the writer's imagination. The concept of the implied reader combines the meanings latent in the text with the reader's realization of these latent meanings in his reading. In *The Act of Reading*, Iser further elaborates his important concept of the "implied reader." He points out that when critics talk about literature in terms of its effects, they invoke two broad categories of reader: the "real" reader and the "hypothetical" reader. The former refers to an actual reader whose response is documented, whereas the hypothetical reader is a projection of all possible realizations of the text. Iser sees both of these concepts as deficient. The documented response of real readers has often been thought to mirror the cultural norms or codes of a given era. The main problem Iser sees with this approach is that any reconstruction of real readers depends on the survival of documents from their era; and the further back we go in history, such documentation becomes increasingly sparser, and we must reconstruct the real readership of a text from the text itself. On the other hand, Iser points out that the "hypothetical" or what is sometimes called the "ideal" reader is often nothing more than a creation of the critic's mind. Moreover, the code of an ideal reader would be identical to that of the author, thereby making reading superfluous. Since the "ideal reader" must encompass all the potential meanings of a text, Iser acknowledges that such a concept might be useful in order to "close the gaps that constantly appear in any analysis of literary effects and responses".

In the 1970s, the reader-response theory quickly spread to the circle of the Anglo-American Criticism. The reader-response critics who achieved brilliant attainments in the world of English language include Norman Holland, Stanley Fish and others. Holland studied reader's response mainly from the angle of psychology. The early Fish advocated a research method named "affective stylistics," emphasizing that a literary text is the existence of time, namely, thinking that a literary text is formed in the time of reading but it is not the object existing in the form of space. Fish held that the meaning of a work is realized in the process of reading and it is the result of the interactions of the reader's expectations, psychological projections, conclusions and judgments. This critical practice often carefully analyzes a text word by word and sentence by sentence, examining the influence exerted by some factors upon the reader's reading psychology. After entering the 1980s, Fish again put forward the concept of interpretative community. He thought that the readers who use the same interpretative strategies form an interpretative community and that the readers' subjective response to a literary work is actually the result of being influenced by the interpretative community to which they belong.

In addition, while the empirical tradition is not yet characterized by a single approach, it is notable for the adoption by some scholars of such methods as stylistics, corpus linguistics, narratology, phenomenology, cognitive psychology, neuropsychology, and evolutionary psychology.

Further Reading

Amacher, Richard & Victor Lange. *New Perspectives in German Literary Criticism*. Princeton: Princeton University Press, 1979.

Bennett, Susan. *Theatre Audiences: A Theory of Production and Reception*. New York: Routledge, 1990.

Eagleton, Terry. Phenomenology, Hermeneutics, and Reception Theory. *Literary Theory*. University of Minnesota Press, 1996, pp. 47–78.

Fortier, Mark. *Theory/Theatre: An Introduction*. 2nd ed. New York: Routledge, 2002.

Hohendahl, Peter Uwe. Introduction to Reception Aesthetics. *New German Critique* 10 (1977): 29–63.

Holub, Robert C. *Crossing Borders: Reception Theory, Poststructuralism, Deconstruction*. Madison: University of Wisconsin Press, 1992.

——. *Reception Theory: A Critical Introduction*. London: Methuen, 1984.

Hunt, John Dixon. *The Afterlife of Gardens*. Philadelphia: University of Pennsylvania Press, 2004.

Iser, Wolfgang. *The Act of Reading: A Theory of Aesthetic Response*. Baltimore: Johns Hopkins University Press, 1978.

——. *The Act of Reading: A Theory of Aesthetic Response*. Baltimore: Johns Hopkins University Press, 1978.

Jauss, Hans R. *Toward an Aesthetic of Reception*. Hampstead: Harvester Wheatsheaf, 1982.

Jauss, Hans Robert. *Aesthetic Experience and Literary Hermeneutics*. Trans. Michael Shaw. Minneapolis: University of Minnesota Press, 1982.

——. *Toward an Aesthetic of Reception*. Trans. Timothy Bahti. Minneapolis: University of Minnesota Press, 1982.

Tompkins, Jane P. *Reader-response Criticism: From Formalism to Post-structuralism*. Baltimore: Johns Hopkins University Press, 1980.

Tyson, Lois. *Critical Theory Today: A User-friendly Guide*. 2nd ed. New York & London: Routledge, 2006.

Bibliography

Cuddon, J. A. *A Dictionary of Literary Terms and Literary Theory*. 5th ed. Malden: Wiley-Blackwell, 2013.

Rice, Philip & Patricia Waugh. *Modern Literary Theory*. New York: Oxford University Press, 2002.

Bressler, Charles. *Literary Criticism: An Introduction to Theory and Practice*. Beijing: Higher Education Press, 2004.

Richter, David H. *A Companion to Literary Theory*. Hoboken: Wiley Blackwell, 2018.

Habib, Rafey. *A History of Literary Criticism: From Plato to the Present.* Oxford: Blackwell Publishing, 2005.

泰勒，温奎斯特. 后现代主义百科全书. 章燕，李自修，等译. 刘象愚，校. 长春：吉林人民出版社，2007.

王治河. 后现代主义辞典. 北京：中央编译出版社，2004.

张中载，王逢振，赵国新. 二十世纪西方文论选读. 北京：外语教学与研究出版社，2002.

朱刚. 二十世纪西方文艺批评理论. 上海：上海外语教育出版社，2001.

Selected Readings

Hans Robert Jauss: "Literary History as a Challenge to Literary Theory"

Wolfgang Iser: "The Reading Process: a Phenomenological Approach"

"The Role of the Reader in Fielding's *Joseph Andrews*"

Chapter Eight

Post-structuralism

Roughly speaking, the Western literary criticism mainly discussed the text of a work and defined the meaning that the text represents till the 1960s. Late in the 1960s, Structuralism became subject to a rigorous and lasting critique of its thinking and method. Post-structuralism is in part an attempt to work out some of the overlooked possibilities, implications and shortcomings of Structuralism and its basis in Saussurean linguistics itself. In a sense, it complements Structuralism by offering alternative modes of inquiry, explanation and interpretation. Post-structuralism questions the assumptions of Structuralism and, as far as literature is concerned, tends to argue that the meaning of any text is indeterminate. It reveals that signification is, in its very nature, unstable. A belief in incommensurate qualities of language (a form of inadequacy) is basic to post-structuralist thinking. Hence the idea of indeterminacy, which is an important element in deconstructive practice and in Jacques Derrida's theory of *différance*. The fundamental position of post-structuralist theory is that meaning is inherently unstable, whereas a structuralist would hold that an explanation/understanding is conceivable and possible, provided that the conventions and codes of any literary text or cultural message are analyzed.

A. Development of Post-structuralism

The true development as a breakthrough of Western literary criticism is Post-structuralism. But the word Post-structuralism is not exact, for it seems to contain not only its continuity but also its overstepping and development of Structuralism and actually marks the end of it. Generally speaking, Post-structuralism is not a school having identical ideas nor an idealistic movement.

None of the most famous scholars such as Michel Foucault, Jacques Derrida, Roland Barthes and others listed under the name of Post-structuralism acknowledges that they have common creeds and methods. They are, however, identical in their doubt about and their subversive attitude toward the tradition of modernity: Foucault's exploration of power and knowledge construction, Derrida's criticism of metaphysics, Barthes' query to the closed construction, and Feminism's criticism under their influence against androcentrism, all these display an anti-traditional posture.

Post-structuralism is often used alternately with postmodernism, which indicates that the "post" turn of theory is often seen as a symptom of the morbid state that it explains, namely, "the postmodern condition," "mimetic era," "crisis" or "the process of meaning dispelling." This confusion of life and theory or a unique field often produces another critical field: Should the "post" theory be read as the analysis of an era (taking the social reality as its referent) or as the fundamental turn of theory (opposing reproduction and reference)? When the study of postmodern culture finds that in the avant-garde paintings, movie, music and narratology there is the same "subversive" spirit, this kind of confusion is further aggravated. Therefore, Post-structuralism is a concept which is very difficult to define.

In the postmodern period, art also takes "the turn of theory" and joins the attack on the developing reality. Though the reference to "truth," stability, the weakening of experience, and meaning are perhaps the themes and the consequences of the post-structuralist discussion and its consequences, the confusion of different fields, for example, the signifier and the signified, events and concepts, is the most conspicuous characteristic of Post-structuralism. Obliterating or at least weakening the difference between different fields, for instance, the signifier and the signified, reading and writing, literature and criticism, etc., can be said a mark of the theory's function in the postmodern period.

The various usages of the prefix "post-" make clear the important meaning of the past (including the theories of Nietzche, Heidegger and Freud, the Western metaphysics, Structuralism, etc.) to the theory of Post-structuralism. Derrida, Lyotard and Barthes all ever constantly turned to this problem, refusing the suggestions to condemn or promote transcending the predecessors. Derrida pointed out that the role of exploration is to recollect the past and it is the rupture of a discourse system. Lyotard thought that all kinds of concepts, such as the so-called new beginning, transcendence or progress, speak of the "hero patterns" in modernity, and are the concepts that the "post" theories hope to replace. Therefore, he described Post-structuralism as the rewriting of modernity and pointed out that the works today must be at least postmodern if they want to be modern. However, what is self-contradictory is that what the "post" theories pay close attention to is only the present *now*.

B. Theory of Post-structuralism

Structuralism exerts great influence upon linguistics and anthropology, especially Saussure's linguistics and Strauss' anthropology though the latter has developed in its own form the analogy with linguistics. The structuralist conception of language is derived from the work of Swiss linguist Ferdinand de Saussure's *Course in General Linguistics* (1916). In this foundational text compiled from lecture notes and posthumously published by his disciples, Saussure presented a concise argument that language is an organized system. As a self-regulating system, language forges its own "reality" instead of being a transparent window on reality, and the relational identity of its elements. Saussure, through displaying language as symbols and symbol system, provided a synchronic basis for linguistic science. A construction consists of the separated signifier and the signified. Language symbols suppose a kind of arbitrary relation between the physical symbols (letters or sounds) and the non-physical concepts (the signified). Because structuralist linguistics divorces itself from meaning but turns to pay close attention to construction, meaning is no longer the intrinsic thing of the expressive factors. The meaning of a symbol can be generated only in its relation with other symbols (different from other symbols). Therefore, meaning exists in the form of language.

Structuralism destroys the modern discourse in two aspects. Firstly, structure stipulates all phenomena—concrete, special, and historical. It seeks acquiring a certain "benefit" outside experience and history. Because it stipulates history, structure transcends history. Thus, structure makes time static, excluding modern concepts (e.g. rejuvenation, progress, etc.) in history. Just as Derrida's criticism indicates, structure as a closed field rejects not only any intrinsic secret but also any external limitation. Secondly, linguistic science (opposite to the individual's speeches) separates meaning from symbols and reconstructs the former as the consequence of the structure's function. Therefore, it displaces the position of the subject of speeches, making it no longer the subject that gives meaning in speeches.

Just as Foucault pointed out, however, Structuralism still keeps its final hallucination, namely, it tries to present the world to consciousness as if it must be read by man. Structuralism maybe has realized the death of the subject of speeches but it is not the death of the speeches that take the subject as the center. The task of post-structuralist theory in various forms is just to break this final hallucination. Therefore, Post-structuralism has transcended the limitation of Saussure's ideas that has already shown itself. The idealistic predecessors of Post-structuralism include Nietzche's "genealogy," Henry Bartaille's "unhealthy part," and Marcel Mauss' "innatism," all of which are the theories that break order and systems and oppose their own discourse with their own concepts. In the general opinion, Derrida was the initiator of the first stage of Post-structuralism. Deconstruction that he advocated in his *Of Grammatology* (1976) and *Writing and Difference* (1978) first directs its spearhead at the basic texts by Saussure and Strauss and subverts the structural concepts that take symbol system as a stable construction.

In the general opinion, Derrida was the initiator of the first stage of Post-structuralism. The term "Deconstruction" Derrida advocated has been introduced from philosophy and literary theory into popular culture and journalistic discourse. Derrida was not as influential as Foucault in France, and his fame came chiefly from the response of the American scholars. The vogue of deconstruction came to the US in the late 1960s, owing particularly to a 1966 conference at Johns Hopkins University on Structuralism. In front of the major structuralists of the day, the little known Derrida read his paper "Structure, Sign, and Play in the Discourse of the Human Sciences" and at the height of Structuralism announced its death. To Derrida, the structure here is a metaphor for any "presence" with a center. It is, to be more precise, the metaphysical tradition of the West (logocentrism) relying entirely on a series of shifts of centers, be it God, truth, man or conscience. "Structure, Sign, and Play in the Discourse of the Human Science" is called the manifesto of deconstruction. The following year, 1967, witnessed his entry onto the international stage of literary and cultural theory, with the publication of his first three books: *Speech and Phenomena*, concerning Edmund Husserl's theory of signs; *Of Grammatology*, whose subject was the "science" of writing; and *Writing and Difference*, which contained important essays on Hegel, Freud, and Michel Foucault. Deconstruction that he advocated in his *Of Grammatology* and *Writing and Difference* first directs its spearhead at the basic texts by Saussure and Strauss and subverts the structural concepts that take symbol system as a stable construction. Later works included *Dissemination* (1972), which included a lengthy engagement with Plato's views of writing and sophistry; *Margins of Philosophy* (1982), which included essays on Hegel's semiology and the use of metaphor in philosophy; *Positions* (1972), containing three illuminating interviews with Derrida, touching on his attitude to Marxism, Hegel, and other issues; *Circumfessions* (1991), an autobiographical work that engages with the text of Augustine's Confessions; and *Specters of Marx* (1994), which looks at the various legacies of Marx.

Proponents of deconstruction refuse to believe that there are any static definition or systematization because the meaning of the terms it employs is capable of flowing. Its color varies with the localized contexts and texts with which it engages. Indeed, deconstruction is often conceived as a method of undermining all tendency toward systematization. However, it is said that numerous concerns and certain heuristic terms can be characterized by deconstruction. In the discourse of structuralist linguistics, deconstruction has found a basic philosophical concept.

This kind of philosophy expresses ideas always by supposing a certain accidental and superficial externality of language. Symbols stipulate the order of philosophy: the signified crops up spontaneously from its own inside, a text is a window of ideas and consciousness, and meaning is stable and can be directly known and fixed in the text.

Derrida's early works mainly reread philosophy and writing, examined the relation between philosophy and linguistics. His concepts of "supplement" and "différance" (derived from the two words: "to differ" and "to defer") borrow Saussure's theory of difference and subvert the metaphysical concept of existence engraved in symbols. He interpreted "absence" as "the trace of existence of absence." Thus, the signifier becomes the supplement of the absent signified, yet it does not present the absent signified but instead it occupies its hollow position. The expressive activity always contains silent function of deferment; expression cannot present but only defer the appearance of the signified. The expressive function of Saussure's binary opposition between the signifier and the signified becomes an unceasing activity of "différance" which is always unfixed and always endless.

Derrida's criticism of symbols has opened a new pattern of text criticism. This pattern is not the change of contents but the analysis of language itself. It re-examines closely the relation between language and truth, fallacy, knowledge, power, reason, desire and the subject of speeches in the whole branch of humanities. Therefore, it is not strange at all that deconstruction exerts great and profound influence upon literary criticism. It has changed the whole field of literary criticism, obscured the difference between fiction and theory, literature and philosophy, reading and writing, critics and writers. Under the influence of deconstruction and Lacan's psychoanalytic theory, a new writing category has appeared: in the set of complicated chains being texts for each other (i. e. the so-called intertextuality), the writing that puts itself in the reading in another time, for instance, Lacan's reading Freud, Derrida's reading Plato and Rousseau, Barthes' reading Balzac.

In the philosophical field of social ideas and science, Foucault presented the method of genealogy, whose consequence is similar with deconstruction. As a discussion of the realm of discourse and its formation, genealogy not only restores the history that the modern subject writes but also displaces this history. In his book *History of Lunacy*, he re-wrote the history of reason, regarding it as a history repressing irrational voice in language. In his later works, Foucault developed the methodology from archaeology to genealogy, finding out the meaning of knowledge subject from within different fields, involving science and epistemology, commandments and punishments, medicine, ethics, sex acts and the techniques of self-expression. These histories examine the complicated relation between discourse and its objects (body, disease, sex acts, order, truth and knowledge) so as to write a genealogy of modern subjects. Finally, these explorations find that discourse has not only the function as a ruler but also the function as an object. As a ruler, it is implied in the relation of powers and controls the object; as an object, it yields to the rule of its own function of discourse. In some essays, for instance, "What Is Enlightenment?" and "Nietzche, Genealogy, History," Foucault also discusses genealogy's influence upon the discourse of exploration itself. He examined the intersectant relation of power, knowledge, and truth, but he looked on them neither as the objects existing outside discourse nor as the abstract concepts of discourse's formation but as the operation of discourse, as the events in discourse and the consequence of discourse.

Barthes' works trace the theoretical turn in every field from Structuralism to Post-structuralism, changing the objects of exploration from works to texts, from statement to interpretative actions, from stories to discourse, from structure to a set of effective discourse activities. Barthes thought that, if a work is a stable and closed structure, which is identical with itself and organizes itself according to a narrative logic that many kinds of texts are transcendental, the text of this work is a place where there is production and diffusing, and a field where there is collision and in which the writer himself is only a visitor or a role of writing and he does not have any special way to know meaning. Everything constantly does multiply signifying but cannot form a final great polymerization or a final structure.

The similar conversion is from statement to interpretation. A text tries its best to create the hallucination of pure contents or pure story (history), thus being doubted as a field of operation activities. Consequently, Post-structuralism abandons the analysis of the meaning hidden inside the text and turns to study the operation activities of language to stipulate the order of its discourse formation. For instance, the theory of movies doubts that the movie text is the function of ideology and movie mechanism, which anticipates, plans, and positions audiences and brings the audience into its seamless text. Thus, the audience, mixed with the subjects of experience, is re-explained as a formation of movie: a position in the text, a function in reading, and an effect in meaning.

Freud's theory of "the unconscious" exerts great influence upon Post-structuralism. His strategy is to shake the discourse mechanism by re-embedding the repressed and excluded voice in the discourse order. In all different branches of learning, this strategy is shared by different post-structuralists. For example, Foucault's *The Order of Things* (1966) reveals the definite unconscious about knowledge while his *History of Madness* (1964) opens out the repressed and irrational voice. This breaks the "master's" position of science and rational discourse. But here there are some problems: the repressed voice can exist in other places but what is more important, it is unable to re-appear in writing. Derrida held that the fundamental change can never emerge in "man" but can only be said by representatives or agents.

Lacan's theoretical mechanism of three parts (imagination, symbols, truthfulness) shows this impossibility: truthfulness is the non-existent object (the signified) that both theory and subject are unable to come into contact with. The price of the subject's identity or the price of existence in language is just disappearance, namely, it is always a mediated (i. e. differanced or differed and deferred) relation with truthfulness.

This difficulty is most obvious in the feminist theory because it wants to restore the excluded women in such dominant discourses as philosophy, criticism and narrative. Under the influence of psychoanalysis and deconstruction, the post-structuralist Feminism longs for this kind of excluded voice in the works of science, philosophy, literature, art and Feminism itself. This longing contains a double task of criticism and reappearance. Feminist Criticism interprets the reappearance of women as a mirror with a double reflection: when these discourses reflect that women suffer from "aphasia," this negated image also has the function of a mirror, reflecting that masculine subject acknowledges himself as a totality. As for this criticism that cannot provide definite identity for women, it shows the difficulty when Feminist Criticism wants to find a system to express its own stand of discourse.

Among Deconstruction, Genealogy, Psychoanalysis and Feminism, each of Post-structuralism theories takes the stand of "turning to linguistics": denying that it has any position of privilege to its object in language. When it acknowledges that there is no such a metalanguage that describes another object with language, a theory denies the demand on reason, writer, scientific objectivity or the demand that forms the basis of a text's contents. A text is no longer an original existence that can be imagined nor a unified manner of existence. Everything begins with or has already been a reappearance or reproduction; meaning is always a reconstruction that is being continually deferred and differed.

Derrida's influence in America and Europe was unparalleled in the latter 20th century. His American disciples included the Yale critics Paul de Man, J. Hillis Miller, and Geoffrey Hartman, as well as Barbara Johnson and, arguably, Harold Bloom. Derrida's essay "Structure, Sign, and Play in the Discourse of the Human Science" (which is called the manifesto of deconstruction), Barthes' essay "The Death of the Author" (which turns the direction of literary criticism), and Paul de Man's essay "Semiology and Rhetoric" (which presents the theory of rhetoric deconstruction) explain clearly the basic views of Post-structuralism from different aspects.

Further Reading

Aitken, Stuart C. & Gill Valentine. *Approaches to Human Geography*. London/Thousand Oaks, Calif.: SAGE, 2006.

Barry, P. *Beginning Theory: An Introduction to Literary and Cultural Theory.* Manchester: Manchester University Press, 2002.

Barthes, Roland. *Elements of Semiology.* New York: Noonday Press, 1968.

Cuddon, J. A. *Dictionary of Literary Terms & Literary Theory.* London: Penguin, 1998.

Derrida, Jacques & Peggy Kamuf, ed. *A Derrida Reader: Between the Blinds*. New York: Columbia University Press, 1991.

Derrida, Jacques. *Writing and Difference.* Trans. Alan Bass. London: Routledge,

Eagleton, T. *Literary Theory: An Introduction.* Oxford: Basil Blackwell, 1983.

Foucault, Michel. *Society Must Be Defended.* Trans. David Macey. Picador: Bertani, Mauro & Fontana, 2003.

Lévinas, Immanuel. *Humanism of the Other.* Chicago: University of Illinois Press, 2003.

Matthews, E. *Twentieth-Century French Philosophy.* Oxford: Oxford University Press, 1996.

Ryan, M. *Literary Theory: A Practical Introduction.* MA: Blackwell Publishers Inc, 1999.

Wolfreys, J. & W. Baker eds. *Literary Theories: A Case Study in Critical Performance.* London: Macmillan Press, 1996.

Bibliography

Cuddon, J. A. *A Dictionary of Literary Terms and Literary Theory*. 5th ed. Malden: Wiley-Blackwell, 2013.

Rice, Philip & Patricia Waugh. *Modern Literary Theory*. New York: Oxford University Press, 2002.

Bressler, Charles. *Literary Criticism: An Introduction to Theory and Practice*. Beijing: Higher Education Press, 2004.

Richter, David H. *A Companion to Literary Theory*. Hoboken: Wiley Blackwell, 2018.

泰勒，温奎斯特. 后现代主义百科全书. 章燕，李自修，等译. 刘象愚，校. 长春：吉林人民出版社，2007.

王治河. 后现代主义辞典. 北京：中央编译出版社，2004.

张中载，王逢振，赵国新. 二十世纪西方文论选读. 北京：外语教学与研究出版社，2002.
朱刚. 二十世纪西方文艺批评理论. 上海：上海外语教育出版社，2001.

Selected Readings

Jacques Derrida: "Structure, Sign and Play in the Discourse of the Human Sciences"
Roland Barthes: "The Death of the Author"

Chapter Nine

Postmodernism

As with Structuralism and Post-structuralism, there is a heated debate over how exactly modernism and postmodernism differ. The two concepts are entirely different, "modernism" being a long-standing category which served as dominant culture of the first half of the 20th century, whereas the term "postmodernism" is an intellectual stance or mode of discourse which has only been a popular phenomenon since the 1980s. Modernism was a radical approach that yearned to bring down much of the structure of pre-20th-century practice in music, painting, literature, and architecture. Postmodernism is a general term used to refer to changes, developments and tendencies which have taken place (and are taking place) in literature, art, music, architecture, philosophy, etc. since the 1950s. It is different from modernism, even a reaction against it. Because it includes almost everything, postmodernism is involved in almost all the fields of humanities and social science such as philosophy, sociology, architecture, painting, music, history, literature, culture, etc. In the discussion about Postmodernism at home, some people often lump the three terms, "Postmodern," "Post-modernity" and "Postmodernism" together. In fact, they express three different concepts though there is an inseparable relation between them. Simply speaking, "postmodern" is a concept of time, referring to the late capitalism, which is also named post-industrial society, information society, the period of transnational capitalism or the era after modernization. Post-modernity is a concept of sociology, indicating the social characteristics of the postmodern period, being involved with many aspects such as the modes of production, the relations of production, the social structure, ideology, etc., and having obvious meanings of history and philosophy. Postmodernism is a concept of styles, referring to the characteristics of the cultural and artistic manifestations in the postmodern period including such categories as architecture, literature, music, painting, movie, TV, etc. Among the three concepts, what is more important is to differentiate post-modernity from postmodernism.

Post-modernity can mean a personal response to a postmodern society, the conditions in a society which make it postmodern or the state of being that is associated with a postmodern society as well as an historical epoch. In most contexts it should be distinguished from postmodernism, the adoption of postmodern philosophies or traits in art, literature, culture and society. In fact, today, historical perspectives on the developments of postmodern art (postmodernism) and postmodern society (post-modernity) can be best described as two umbrella terms for processes engaged in an ongoing dialectical relationship, the result of which is the evolving world in which we now live.

A. Post-modernity

Post-modernity is a concept wide in range and rich in more social, historical and philosophical meanings while postmodernism is comparatively narrow, indicating emphatically cultural and aesthetic characteristics. Post-modernity (or the post-modern condition) is the economic or cultural state or condition of society which is said to exist *after* modernity. Some schools of thought hold that modernity ended in the late 20th century—in the 1980s or early 1990s—and that it was replaced by postmodernity, while others would extend modernity to cover the developments denoted by post-modernity, while some believe that modernity ended after World War II. The idea of the post-modern condition is sometimes characterized as a culture stripped of its capacity to function in any linear or autonomous state as opposed to the progressive mind state of modernism.

As for such grand narratives as truth, reason, science, progress and universal liberation, because they are considered the basic characteristics of modern thoughts since the Enlightenment Movement, post-modernity means the end of modernity. To post-modernity, those expectations are challenged and considered hallucinations from the very beginning because they cause all kinds of historical possibilities to fall into the trammels of concepts. This "autocratic system" of modernity rudely destroys the complexity and variety of the true history, ruthlessly abolishes differences, changes all "the Otherness" into oppressive identity, and often displays a kind of totalitarian politics. Those grand narratives are some elusive things which, through swaying the possible ideals before people, divert people's attention to political changes. They contain dangerous beliefs of absolutism and believe that the changeable ways of life and cognition can be based on a certain ultimate, undoubted and single principle: reason or historical law, technique or the mode of production, political utopia or universal humanity.

Contrary to modernity, to post-modernity that opposes the theory of basis, people's way of life is relative, uncertain, formed by purely cultural set rules and tradition, and has no origin that can be commonly recognized or the grand goals; most of the so-called "theories" only state these inherited customs and an exaggerative way of mechanism. According to the ideas of post-modernity, people are unable to reasoningly find their activities not only because there are different, conflicting, unmeasurable reasons but also because any reason that people can present is always formed in the contexts of pre-reason's power, belief, interest or desire which themselves cannot be the subjects that reason unfolds before people's eyes. To post-modernity, in human life, there is not totality that contains everything, nor united reason or fixed center; the only thing that does exist is the diversities of culture or narration. These diversities cannot be ranked by orders and degrees nor be differentiated as good or bad and thus they must respect the "Otherness" that does not exist in their own ways of act and that can not be destroyed. Knowledge is relative to cultural contexts. Therefore, to claim to know the "true colors" of the world can only be a vain hope because people's understanding is always a one-sided and biased explanation and the world itself is not specially designated. In other words, truth is the product of explanation, facts are the formation of discourse, objectivity is only the disputable explanation that has already got power, while man as the subject is a fabrication which is completely identical with the reality that he is thinking about or a self-split entity without any fixed quality or nature.

B. Postmodernism

Postmodernism is a "mood" expressed theoretically across a diverse range of theoretical discourses, involving a focus on the collapse of grand narratives into local incommensurable language games or "little narratives," a Foucauldian emphasis on the discontinuity and plurality of history as discursively produced and formulated, and a tendency to view the discourses of Enlightenment reason as complicit with the instrumental rationalization of modern life. The historian Arnold Toynbee first used the term in 1947 to describe the current, fourth and final, phase of Western history, dominated by anxiety and irrationalism. In the contemporary version, there is no longer a transcendent space from which to offer a critique of this culture: only disruption from within, micropolitics, parody and fragmentation. Postmodernism wages war on totality. Postmodernists claim the exhaustion of all meta-narratives which claim to legitimate foundations for truth, though some surreptitiously import new foundationalism (the body, the aesthetic, desire). History becomes a plurality of islands of discourse arising out of the institutionally produced language which we bring to bear on it. Or it is a network of agonistic language games where surface phenomena can no longer be "explained" as the manifestations of deeper underlying truths. Absolute systems of knowledge give way to contingencies and ironies, and aesthetic fictionality displaces philosophical certainty.

Postmodernism can be said a cultural form adapting itself to post-modernity. The typical postmodernist artistic works are random, eclectic, mixed, centerless, uncertain, incoherent, pieced together, and imitative. They are loyal to the principles of post-modernity, abandoning the metaphysical depth, seeking a kind of artificial depth, and as a result they are rich in playfulness and pleasure-seeking, but short of emotions, having only the superficial or temporary intensification. Postmodernism doubts all the truths that have already recognized, so its forms must be ironic and its epistemology relative. It denies all the efforts that attempt to reflect the stable reality, so it must consciously insist on a formal existence or an existence on the linguistic level. It knows that its fabrication is short of basis and grounds and therefore it must show off its ironic consciousness to this fact so that it can maintain a kind of negative truthfulness. Because it worries about the isolated identity and takes precautions against absolute origins, postmodernism emphasizes the nature of "texts being involved in each other" or of "intertextuality." The works that postmodernism parodies and processes are merely this kind of process themselves. A part of the things that it parodies is the history of the past. But this history is no longer the linear causal chains that produce the "present." It is the "present" that exists in a kind of eternity because a vast amount of materials get away from their own contexts and combine themselves with the contemporary times. Finally, the postmodern culture dislikes the fixed dividing lines or categories that differentiate "the high-class art" from the "popular art." It deconstructs these dividing lines through producing imitations, consciously produces popular works and makes itself a commodity that can be joyfully consumed. Like Benjamin's "mechanical copy," postmodernism tries hard to break the frightening atmosphere of the high-class modernist culture with more popular art, doubts all the so-called prerogative or essential value grades. In the postmodernist culture, there is not any differentiation between the good and the bad, the high and the low, but what does exist in it is only difference. Because postmodernism seeks to surmount the fence between art and the ordinary life, some people think that postmodernism is the revival of the radical avant-garde because the traditional avant-garde ever also sought such a goal. Indeed, in advertisements, fashions, ways of life, shopping centers and mass media, aesthetics and techniques have already penetrated each other and politics has been transformed into an aesthetic landscape. However, postmodernism regards the traditional aesthetic judgments beneath its notice and this view exerts obvious influence in Cultural Studies. Since the 1980s, Cultural Studies often do not respect the value differentiation between the classical works and the popular art and even not consider the value differentiation between sonnets and soap operas.

As we know, the dispute about post-modernity and postmodernism exists all the time and its forms are varied. According to the statements in the book *Time-Space Compression and the Postmodern Condition* (1989) by David Harvey, postmodernism is a historical response to the crisis of capitalist over-accumulation. The signs of this crisis include the split of the central subject; the loss of referential objects; the collapse of the relation between the moral judgment and the scientific judgment; images having the advantage of narration; aesthetics having the advantage of ethics; temporariness and fragmentation exceeding eternal truth and united politics. Harvey pointed out that Reagan's economics and image production of sorcery type can be said the epitome of postmodernist view. According to this point of view, the problems such as homelessness, advancedness, the poverty intensifying day by day and the loss of ability all can be explained away through resorting to the traditional values such as self-reliance, pioneering individualism, sacred family and religion. The scribbling sceneries in the street, the corruption in the city, miserable events, etc. become the strange and rolling backgrounds of media's camera lens; poverty, disappointment and despair become the sources of aesthetic pleasure or the marks of the "Otherness" and difference.

1. Jürgen Habermas

A major moment in the history of postmodernism is the influential paper "Modernity—an Unfinished Project" delivered by the contemporary German theorist Jürgen Habermas in 1980. For Habermas, the modern period begins with the Enlightenment, that period of about one hundred years, from the mid-17th to the mid-18th century, when a new faith arose in the power of reason to improve human society. Such ideas are expressed or embodied in the philosophy of Kant in Germany, Voltaire and Diderot in France, and Locke and Hume in Britain. In Britain the term "The Age of Reason" was used (until recently) to designate the same period. The so-called Enlightenment "project" is the fostering of this belief that a break with tradition, blind habit, and slavish obedience to religious precepts and prohibitions, coupled with the application of reason and logic by the disinterested individual, can bring about a solution to the problems of society. This outlook is what Habermas means by "modernity." The French Revolution can be seen as a first attempt to test this theory in practice. For Habermas, this faith in reason and the possibility of progress survived into the 20th century, and even survived the catalogue of disasters which made up that century's history. The cultural movement known as modernism subscribed to this "project," in the sense that it constituted a lament for a lost sense of purpose, a lost coherence, a lost system of values. For Habermas, the French Post-structuralism thinkers of the 1970s, such as Derrida and Foucault, represented a specific repudiation of this kind of Enlightenment "modernity." They attacked, in his view, the ideals of reason, clarity, truth, and progress, and as they were thereby detached from the quest for justice, he identified them as "young conservatives." For Lyotard, the Enlightenment whose project Habermas wishes to continue is simply one of the would-be authoritative, "overarching," "totalising" explanations of things-like Christianity, Marxism, or the myth of scientific progress. These "metanarratives" ("super-narratives"), which purport to explain and reassure, are really illusions, fostered in order to smother difference, opposition, and plurality.

2. Jean-Francois Lyotard

Jean-Francois Lyotard praised that postmodern condition has realized the true spirit that modernism imagined. He opposed Júrgen Habermas' censure on postmodernism and rejected the idea that postmodernism betrays the ideals of the Enlightenment Movement, for instance, the objective science, the universal morality and law, and the independent art, etc. He denied the world outlook that originates from Hegel's totality, pointing out that that world outlook leads to an organically total and transcendental mirages imposed by the state's violence. To him, modernity to an individual is equal to terrorism. Therefore, he insisted on eliminating the concept of the self-recognized subject, dispelling the single historical aim and replaces them with the nihilism of Nietzche type or conceptualism. To be more exact, he advocated a kind of neo-Kantian aesthetics about sublimity to reproduce the things that cannot be reproduced, metaphorically indicating the things that cannot be reproduced but can be imagined. Lyotard negated the sense of nostalgia for totality and identity and denies the compromise between concept and feeling. He loudly appealed to the public to make war upon totality; witness the things that cannot be reproduced; push forward differences and save the honors of famous persons.

Lyotard's *The Postmodern Condition* (1984) has proved the major focus for debates on cultural postmodernism. Drawing first on Nietzsche's critique of the totalizing claims of reason as being without moral or philosophical grounds, and second on Wittgenstein, Lyotard argued that the criteria regulating the "truth claims" of knowledge derived from discrete, context-dependent "language games", not absolute rules or standards. For Lyotard, the postmodern is not an epoch, and less a periodizing concept than a mode. The postmodern mode proceeds without predetermined criteria or rules, since these are discovered rather than assumed. By analogy this will also apply in the political arena, and to a working through to notions of "postmodern" justice. It is here, however, in the consideration of social and political complexities, that Lyotard's thought is found by some to be at its weakest or most ambiguous. For while on the one hand, in common with deconstruction generally, it can be said to authorize a consciously decentred "postmodern" micro-politics, alert to heterogeneity, the local, provisional and pragmatic in ethical judgements and conduct, it can be read, on the other hand, as sponsoring an unconnected relativism, high on rhetoric and low on proposals for concrete social action.

3. Jean Baudrillard

Jean Baudrillard's early work questioned the tenets of both Marxism and Structuralism. Having argued for the dominance in modern capitalist societies of consumption over production and of the signifier over the signified, he turned his attention to a critique of technology in the era of media reproduction, and has come to repudiate all models which distinguish between surface and depth or the apparent and the real. Baudrillard's first influential work, *Simulacra et Simulation* (1981), explores this depthless world of unreflecting images. According to Baudrillard, signs no longer correspond to, or mask, their "real-life" referent but replace it in a world of autonomous "floating Signifiers"; there has been "an implosion of image and reality". Experience everywhere is now derivative and literally superficial, and has achieved its final "utopian" form in the instantaneous abundance and banality of the "cultureless" society of the United States, quintessentially in Disneyland. Baudrillard's writings through the late 1980s and into the 1990s (including *America*, *Fatal Strategies*, *The Illusion of the End*) have been increasingly nihilistic. He sees postmodernity repeatedly in terms of the disappearance of meaning, of inertia, exhaustion and endings, whether of history or subjectivity.

4. Fredric Jameson

Fredric Jameson thought that postmodernism is the intrinsic logic of the late capitalist culture, and the penetration of the commercial forms into the culture itself, and in short the commercialization of culture and the culturalization of commerce. To Jameson, postmodernism expresses an entirely new social location of art. He thought that postmodernism is not a problem of themes, nor a problem of subjects but a problem of art's going into the world of commodity production. Jameson's explanation is related with Marxism and he holds that the period of the global and transnational capitalism marks a new period of capitalist development. Therefore, postmodernism is a cultural form of the late capitalist period at present, which is quite similar to that realism was the artistic form specially in the development stage of capitalist industry and modernism corresponded to the period of imperialism and monopoly capitalism.

While stating postmodernism, Jameson emphasized that the unification of economy and culture is identical with the modernist view of Adorno and the Frankfurt School as well as strongly opposite to it. To Theodor Wiesengrund Adorno, the commercialization of art marks finally dispelling any independent critical views. That is to say, it is hard to criticize the dominant forms in the economic development by proceeding from the independent view. But to Jameson, the complete unification of the cultural production and the economic production makes it possible to realize the cultural politics that helps culture intervene economy fundamentally.

Jameson thought that, if the first cultural response to capitalism is realism which aims at providing the expression form to understand this new period of economic development, modernism is to acknowledge that this expression itself yields to social and economic forms which will make the understanding of the expression relative according to the readers who are constantly changing. Jameson pointed out that, after it lost its innocence about expression, modernism tries to devise the form that determines its own readers and project an imaginary world in one's own mind to the future that is not yet intervened by any commodity forms. Just because of this, the history of modernism obviously has the initiatory position of new forms and a kind of ethics of the avant-garde. Whether it is an aesthetic or political form, this ethics will look attentively at future and seek ideal readers of Joyce type or proletariat. Jameson considered that quite early before Ardorno's cultural analysis modernism formed a field opposing commerce from structure. It projected itself into the realistic efforts whose premise is based on perfect future people who will become the ideal readers of the ideal art.

In the modernist architecture, this tentative idea is the most obvious but its insufficiency shows itself also the most clearly. Jameson held that architecture is always a field that is the most able to express the combination of art with economy, so it is also a neuralgia point of the modernist decay just as the proposition of Frank Lloyd Wright meets the reality of the postindustrial city. Just out of this consideration, Jameson's analysis of postmodernism often lays special emphasis on the disputes about architecture in the late 1970s. But he pointed out that, if architecture is the traditional art that has greatest difficulty to break away from economy, movie is the postmodern art (of course it is also hard to fully understand its separation from the first development stage of capitalism)—movie is a product of the most complicated form of industrial production.

Thus, Jameson considered that people must take the historical paradox into consideration: movie, this kind of postmodern medium, summarizes the basic aesthetic development of realism/modernism/postmodernism. The classical Hollywood movies expressed realism, the

European movies in the 1950s and 1960s reproduced all kinds of contradictions and paradoxes of modernism (the French movie director Jean-Luc Godard's movies were its models), and the fully developed postmodern movies did not appear until the early 1970s. The postmodern movie is such kind of movie: the dividing line between high-level art and low-level art (which is often uncertain) has more or less disappeared and culture and economy repeatedly cross at all levels of the two fields. Though it is not a universal form, this kind of movie at least provides more possibilities to combine the oldest regional artistic tradition with the most contemporary global advertisement movement than the other media. Jameson pointed out that this is a cultural form, it is penetrated at all levels by the usual practice and paradox in marketing or by a kind of postmodern practice, so it is shaking between the passive reproduction and the actively re-molding of the audience. Therefore, if the realistic politics contains reformism (in which the understanding of the society directly leads to the social control) and the modernist politics is avant-garde (in which the future tendency of the institution provides the basis for political act), what is actually the postmodernist politics is not yet clear. Anyway, what is very obvious is that it will link the increasing microcosmic political level and those almost paralyzed excitements to the global forms.

In Jameson's opinion, the contemporary movies can be said the most postmodern artistic form (here including the relation between them and rock music and TV) and thereupon we may use this artistic form to make the most effective analysis of the political unconscious at present. He thought that the analysis can be carried out in three aspects: space, representation and allegory. The most important is the change of "images."

To postmodernists, we live in a pluralized culture surrounded by a multiplicity of styles, knowledge, stories that we tell ourselves about the world. To attempt to impose an overarching narrative on such experience is to perpetuate the violence of modernity with their exclusions and terrors. The relativization of styles which is postmodernism, throws into doubt the claims of any one discourse or story to be offering the "truth" about the world or an authoritative version of the real. Issues of ethics, law, equality and authority become deeply problematic in such a context: How is one to legitimate knowledge and where to locate value? Central to the "postmodern condition" is a recognition and account of the way in which the "grand narratives" of Western history, and in particular of enlightened modernity, have broken down. Counter-Enlightenment, of course, is as old as Enlightenment itself but, whereas in Romantic thought the critique of reason is accompanied by an assertion of an alternative foundationalist paradigm based on imaginative knowing and the truth of the human heart, postmodernists claim abandonment of all metanarratives which claim to legitimate foundations for knowledge or truth. As Lyotard argued in his book, *The Postmodern Condition* (1984), that instrumental conceptions of reason and belief in "totalities," systematic metaphysical systems, had produced totalitarianism, reigns of terror, postmodernism welcomes the collapse of grand theory and of legitimating metanarratives and advocates context-specific agon, heterogeneity, and difference.

Further Reading

Anderson, Perry. *The Origins of Postmodernity*. London: Verso, 1998.

Bauman, Zygmunt. *Liquid Modernity*. Cambridge: Polity Press, 2000.

Bertens, Hans. *The Idea of the Postmodern: A History*. London: Routledge, 1995.

Brass, Tom. *Peasants, Populism and Postmodernism*. London: Cass, 2000.

Callinicos, Alex. *Against Postmodernism: A Marxist Critique*. Cambridge: Polity, 1999.

Featherstone, M. *Consumer Culture and Postmodernism*. London/Newbury Park, Calif.: Sage Publications, 1991.

Giddens, Anthony. *Modernity and Self Identity*. Cambridge: Polity Press, 1991.

Goulimari, Pelagia. *Postmodernism. What Moment*? Manchester: Manchester University Press, 2007.

Greer, Robert C. *Mapping Postmodernism*. IL: Intervarsity Press, 2003.

Groothuis, Douglas. *Truth Decay*. Downers Grove, Illinois: InterVarsity Press, 2000.

Harvey, David. *The Condition of Postmodernity: An Enquiry into the Origins of Cultural Change*, 1989.

Hassan, Ihab. *The Postmodern Turn: Essays in Postmodern Theory and Culture*. Columbus: Ohio State University Press, 1987.

Hutcheon, Linda. *The Politics of Postmodernism: History, Theory, Fiction*. London: Verso, 1988.

Jameson, Fredric. *Postmodernism, or, the Cultural Logic of Late Capitalism*. London: Verso, 1991.

Lyotard, Jean-François. *The Postmodern Condition: A Report on Knowledge*. Mancheter: Manchester University, 1984.

McHale, Brian. *Postmodernist Fiction*. London: Routledge, 1987.

——. *Constructing Postmodernism*. NY & London: Routledge, 1992.

Bibliography

Cuddon, J. A. *A Dictionary of Literary Terms and Literary Theory*. 5th ed. Malden: Wiley-Blackwell, 2013.

Rice, Philip & Patricia Waugh. *Modern Literary Theory*. New York: Oxford University Press, 2002.

Bressler, Charles. *Literary Criticism: An Introduction to Theory and Practice*. Beijing: Higher Education Press, 2004.

Barry, Peter. *Beginning Theory: An Introduction to Literary and Cultural Theory*. Manchester: Manchester University Press, 2017.

Selden, Raman, Peter Widdowson, Peter Brooker. *A Reader's Guide to Contemporary Literary Theory*. 5th ed. Great Britain: Pearson Longman, 2005.

泰勒，温奎斯特. 后现代主义百科全书. 章燕，李自修，等译. 刘象愚，校. 长春：吉林人民出版社，2007.

王治河. 后现代主义辞典. 北京：中央编译出版社，2005.

张中载，王逢振，赵国新. 二十世纪西方文论选读. 北京：外语教学与研究出版社，2002.

朱刚. 二十世纪西方文艺批评理论. 上海：上海外语教育出版社，2001.

Selected Readings

Jonathan Arac: "An Introduction: Postmodernism"

Patricia Waugh: "Postmodernism and Feminism?"

Fredric Jameson: "The Adventures of the Sign"

Volume 2
下卷

陈世丹　王小会　黄　贺　著

Chapter Ten

Feminist Criticism

Feminist Criticism is a development in critical theory and in the evaluation of literature which was well under way by the late 1960s and which has burgeoned steadily since. For the recent fifty years, Feminism has been one of the most vigorous trends of thought. Its influence involves many aspects including philosophical ideas, social theories, politics, anthropology, literature, art, and a variety of Cultural Studies. It is an attempt to describe and interpret (and reinterpret) women's experience as depicted in various kinds of literature—especially the novel, and, to a lesser extent, poetry and drama. It questions the long-standing, dominant, male, phallocentric ideologies (which add up to a kind of male conspiracy), patriarchal attitudes and male interpretations in literature (and critical evaluation of literature). It attacks male notions of value in literature—by offering critiques of male authors and representations of man in literature and also by privileging women writers. In addition, it challenges traditional and accepted male ideas about the nature of women and about how women feel, act and think, or are *supposed* to feel, act and think, and how in general they respond to life and living. It thus questions numerous prejudices and assumptions about women made by male writers, not least any tendency to cast women in stock character roles.

Feminism is related with the Women's Movement. In the late 1960s in the West appeared the increasingly rising women's liberation movement that put forward very radical propositions and demanded thoroughly changing the existing world, which was called the "Radical Feminism." Later, especially in the middle of the 1970s, important changes happened to its propositions. Feminism began to be related with culture and ideology and gradually formed the "Cultural Feminism," involving all fields of culture naturally including literature and literary criticism. The "Radical Feminism" presents equality of men and women and women's liberation, and regards the problem of sex as a social and political problem, thus leading to the change of women's consciousness and arousing women's social enthusiasm. The "Cultural Feminism" stresses liberating women from under the oppression of the so-called "masculine value" and creating a substitutive culture according to "feminine value," whose nature is a moral and anti-mainstream-culture movement and whose aim is to change women's images.

On the whole, Feminist Criticism may be divided into three stages: in the first stage it mainly attacks men's sexual discrimination; in the second stage, it studies women's literary works as the focus of its work; in the third stage, it focuses its attention on the theoretical study of literature, criticism, psychology and culture.

Actually, Feminism was created by the women in the circles of literature and academe, including writers, editors, social activists, university graduate students, teachers, and professors. In the late 1960s, these people joined the Women's Liberation Movement, showing their strong sympathy and sympathetic response to all kinds of propositions, demands and social efforts of the Women's Movement. For example, the first important work of Feminist Criticism—Kate Millette's *Sexual Politics* (1970)—is not only a work of literary criticism but also a political treatise full of fervor. Most feminists think that just because of the Women's Movement they begin to pay attention to the relation between their works and their own life and the difference between their psychological identity and the actual intentions, also notice their limited and secondary function as heroines in fictions, women writers or women scholars. They emphasize women's own life experience and literary experience, and wake up women's consciousness with a kind of "transforming experience."

Therefore, in its first stage, Feminist Criticism focused its attention on revealing the distortion and depreciation of women in literary practice, for instance, the patternized women images as angels or demons in literature, the word humiliation to women in classical and popular works, the exclusion of women writers in the history of literature, etc. Through stressing the relation between the literary maltreatment and the social maltreatment of women, feminist critics strengthened their position and aroused people's attention to them. Their efforts changed the atmosphere of literary response and made readers have doubt about all kinds of characteristics of anti-feminism. In the 1980s, even men critics also noticed that because of their high sensitivity they could no longer ignore or forgive the distortion and depreciation of women in literature. Thus, changes began to happen to the interests in and evaluation of classical works.

In the second stage of Feminist Criticism, feminists found that there was a literature belonging to their own. This kind of literature has the continuity of history, the identity of subjects, and important values in artistry but has been all the time being drowned because of the dominance of masculine values over the culture. Thereupon, Feminist Criticism emphatically explores women literary works, describes the map of women's imagination, analyzes women's plot structure, and makes women literature a special exploration field unfold before people's eyes. This effort leads to the re-discovery and re-reading of women literary works in all historical periods in all countries. Consequently, large numbers of women writers once more saw the light of day, their letters and diaries were published, the critical biographies studying the relation between the personal talent of women and the literary tradition were continually published, and the continuity in women writing was for the first time recognized. These works not only describe the development of women literature but also theoretically explain the situation of women writers, their worries, their experiences, and the re-writing of the masculine myths in their works. The methods, concepts and insights embodied by these works which are examined, revised, supplemented and developed by feminists form a systematic narration of the history of women literature, unfold before people's eyes the changes of women writing for two hundred years, and explain women's social, psychological and aesthetic experiences in the man-governed culture. The images, subjects and plots which are formed by these works appear again and again.

This development led to the appearance of women's aesthetic concept emphasizing women literary consciousness. Proceeding from a special women's psychology, this aesthetic concept examined a kind of women culture that had been all the time neglected but now should be restored, women's language, the style and the form of women literature. However, there was controversy on the exact nature of women's aesthetic concept at the very beginning. In the 1970s, it was often recognized as the consciousness of women's Lesbian love or separationist politics of Lesbian love. Therefore, the images of women fighters of Amazon in Greek mythology were often used as the symbols of creative power of the independent women. The woman poet Adrienne Rich ever pointed out that every woman is driven by the power of women and attracted by powerful women, and seeks a literature expressing that energy and strength—this is the Lesbian love on every woman. Just this kind of love impels us to feel in the way of imagination, express in the way of language, and grasp the whole relation between woman and woman.

However, many feminists opposed this concept of Lesbian love and opposed the concept of women's identity expressed only through one literary style. Therefore, in the 1980s, the aesthetic concept of Lesbian love was split off from women's aesthetic concept and became a special Feminist Criticism while feminist critics turned their attention to the analysis of the mother-daughter relation, replacing the Amazon women fighters with the images of mothers. Some critics studied the metaphor of childbirth in the activities of artistic creation but some presented that women's writing is characterized by the women's poetics that defines beginnings and origins, namely, it relies on the relation between daughter and mother. This change of focus is identical with the study about motherhood in other fields, which finally caused that Feminist Criticism and anthropological study penetrated each other.

On the other hand, the man's power system still exists in the theory of literary criticism. Hence, the effort to explain the difference of women's writings as an aesthetic expression led to the interest in psychoanalysis and aesthetic theories. In addition, the study of the process of women's writing made feminists challenge the theoretical tentative ideas of the traditional literary criticism and question the division of literary history into periods. However, if they attempted to create their own critical concept, they had to consider the formation of other critical theories and the relation between them and other theories. Therefore, in the third stage of Feminist Criticism, feminists demanded not only that women's writing should be recognized but also that the generally recognized theoretical tentative ideas about writing and reading should be revised because they thought that all these were based on man's literary experiences.

Of course, this theoretical demand was closely related with the rise of all kinds of thoughts since the 1960s. Phenomenology, psychoanalytic theory, Structuralism, semiotics, reception theory, deconstruction, Post-structuralism and new Marxism all exerted more or less influence upon Feminism; Lacan's new Freudian psychoanalytic theory, Barthes' Structuralism, Derrida's deconstruction, and Foucault's discourse theory even had instructive function to some feminists. Consequently, because of the interaction of many theories, in the late 1980s, Feminism presented the tendency toward split and variety. Among the later variety of Feminist Criticisms, the most conspicuous were French Feminist Criticism, Black Feminist Criticism, and the Materialistic Feminist Criticism. French Feminist Criticism stresses the relation between women and language, pays close attention to feminist formation in language, philosophy, psychoanalysis and other discourse systems, and holds that breaking the traditional women discourse is a political action that expresses objection. Black Feminist Criticism emphasizes struggles in many aspects: it opposes the Whites, racism (including White women feminists' racism), opposes the economic rule and exploitation (including the Black man's exploitation), and opposes the Blacks and the Whites' sexual discrimination including family violence. In short, Black Feminist Criticism maintains to oppose at the same time racial discrimination, sexual discrimination, the violence of the opposite sex, and class oppression. The Materialistic Feminist Criticism insists on examining the material condition, proceeding from the deep conscious (or the unconscious) of psychology, and discusses how the social arrangement (including the degrees of sexual distinction) under such material conditions has been developed and how it determines women's imaginations. The Materialist Feminist Criticism considers that people should attach importance to all the aspects of social life, bring women's specific function in the society into full play, and form a new relation between men and women.

Further Reading

Baron, Dennis. *Grammar and Gender.* New Haven: Yale University Press, 1986.

Cameron, Deborah. *The Feminist Critique of Language: A Reader.* 2nd ed. London: Routledge, 1998.

Dasilva, Fabio B. & Matthew Kanjirathinkal. *Her Voices: Hermeneutics of the Feminine.* Lanham: University Press of America, 1996.

De Lauretis, Teresa, Andreas Huyssen & Kathleen Woodward. *The Technological Imagination: Theories and Fictions.* Madison: Coda Press, 1980.

Felman, Shoshana. *What Does a Woman Want? Reading and Sexual Difference.* Baltimore: Johns Hopkins University Press, 1993.

Fendler, Susanne. *Feminist Contributions to the Literary Canon: Setting Standards of Taste.* Lewiston: Edwin Mellen Press Ltd., 1997.

Fisher, Jerilyn & Ellen S. Silber. *Analyzing the Different Voice: Feminist Psychological Theory and Literary Texts.* Lanham: Rowman and Littlefield, 1997.

Florence, Penny & Dee Reynolds. *Feminist Subjects, Multi-Media: Cultural Methodologies.* Manchester: Manchester University Press, 1995.

Gilmore, Leigh. *Autobiographies: A Feminist Theory of Women's Self-Representation.* Ithaca: Cornell University Press, 1994.

Godard, Barbara. *Bibliography of Feminist Criticism.* Montreal: ECW Press, 1987.

Hedges, Elaine & Shelley Fisher Fishkin. *Listening to Silences: New Essays in Feminist Criticism.* Oxford: Oxford University Press, 1994.

Hill, Alette Olin. *Mother Tongue, Father Time: A Decade of Linguistic Revolt.* Bloomington: Indiana University Press, 1986.

Hohne, Karen & Helen Wussow. *A Dialogue of Voices: Feminist Literary Theory and Bakhtin.* Minnesota: University of Minnesota Press, 1994.

Humm, Maggie. *Practicing Feminist Criticism: An Introduction.* Coleshill: Harvester Wheatsheaf, 1995.

Humm, Maggie. *A Reader's Guide to Contemporary Feminist Literary Criticism.* Coleshill: Harvester Wheatsheaf, 1994.

Kaplan, Carla. *The Erotics of Talk: Women's Writing and Feminist Paradigms.* Oxford: Oxford University Press, 1996.

Kramarae, Cheris. *The Voices and Words of Women and Men.* Amsterdam: Elsevier Science &

Technology, 1980.

Kuribayashi, Tomoko & Julie Tharp. *Creating Safe Space: Violence and Women's Writing.* Albany: State University of New York Press, 1998.

Lakoff, Robin. *Language and Woman's Place.* San Francisco: Robin Lakoff, Harper Colophon Books, 1975.

McConnel-Ginet, Sally, Ruth Borker & Nelly Furman. *Women and Language in Literature and Society.* Westport: Greenwood Pub. Group, 1980.

Meese, Elizabeth A. *Crossing the Double-Cross: The Practice of Feminist Criticism.* Chapel Hill, North Carolina: University of North Carolina Press, 1986.

Miller, Casey & Kate Swift. *Words and Women.* New York: Harper Collins, 1991.

Miller, Jane. *Seductions: Studies in Reading and Culture.* Cambridge: Harvard University Press, 1991.

Miller, Nancy K. *Getting Personal: Feminist Occasions and Other Autobiographical Acts.* London: Routledge, 1991.

Miller, Nancy K. *Subject to Change: Reading Feminist Writing.* New York: Columbia University Press, 1988.

Mills, Sara. *Feminist Readings/Feminists Reading.* Charlottesville: University Press of Virginia, 1989.

Mills, Sara. *Feminist Stylistics.* London: Routledge, 1995.

Moers, Ellen. *Literary Women.* Oxford: Oxford University Press, 1985.

Mora, Gabriela & Karen S. *Theory and Practice of Feminist Literary Criticism.* Tempe: Bilingual Review Press, 1982.

Morris, Pam. *Literature and Feminism: An Introduction.* Oxford: Blackwell Publishers, 1993.

Parker, Alice A. & Elizabeth A. *Feminist Critical Negotiations.* Amsterdam/Philadelphia: John Benjamins Publishing Company, 1992.

Radner, Joan Newlon. *Feminist Messages: Coding in Women's Folk Culture.* Champaign: University of Illinois Press, 1993.

Roe, Sue, Susan Sellers, Nicole Ward Jouve & Michele Roberts. *The Semi-Transparent Envelope: Women Writing—Feminism and Fiction.* London: Marion Boyars, 1994.

Sellers, Susan. *Feminist Criticism: Theory and Practice.* Toronto: University of Toronto Press, 1991.

Thorne, Barrie & Nancy Henley. *Language and Sex: Difference and Dominance.* Rowley: Newbury House Publishers, 1975.

Warhol, Robyn R. & Diane Price Herndl. *Feminisms: An Anthology of Literary Theory and*

Criticism. New Brunswick: Rutgers University Press, 1991.

Waxman, Barbara Frey. *From the Hearth to the Open Road: A Feminist Study of Aging in Contemporary Literature*. Westport: Greenwood Pub. Group, 1990.

Yaeger, Patricia. *Honey-Mad Women: Emancipatory Strategies in Women's Writing*. New York: Columbia University Press, 1988.

Van Zoonen, Liesbet. *Feminist Media Studies*. Thousand Oaks: Sage Pub., 1994.

Bibliography

Cuddon, J. A. *A Dictionary of Literary Terms and Literary Theory*. 5th ed. Malden: Wiley-Blackwell, 2013.

Rice, Philip & Patricia Waugh. *Modern Literary Theory*. New York: Oxford University Press, 2002.

Bressler, Charles. *Literary Criticism: An Introduction to Theory and Practice*. Beijing: Higher Education Press, 2004.

泰勒，温奎斯特. 后现代主义百科全书. 章燕，李自修，等译. 刘象愚，校. 长春：吉林人民出版社，2007.

王治河. 后现代主义辞典. 北京：中央编译出版社，2004.

张中载，王逢振，赵国新. 二十世纪西方文论选读. 北京：外语教学与研究出版社，2002.

朱刚. 二十世纪西方文艺批评理论. 上海：上海外语教育出版社，2001.

Selected Readings

Elaine Showalter: "Toward a Feminist Poetics"

Sandra M. Gilbert: "What Do Feminist Critics Want? A Postcard from the Volcano"

Hélène Cixous: *The Newly Born Woman*

Virgina Woolf: "A Room of One's Own"

Chapter Eleven

New Historicism

New Historicism is relatively new in literary studies and literary theory. The practice of the approach has been described under the name of the "historical method." There are many kinds of historical methods, such as those belonging to Marxist method and Jauss's reception theory. At its simplest, the historical method is interested not in asserting the transcendent or autonomous aesthetic value of literary texts but, to use Marxist terminology, in researching the contexts of their production, consumption and status. It would be certainly true to say that the "New Historicists" are opposed, above all, to the pure formalism of the Anglo-American New Criticism, Structuralism, Post-structuralism and Hermeneutics as approaches to literature. They also oppose the old Leavisite preoccupation with moral value, and implicitly question the way that the literary canon in schools and universities has been arrived at, namely through exclusion and suppression. New Historicism is a form of literary theory whose goal is to understand intellectual history through literature, and literature through its cultural context, which follows the 1950s field of history of ideas and refers to itself as a form of "Cultural Poetics." It was first developed in the 1980s, primarily through the work of Stephen Greenblatt, critic and Harvard English Professor, and it exerted widespread influence in the 1990s. The term, New Historicism, was coined by Greenblatt when he "collected a bunch of essays and then, out of a kind of desperation to get the introduction done," and "wrote that the essays represented something I called a 'New Historicism.'"① In *The New Historicism* (1989), H. Aram Veeser noted and summarized some key assumptions that continually reappear in New Historicism: that every expressive act is embedded in a network of material practices; that every act of unmasking, critique and opposition uses the

① Stephen Greenblatt, *Learning to Curse*. London & New York: Routledge, 2007, p. 197.

tools it condemns and risks falling prey to the practice it exposes; that literary and non-literary texts circulate inseparably; that no discourse, imaginative or archival, gives access to unchanging truths or expresses inalterable human nature; that [...] a critical method and a language adequate to describe culture under capitalism participates in the economy they describe.①

A. The Rise of New Historicism

New Historicism, a thought of Cultural Criticism, first appeared at the beginning of the 1980s and then spread to England and Australia. Its formation was the result of the joining of multiple thoughts. Firstly, it is the logic of the development of deconstructionism itself. The rise of deconstructionist movement in the 1960s and 1970s destroyed structure with "nihility" of texts as its purport. Just as an element of disintegration of Structuralism—denial of itself, that is, "deconstruction of deconstruction," deconstructionism's subversion of all texts inevitably leads to the subversion of its own base at last. Deconstructionism's criticism of "logocentrism" continually pushes itself to the borders and finally goes beyond the jail that it draws for itself. There are two borders of the jail, one being the barrier between text and meaning, the other being the barrier between text and its external reality or history. Thus, Post-structuralism in the late 1970s, especially Michel Foucault who broke through the durance of the simultaneous, inclined to "diachronic" examination of texts.

Secondly, it is "new historiography," especially the one represented by Hayden White's "metahistory." Since World War II, the changes of "new historiography" in the field of historical study in the West come down to two main aspects: one is that the field of vision has been broadened from important political events and personages to common events and personages in a given period; the other is that the positivist historical objectivism of old historiography inclines to historical relativism of subjectivism. This sort of changes and the concepts of historical textualism and intertextuality of New Historicism in literary criticism happen to have the same view. The so-called historical textualism means that it is through "texts," that is, the documents and historical materials left by history or recorded by people then or later, through this sort of textual manner that history has "dialogues" with contemporary people. The so-called "intertextuality" is a main characteristic of the criticism of New Historicism. It means that on the one hand it implies that there is a relationship of interaction between history (objective facts) and texts (narrative documents); and on the other hand there is a relationship of shining-upon-each-other between

① H. Aram Veeser, *The New Historicism*. New York & London: Routledge, 1989, "Introduction," p. xi.

texts in different nature such as politics, philosophy, economy, religion, law, literature, art, etc. This new historiography regards history as "all the activities of the people in the past" without localization with only great political events, which means in New Historicism that the literary texts and other historical texts conform to and communicate with each other. Hayden White, professor of history of the University of California in the United States, negates the "innocent" idea that people could grasp the precise historical truth. He treats historical documents and literary texts equally or simply regards historical texts as "literary fictions," emphasizing the narrativeness and poeticalness of history, and thus blurring the relationship between the historical objectivity and the present subjectivity, and the line of demarcation between non-historical texts (literary texts) and the historical texts (non-literary texts).

Thirdly, it is the Cultural Materialism in England. "Cultural Materialism" was initiated by Raymond Williams and it represents British eclecticism. In their works, the scholars of "Cultural Materialism" combined literary texts with the researches of history, society and English language, attempting to historically study these problems by using Marxist views of classes and class struggles. While comparing New Historicism with British Cultural Materialism, Louis Adrian Montrose, one of the representatives of British New Historicism, pointed out that the center of gravity to which American New Historicism pays attention lies in the "reconstruction" of the field of social culture in which the initial texts of the Renaissance were produced. Of course, this sort of "reconstruction" is based on the function of the "now" to the "past" in the relation of New Historicist view. Relatively speaking, in England, people more emphasized how the "now" makes use of the "now's" description of the "past."

Fourthly, it is Marxism and the other criticisms which keep close relation to Marxism and could be called its "periphery" such as Feminism, Black people's critical theories, etc. It is also influenced by Louis Althusser's ideological plural-determinism, Jürgen Habermas's theories of communication and his reconstruction of historical materialism, Mikhail Bakhtin's theories of dialogism, etc. Therefore, New Historicism itself is a very complex thought of literary criticism with external and interior "pluralisms."

In the past, the research of the texts of Renaissance in Europe and America followed the close-reading method of "the New Criticism" since the 1940s, and the influence of Structuralism did not yet form a vogue. No doubt, the flourishing of New Historicism brought a new strong wind to the self-reference of the oppressive textualism. Observing from the specific political background, this turn means that the political movement with students and intellectuals who were against the Vietnam War and counterworked against the authorities as its main body under the influence of Marxism and "the New Left" in the 1960s and the 1970s went from streets to studies.

Most of the members of the movement engaged in the operation of New Historicism were students who were involved in the political movement. Like deconstruction that turned from the subversion of the state apparatus to the subversion of language, the operation of New Historicism is full of the terms such as power, consolidation, subversion, and offering amnesty and enlistment to rebels. Therefore, some people regard New Historicism as the product of "the disillusion of the Left."

In the concrete operation, the criticism of New Historicism often mixes the texts of history and literature with the thick description of anthropology and the historical anecdotes or makes use of a subject to elaborate its own ideas by right of the discovery of new materials, for instance, a poem by William Shakespeare, to do the "practice of discourse" in discursion. Its main point of excitement and its final aim do not lie in history itself nor in the aesthetic things themselves, but still in the aspect of ideology or politics, that is, Michel Foucault's operation of "discourse—text—power." Stephen Greenblatt's *Renaissance Self-Fashioning: From More to Shakespeare* (1980) studies 6 English poets from More to Shakespeare in the 16th century. Based on the view that sees "the great art" as "the extremely sensitive record for complex struggles and cultural harmony," the work deals with humanism the old question—man's "self-fashioning" and "self-cancelling" as the center and makes "bidirectional investigation" of "the social presence in the literary textual world and the influence of social presence on literature" through "the interaction of the complex meanings in a given culture." "Self-fashioning" indicates the acquirement of a sort of unobvious modalities such as the distinctive personality, the individual expression of the world, and the consecutive style for an understanding and action. Greeblatt points out that "self-fashioning" is not acquired in the same direction as obey but the other way round it is acquired in the converse via the things regarded as heresy, strange, and hateful. The alien image is recognized through permeation of authoritative consciousness and appears as its opposite. The authority of one man is just the alien of another and any side of them is replaced immediately as soon as it is ruined. Authority and the alien self will internalize obedience and destruction in human nature and sometimes the threatening experience of authority will cause self to be obliterated or lost. Therefore, self-fashioning develops in the conflict between the alien "self" and the power or the authoritative force and it happens at the moment when an authority encounters with the alien self, and the force produced in the process of the encounter means attack to both the authority and the alien self; accordingly, any acquired personality always contains the evidence that subverts or bereaves itself.

B. Basic Ideas of New Historicism

Relatively speaking, it is new just in comparison with traditional historicism. In the aspect of history, traditional historicists pay close attention to historical events themselves. New Historicists are not very interested in historical events themselves. The object that they study is how the historical books, historical fictions, documents and references, folk legends, literary works, etc. then and afterwards reflect, record, and explain the historical events, from which they will know the politics, thoughts, and cultural backgrounds then and there that they reflect.

1. History Is Also a Text

To New Historicists, historical events and personages are the objects of explanation, history in essence is linguistic explanation, and this kind of narrative discourse has inevitably subjective, imaginary and fictive elements. They pointed out that the understanding of and the commentary on historical events and personages are to a great extent determined by the subjectivity of the person who writes the history while his subjectivity is again to a great extent determined by his own concepts of politics and thoughts and also by the discourse in the dominant position and the cultural background.

After the 1960s, the traditional historicism was attacked by Structuralism and Post-structuralism. Such structuralists as Foucault and others held that "history" is not an objective existence any more, and the objectivity or truthfulness is only a fantasy; since history is also a text, it is likewise an object of explanation. Hayden White, professor of the University of California of the United States, said that history as a form of narrative discourse has fictitious elements. Thus, history that considers itself to be "true" all along loses its truthfulness before New Historicists.

New Historicists thought that many history books, either written by the scholars of the ruling class or examined by the specially established agency of the ruling class, represent the views of the ruling class and cannot reflect the true history. Just because of this, New Historicists turned their eyes to the things unheard of, anecdotes, legends, jokes, unofficial history, ballads, etc. said or written by the classes and communities that are marginalized by the ruling class.

Such thinkers as Heidegger, Sartre, Foucault and others subverted the authoritativeness, truthfulness and mysteriousness of the historical texts before the rise of New Historicism. In the past, people usually thought literary texts were fictitious and historical texts were authentic and the true historical events. Now, the fictitiousness of historical texts has been revealed and thus the dividing line between literature and history has been more obscure. It is naturally well-reasoned that literature and history are open to each other. This is the difference between New Historicism and traditional historicism in the aspect of studying history.

2. The Study of Literary Texts Must Be Combined with the Study of the Content

When they study a certain literary work, traditional historicists always tried to reproduce the writer's original intention, world outlook, and the cultural background when he was writing. What they paid close attention to were editions, proofreading notes, the writer's autobiographies, the biographies about the writer, etc. New Historicists considered that this kind of research method is similar to historical study, neglecting the characteristics of literature itself. They advocated to know the society when the work was being written in the literary work, combining the study of the text with the study of the context (i. e. the society or the cultural background). Just as Stephen Greenblatt said in his famous work *Renaissance Self-fashioning: From More to Shakespeare*, New Historicism wants to go deep into the social existence in the world in a literary work and the social existence that the work reflects.

New Historicism divides the context into three levels: 1) The context of writing, namely the writer's original intentions, autobiography, reminiscences, the biographies, diaries, files and references about the writer, and the political, social and cultural background when the writer was writing; 2) The context of reception, namely, how different readers, organizations and agencies, and communities read and interpret the same work; 3) The context of criticism, namely, the critic's background of criticism.

3. New Historicism Is Trans-disciplinary Study

Greenblatt first used the term "New Historicism" in an essay published by a special issue of *Genre* in 1982. Later, he changed to use "cultural poetics" because New Historicism regards the whole culture as the object of study and thinks that there is a relation that cannot be broken between history and culture and there are many places where they are open to each other. Just as many critics say that New Historicism is a phrase without an adequate referent. It not only studies history, literature, art, and culture but also involves such different branches of learning as Marxism, psychology, anthropology, etc. Therefore, some critics call it "trans-disciplinary study" or say that it is not a critical theory but a critical method. About New Historicism, the opinions vary in the critical circles, even inside New Historicists the ideas are different, and the scholars called "New Historicists" also often publish different and even mutually contradictory views.

Edward Pechter published his essay "New Historicism and Its Grievance: Drama's Dramatization in Renaissance Period" in the issue 102 of *PLMA* (1987) in which he said by parodying the phrase in *Manifesto of Communist Party*: A ghost is loafing about in the circles of critical theories, a ghost named New Historicism. He thought that though it contains many critical practices, New Historicism's core is "a Marxist critical theory." His views were opposed by other critical theorists. Some critical theorists who called themselves Marxists not only denied New Historicists' being Marxists but also criticized their escaping from political participation. Louis Montrose, another famous New Historicist, the professor of the University of California at San Diego, published an essay entitled "Cultural Poetics and Politics" in 1986 which points out: One of the purposes of New Historicism is to re-describe the relation between texts and the cultural institutions that produce them. He said that New Historicism aims at exploring the factors of politics and power in the texts because, when a writer writes, his concepts of thought are inevitably controlled or influenced by all kinds of power agencies and their discourses.

New Historicism, receiving the views of Foucault and Althusser, thinks that social agencies, especially their discourses, shape man's "experiences." Foucault stressed that discourses always root in social agencies and that social and political powers can only be carried out through discourses. Greenblatt, taking English literature (especially drama) in the 16th century for example, thought that if you want to know the literary works during the English Renaissance period you must relate the literary works with the power agencies of the House of Tudor (1485–1603) and the culture in that period.

During the periods of the House of Stuart (1603–1649, 1660–1714), the situations that the monarchical power was usurped or passed into others' hands often took place. This is an important subject of English drama (represented by Shakespeare's drama), especially of historical plays and tragedies, in the era of Renaissance. New Historicists such as Greenblatt, Montrose and others see the House of Tudor's worries about the loss of power in these plays. Before the uprising of Essex took place in London in 1601, *Richard I* with the subversion of the royal court's power as its theme was performed on the stage. Queen Elizabeth then acknowledged that the *Richard II* in the play insinuated her and complained that this tragedy had been performed at theaters and squares as many as 40 times.

What New Historicists considered important is just the politicalization of the drama during the English Renaissance period. To them, history and literature are the stories of power and political relations. About how to explain *Richard I*, different people have different views. Some people thought that it warns the subjects of the feudal ruler: "Don't rebel. Rebels will come to no good end." But others held that it aims at non-deifying the power of the royal court and has the dramatic effect to call on the common people to subvert the royal court. This is just why Queen Elizabeth is heavyhearted about the performance of the play.

Thus, just as Thomas Carlyle, English famous essayist, historian, and philosopher, said that the history of poetry is the quintessence of the history of a country, it is clear that culture and literature cannot be separated from politics, power, and history.

Because Humanism gave birth to a new culture different from the Middle Ages, the literature during the Renaissance period becomes the point of special emphasis of New Historicists' literary study. Renaissance inherited from ancient Greece and Rome classicists' practice of attaching importance to the social, political and aesthetic effects of literature and art. If we want to explore and study the relation between literature and history, society, politics, and power, if we want to know whether literature not only reflects historical facts and contexts but also participates in the historical development and politics, that is, if we want to know the interaction between literature and society, history and contexts, then the literature during the Renaissance period is an ideal object of study. New Historicists also thought that aesthetic statement embodied the market relations. They compared the drama during the Elizabethan period with market capitalism and claimed that all the products of the society circulate on the stage. They saw the circulation between statements of the actors on the stage as the transaction at the monetary market.

Identifying the works of literature and art with commodities and money reflects the enormous controlling and penetrating powers and the expanding of the commodity consciousness. English "Cultural Materialism" opposes this view though Cultural Materialism and New Historicism hold same arguments in many issues (e.g. the relation between texts and contexts, the construction that texts express power relations, the importance of discourse, and the relation between discourse and powers).

New Historicists thought that the writer of none of any texts (no matter they are historical or literary) can boldly declare that his text has pure originality because any text is written by consulting other texts that we have already had. This intertextuality of texts cannot be denied. There is no fixed, immutable and universal standard for the meaning of texts. It changes along with the change of time and place and it is always in the changing state. Greenblatt said that it is for "having dialogues with the dead" that he advocated the research method of New Historicism, that is, people nowadays should start with the cultural contexts now and here to explain the texts then and there, from which they will see the different explanations in the different cultural contexts.

The appearance of New Historicism shows the re-rise of historical criticism in literary study. For many years, all kinds of theories of formalism paid close attention to the text noumenon, abandoned the consideration of society and history, and went to one-sidedness and extremity, thus causing the New Criticism to rule the circles of critical theories alone for years. New Historicism and Cultural Materialism make literary return from the narrow and small world of texts to the broad social and cultural space, combining texts with contexts, which has something to recommend it.

In 1986, J. Hillis Miller, American critic, later deconstructionist, took up the post of Chairman of Modern Linguistics Association (MLA) in the United States. A passage in his inaugural speech more or less shows the wind direction of the circles of American critical theories when New Historicism appeared. He said in his speech that in the past few years the literary study experienced a sudden change, almost completely shook off theories, that is, it no longer paid attention to language noumenon but correspondingly turned to history, culture, society, politics, institution, the limitations of classes and sexes, social background and material basis.

New Historicism has restored the historical dimension obliterated by all kinds of formalist critical theories and ended the scenery of formalism in the circles of critical theories for years. Undoubtedly, its method of literary study considering both forms and contents is desirable. However, it has all sorts of shortcomings. The most obvious one is that when historical facts and fabrications are confused, history loses its objectivity and authenticity and changes into an earth ball for anybody to rub and pinch. Though the subjectivity and fictitiousness of history exist in reality, what we should emphasize are still history's respect for facts and history's objectivity.

Further Reading

Armstrong, Nancy & Leonard Tennenhouse. *The Violence of Representation, Literature and the Violence*. London & New York: Routledge, 1989.

Foucault, Michel. *Discipline and Punish.* New York: Vintage Books, 1979.

Greenblatt, Stephen. *Renaissance Self-Fashioning*. Chicago: University of Chicago Press, 1980.

Lentricchia, Frank. *Criticism and Social Change*. Chicago: University of Chicago Press, 1983.

Moore, Bruce. *The Australian Concise Oxford Dictionary.* Oxford: Oxford University Press, 2004.

Murfin, R. & S. Ray. *The Bedford Glossary of Critical and Literary Terms.* Boston & New York: Bedford Books of St Martins Press, 1998.

Orgel, Stephen. *The Authentic Shakespeare*. London: Routledge, 2002.

Rice, P. & P. Waugh. *Modern Literary Theory: A Reader.* Melbourne: Edward Arnold, 1989.

Veeser, H. Aram. *The New Historicism*. London: Routledge, 1989.

White, Hayden. *Metahistory: The Historical Imagination in Nineteenth-Century Europe.* Baltimore: The Johns Hopkins University Press, 1973.

——. *Tropics of Discourse: Essays in Cultural Criticism*. Baltimore: The Johns Hopkins University Press, 1978.

——. *The Content of the Form: Narrative Discourse and Historical Representation*. Baltimore: The Johns Hopkins University Press, 1987.

——. *Figural Realism: Studies in the Mimesis Effect*. Baltimore: The Johns Hopkins University Press, 1999.

——. *The Fiction of Narrative: Essays on History, Literature, and Theory, 1957–2007*. Baltimore: The Johns Hopkins University Press, 2010.

Bibliography

Cuddon, J. A. *A Dictionary of Literary Terms and Literary Theory*. 5th ed. Malden: Wiley-Blackwell, 2013.

Rice, Philip & Patricia Waugh. *Modern Literary Theory*. New York: Oxford University Press, 2002.

Bressler, Charles. *Literary Criticism: An Introduction to Theory and Practice*. Beijing: Higher Education Press, 2004.

泰勒，温奎斯特. 后现代主义百科全书. 章燕，李自修，等译. 刘象愚，校. 长春：吉林人民出版社，2007.

王治河. 后现代主义辞典. 北京：中央编译出版社，2004.

张中载，王逢振，赵国新. 二十世纪西方文论选读. 北京：外语教学与研究出版社，2002.

张进 . 新历史主义文艺思潮通论 . 广州：暨南大学出版社，2013.

张进 . 新历史主义与历史诗学 . 北京：人民出版社，2021.

张京媛 . 新历史主义与文学批评 . 北京：北京大学出版社，1993.

朱刚. 二十世纪西方文艺批评理论. 上海：上海外语教育出版社，2001.

朱静 . 格林布拉特新历史主义研究 . 北京：人民出版社，2015.

• Selected Readings •

Stephen Greenblatt: “Towards a Poetics of Culture”

Lois Tyson: “New Historicism”

Hayden White: “The Historical Text as Literary Artifact”

Chapter Twelve

Post-colonial Studies

Post-colonialism (covering the terms "post-colonial studies," "post-colonial theory" and "post-colonial literature") is an interdisciplinary academic field devoted to the study of European colonialism and its impact on the society, culture, history and politics of the formerly colonized regions such as the African continent, the Caribbean, the Middle East, South-Asia and the Pacific. The term "post-colonialism" was first used by historians after World War Ⅱ to refer chronologically to the post-independence period. Since the 1990s, in the contemporary field of critical theories in which each of the schools rules its own domain, the literary critical theory of post-colonialism is a decisive force. Literary critics use the term post-colonialism as an oppositional reading practice to study the effects of colonial representation in literary texts. The field has its roots in anticolonial writings, such as the Négritude movement and related works by Aimé Césaire, Léopold Sédar Senghor and Frantz Fanon, and in colonial discourse analysis inaugurated by Edward Said's *Orientalism* (1978). Other prominent post-colonial theorists include Homi Bhabha, Marxist critics such as Aija Ahmad, Robert J. C. Young and Neil Lazarus, and feminist critics such as Gayatri C. Spivak and Anne McClintock. To many critics, post-colonialist literary criticism roughly follows such two lines as: 1) starting with social and historical background, to interpret literary works (the so-called post-colonial literature refers to those works that critically rethink the colonialist relations) and discuss the social and historical influence exerted by them; 2) to re-interpret the classical literary works having something to do with the colonialist activities (usually proceeding from the perspective of Post-structuralism, to deconstruct the colonialist discourse contained in them).

As a cultural and political discourse, to trace it to its social source, in Eagleton's words, post-colonialism reflects the historical change of the Third World's revolutionary nationalism that began to decline from the 1970s to the post-revolutionary conditions. In fact, it is also a deep rethinking and criticism done on the Western colonialism that has already ended and is characterized by armed aggression and economic plunder and neocolonialism which is quietly going on with economic and cultural penetration as its main device. In the source of thought, it has a complicated theoretical relation with Post-structuralism, etc.: the discourse analysis of Post-structuralism and its criticism of the theory of European centrism provide analytic strategy and perspective for post-colonialist criticism; in turn, post-colonialist theory throws a layer of political coat on Post-structuralism that separates itself from social reality. No wonder, there is someone who says that the post-colonialist thought is the last shelter for postmodernism. Postmodernism uses the post-colonialist thought to defend its own cynicism and behavior obsessed with material consumption; Western Marxism, especially Antonio Gramsci's theory of hegemonism and Louis Althusser's theory of ideology, not only provide theoretical tools for post-colonialism but also deepen its political connotation against colonialist discourse. These complicated thought relations form the situation in which the theories of different schools shuttle back and forth in different critical domains.

A. Basic Ideas of the Post-colonialist Works

In the powerful and dynamic anti-colonialist political movement, emerged a lot of works that culturally criticize and resist colonialism. They provide a sum of rich reference resource frequently used by post-colonialism. In his anti-colonialist works such as *Black Skin, White Masks* (1952), *The Dying Colonialism: The Fifth Year of Algerian Revolution* (1959), *The Wretched of the Earth* (1961, the phrase was taken from "The Internationale" by Eugene Pottier: "Arise, the wretched of the earth."), etc. written in the Algerian struggles against French colonialists, Frantz Fanon deeply analyzed all kinds of devices of cultural control adopted by European colonialists in the course of carrying out colonialism and the serious consequences caused in the colonies. At the same time, starting with language, ideology, knowledge, etc., he explained all kinds of anti-colonialist strategies on the cultural level. Fanon analyzed the Black national culture and art that the Black people had formed under the colonialist rule for a long time. In his opinion, the Black national culture and art had experienced three periods of development: firstly, blindly absorbing colonialist culture; secondly, beginning to unearth consciously the resources of its national traditional culture; thirdly, directly joining the struggles for national liberation by using literature and art. He thus revealed Black people's servile state of mind in bemeaning themselves and being eager to be recognized by the White people. What he had done gave great inspiration for the later generation who would explain the post-colonialist literature and culture.

Strictly speaking, Fanon's works belong to the category of political theories while the person who really is a forerunner of the post-colonialist cultural theories and produces the effect of rousing the deaf and enlightening the benighted is Palestinian-American scholar Edward Said. The specific space of "post-colonialism," however, was first articulated in Edward Said's book *Orientalism*. Like "postmodernism," the term has come to refer both to a condition (here post-coloniality) and to the discourses which theorize the condition. His representative work *Orientalism* sorts out, examines the study tradition of Orientalism in Europe (mainly in Britain and France) since the 18th century, and excavates a whole set of hegemonist discourse explaining Oriental society which runs through that tradition. This kind of discourse manifests itself as a concept system which controls Western people's opinions about the Orient and closely coordinates Europeans' colonialist activities in the East, thus having legalized colonialism. To Said, the term "Orientalism" has three layers of meaning. Firstly, it refers to a branch of learning, the research activity carried out by the European research workers including such professional academic people as historians, sociologists, anthropologists and philologists and others, and also the experts in the government who gave counsels for colonialist affairs. Secondly, it is a thinking pattern established on the basis of the differentiation between the "Eastern" and "Western" ontology and epistemology, that is, a state of mind that the West imagines the East as its own opposite side and holds the idea that those who do not belong to our nation must be disloyal. Thirdly, the most important meaning of using the term to express indicates a well-knit system of discourse which supports and controls the West's thinking, imagination and description of the East. In this book, Said made use of Foucault's method of discourse analysis. To Foucault, discourse is a highly surveillant and manipulative system which controls and stipulates the statement patterns and devices of the people in a specific society; discourse always relates to power and is devoted to maintaining the dominant social system. Orientalism is just this kind of cooperative system hidden in the study of Orientalism that aims at stabilizing colonial relations and acts in collusion with colonial forces to deal with the Orient. In the discourse of Orientalism, the Orient always appears as an image of the Other opposite to the West. Under the pens of Orientalists, the Eastern society becomes a pronoun for such fixed images as barbarism, backwardness, autocracy, and corruption, awaiting the European civilization to save; thus the Oriental people become the same clan that is lowly, cowardly, deceitful, dissolute, indulging in sexual pleasures, short of reason, and awaiting to be enlightened by education, on the basis of which the authority of Europe and the positive images of Europeans have been established and prominently manifested. Hence, the concept that the West is superior to the Orient and should place itself above the Orient has accordingly become an indisputable truth. Flaunting the banner of this truth, the colonial rule can high-soundingly follow its own way. The discourse of Orientalism is penetrated with a strong argument for European centrism. It regards the European culture as a criterion or as an absolute criterion to measure other cultures.

In the other important work by him, *Culture and Imperialism* (1993), Said expanded the line of sight of *Orientalism*, no longer focusing only on the Middle Eastern regions but trying to describe the relation between the modern Western land and its overseas colonies. In the book, Said examined those forms of Western scholarship and cultural representation which codified knowledge about non-metropolitan cultures under colonial control. The book drew eclectically on Foucauldian Post-structuralism and on the Gramscian concept of hegemony in order to demonstrate that Europe's construction of the orient is a paradigm of all colonial and imperial structures. In each case, the mysterious and duplicitous "Other" which is the colonized culture functions as a means of stabling and affirming the identity of the imperialist power. Said's book emphasizes the centrality of cultural representation in this process. If colonized peoples are to become subjects of history then "post-colonialism" must strengthen as well as analyze the discursive process of resistance to colonialist perspectives. In his own analysis of Conrad, Said showed how imperialism maintains power through the designation of a discursive space which makes silent and invisible all those perspectives which are excluded by and from its frame. He showed, through analysis of Conrad's representation of Africa, how the construction of "them" is necessary for the affirmation of "us."

By using a very great length, Said analyzed the function that the English novels bring into play in legalizing imperialism, and revealed the accomplice relation between cultural forms and the overseas colonial activities of imperialism, with which he illustrated that literature joins the European overseas expanding. He pointed out that an extremely important purpose that the great realistic fiction in Europe has realized is that it has quietly obtained the social approval of European overseas expanding, and that in the fiction, the overseas colonies not only provide background for the works but also become an important device of the novelists to dissolve realistic conflicts. They are either the good places where the protagonists who were frustrated at their native land make a great fortune and then go back to their hometown in silken robes or the ideal paradises where the protagonists, who were hurt by emotions and escaped far from the disputes of human affairs at home, restart their life. Even those works that have no direct relation with the colonial actions of the British Empire, for instance, the novels by Fielding, Richardson,

Sterne and others, also reflect the values similar with colonialism: the protagonists develop the spirit of hard struggle to overcome difficulties and obstacles and patiently establish power through the technique of combining principles with benefits.

Homi Bhabha and Gayatri Spivak also showed similar preoccupation with relations between power and knowledge in the construction of "Otherness" and, in particular, in the construction of the colonial Subject. In different ways, both Spivak and Bhabha articulated anxieties about voice and authority in the context of colonial and post-colonial discourses. Bhabha's subject is the ambivalence of colonial discourse. When discourse is translated into a colonial context, the result is mimicry which constitutes both resemblance and menace, a kind of hybridization which exposes the lie of universalism that underwrites colonial authority. Spivak too addresses the problem of voice and authority for the post-colonial intellectual in terms of ambivalence. To be a teacher of English in a post-colonial context is to occupy a marginal position where, ironically, the only power accrues from one's facility as a speaker of a Western liberal discourse. Again the post-colonial intellectual appears in a situation that is somewhere between mimicry and mockery, where the menace of mimicry lies in its dualism in disclosing the ambivalence of colonial discourse and thereby disrupting its authority.

B. Natural Relation Between Post-colonialism and Feminism

Post-colonial critics are concerned with the impact of colonialism generally, including its relationship with issues such as gender and class; they challenge how colonialists constructed colonized regions and people as inferior, and also examine how colonialism affected the colonizing nations. They are interested in the wider idea of imperialism: how particular nations construct relationships that secure their superiority. There is a natural relation between Post-colonialism and Feminism and there is an intrinsic similarity between women and the colonial nations. They are both in the marginal positions and are both regarded as the dissident Others. They both study and defend the Others who are marginalized inside the oppressive structure (of colonialism and patriarchy). The early Feminist Criticism, like the early post-colonialist criticism with nationalist nature, tried to reverse the oppressive dominant structure, that is, replace men's discourse with women's discourse and replace European centrism with clan-group centrism. As the theoretical discussion went deep and the critical practice accumulated, they abandoned these simple practices. In the theoretical orientation, they tended more and more to the post-structuralist train of thought and tried to break the foundation that the authorities of patriarchy and colonialism rely on for existence: binary opposition. These natural affinities lead to the frequent exchange and communication between post-colonialism and feminism. Many women post-colonialist critics are at the same time also feminist critics, among whom Gayatri Spivak, Bengalese-American scholar, is the most famous. In her essay, "Can the Subaltern Speak?" she explained the concept of the subaltern that was put forward first by Gramsci. Spivak used "the subaltern" to refer to those oppressed submissive class in the marginal social position. She used the system that widows die for their dead husbands in India for example to illustrate that in the history books stating such a phenomenon we are unable to hear the real desires of "the subaltern" women. The White colonialists parade that abolishing the system that women die for their dead husbands is a magnanimous act undertaken for the public good by the Whites who are saving the brown women out of the control of the brown men. However, the upholders of patriarchy who advocate to restore this system in the Indian land explain it away by saying that women actually want to die. None of these voices represents the voice of "the subaltern" women deeply under the double oppression. The answer to this problem is inevitably negative. When we extend the view about the problem to the whole colony, we have no difficulty to come to the following conclusion: the true ideas in the hearts of the colonial people, no matter they are men or women, are unable to be stated in the world full of colonial discourses, they all become the silent Others. In "Three Women's Texts and a Critique of Imperialism," a comparatively typical Post-colonialist critical essay, Spivak re-interpreted *Jane Eyre*, a classical text of Feminism, analyzed its sequel *Wide Sargasso Sea*, a novel by English novelist Jane Reese who was born in Dominica. Feminist Criticism usually thought that *Jane Eyre* establishes a lofty feminist image that has strong personality and is full of independent and initiative spirit. But Spivak reveals a hidden standard colonial discourse, pointing out that Jane Eyre's personal insight is improved and this lofty image is established at the cost of Bertha Mason, Rochester's wife, the mad woman who is confined in the attic. Under Charlotte Bronttë's pen, Bertha Mason was born in the colony, a descendant of the Creole, on her face there are patches black and white, the room which she lives in seems to be a den of animals, her body embodies the colonial people's fixed images in the eyes of the White colonialists: mad, indulging in excessive drinking, lewd and fond of violence.

C. Theory of Hybridity of the Post-colonialist Culture

The early post-colonialist literary criticism emphasized the uniqueness of the original inhabitants' cultural identities in colonies and regarded reconstructing pure cultural identities as the important contents of the collective political resistance. But the recent development of the post-colonial cultural theory queries this early idea. In his work, *The Location of Culture* (1994), Homi K. Bhabha, English scholar, another representative figure, who is a Persian brought up in India, presented the "hybridity" theory of post-colonial culture which exerts a great influence. Most post-colonialist critics think that, in the post-colonial culture, between the original inhabitants' culture and the colonialists' culture in colonies emerges a complicated state that there is "I" in "you" and "you" in "I," which is quite an advantage of symbiosis of plural cultures. This phenomenon indicates that in the contact of cultures, the one-way process that the colonialists' culture completely puts an end to the tradition of the colonized culture did not appear. On the contrary, just in the intense cultural conflicts, some unique things of the culture of the colonized have toughly remained and become an important component part of the new cultural formation. The appearance of the phenomenon of cultural hybridity is not established on the basis that the independent cultural tradition of the original inhabitants completely disappears but is related with the continual existence of these cultural traditions and the constant absorption of the foreign influence. As for this, the hybridity of the post-colonial culture also has the meaning to resist the assimilation of the colonial culture. However, it is not difficult to see that in the process of the unequal exchange of cultures in the post-colonial society, the traditional culture of the original inhabitants is in the weak position from the beginning to the end, more playing a passive role having no alternative.

Post-colonial critics use literature as a prime example of how colonial ideas are transmitted through writing, which often involves a rewriting of colonial Western texts in order to expose the biases operating in what is claimed to be universal humanism. Post-colonial literature seeks to reclaim self-representation from stereotypical portrayals in colonial literature and colonial discourses, and to do so they often use the "writing back" paradigm, or a rewriting of Western "master" texts. They imagine silenced and suppressed histories—of slavery and colonialism—and endeavor to come to terms with the trauma of the Middle Passage. They are often engaged with the problems of identity (individual or national) that have resulted from the cultural disruptions initiated by colonialism (disempowerment, dislocation, diaspora, migration). The term "postcolonialism" has been a subject of much debate among scholars. It may imply that colonialism is over when it is not, and it often tends to homogenize into a single category cultural experiences that are very different. Some scholars debate whether "post-colonialism" is a useful term for White settler colonies like Canada, Australia and New Zealand, whether it should be used to refer to countries such as Ireland, and most recently, the former Communist countries of eastern Europe. Finally, the term defines all world cultures by their relationship to European colonialism, and so obliquely perpetuates the European belief in its own centrality. Anyway, post-colonialism has also provided timely critiques of the continuing legacies of colonialism in both the colonized and colonizing nations. As Sara Ahmed usefully pointed out in her book *Strange Encounters*: *Embodied Others in Post-Coloniality* (2000), post-colonialism opens up the complexity of the relationship between the histories of European colonization and contemporary forms of globalization, which can be considered the affirmative evaluation of post-colonialism's contribution to the world culture.

Further Reading

Ahmed, Sara. *Strange Encounters: Embodied Others in Post-Coloniality*. London: Routledge, 2000.

Bhabha, Homi. *Nation and Narration*. London: Routledge, 1990.

Bassnet, Susan & Harish Trivedi. *Post-colonial Translation*, *Theory and Practice*. London: Routledge, 1999.

Fanon, Frantz. *The Wretched of the Earth*. New York: Grove Press, 1963.

——. *Black Skin White Masks*. Trans. Charles Lam Markmann. New York: Grove P, Inc., 1967.

Gregory, Derek. *Dictionary of Human Geography*. Hoboken: Wiley-Blackwell Publishing, 2009.

Hart, Jonathan & Terrie Goldie. Post-colonial Theory // *Encyclopedia of Contemporary Literary Theory*: *Approaches*, *Scholars*, *Terms*. Eds. Irene Rima Makaryk, Linda Hutcheon, & Paul Perron. Toronto: University of Toronto Press, 1993.

Spivak, Gayatri Chakravorty. "Can the Subaltern Speak?" // Cary Nelson and Larry Grossberg. *Marxism and the Interpretation of Culture.* Urbana: University of Illinois Press: 271–313.

Young, Robert. *Postcolonialism: A Very Short Introduction*. Oxford: Oxford University Press, 2003.

Sadiki, Larbi. *The Search for Arab Democracy*: *Discourses and Counter-Discourses*. India: C. Hurst & Co. Ltd., 2004.

Said, Edward. *Orientalism*. New York: Pantheon, 1978.

——. *The World, the Text, and the Critic*. Cambridge: Harvard University Press, 1981.

Spivak, Gayatri Chakravorty (1990). Can the Subaltern Speak? (PDF). Archived from *The Original* (PDF) on January 5, 2012.

Bibliography

Cuddon, J. A. *A Dictionary of Literary Terms and Literary Theory*. 5th ed. Malden: Wiley-Blackwell, 2013.

Rice, Philip & Patricia Waugh. *Modern Literary Theory*. New York: Oxford University Press, 2002.

Bressler, Charles. *Literary Criticism: An Introduction to Theory and Practice*. Beijing: Higher Education Press, 2004.

李应志，罗钢 . 后殖民主义：人物与思想 . 北京：北京师范大学出版社，2015.

扬. 后殖民主义与世界格局 . 容新芳，译 . 南京：译林出版社，2013.

泰勒，温奎斯特. 后现代主义百科全书. 章燕，李自修，等译. 刘象愚，校. 长春：吉林人民出版社，2007.

王治河. 后现代主义辞典. 北京：中央编译出版社，2004.

张中载，王逢振，赵国新. 二十世纪西方文论选读. 北京：外语教学与研究出版社，2002.

朱刚. 二十世纪西方文艺批评理论. 上海：上海外语教育出版社，2001.

Selected Readings

Edward Said: "Culture and Imperialism: Introduction"

Gayatri Spivak: "Three Women's Texts and a Critique of Imperialism"

Chapter Thirteen

Gender Studies

Gender Studies is an interdisciplinary field that focuses on the complex interaction of gender, race, class and sexuality in social relations, institutions, and systems. It includes gay, lesbian and queer studies (or criticism), is a manner that parallels African-American studies and women's studies, seeks to advance the interests of lesbian, gay and queer (and often also bisexual and transgendered) people by contributing intellectually to a lesbian, gay and queer movement, and is informed by resistance to homophobia and heterosexism. For Gender Studies, there is a number of topics, the most salient of which are the emergence of sexual identities—in particular, how these have been constructed by capitalist economics and medical discourse; the recovery of gay, lesbian and queer texts and histories which have often been obscured by mainstream literary criticism and official heritage discourse—the homoeroticism pervaded much World War I poetry or the queerness of the Bloomsbury Group; gay, lesbian and queer literary and cultural representations—from detecting covert homosexual desire in ostensibly mainstream texts to evaluating identifiably gay, lesbian and queer narratives. The field of Gender Studies draws upon a number of recent intellectual developments. Firstly, Feminist Criticism, particularly Lesbian Feminist Criticism, emerged as a distinct strand in the 1970s in the result of mainstream Feminism's sidelining of lesbian experience. Secondly, New Historicism and Cultural Materialism have been crucial for understanding sexuality as a historical and social construction and for helping to conceive of ways in which texts might lend themselves to alternative readings by sexual dissidents. Finally, queer theory, an anti-essentialist approach to sexuality and gender draws heavily on post-structuralist thinking.

Gay and lesbian theories originated, like Feminist Criticism and Black Criticism, not in academic institutions, but in the radical movements of the 1960s. The birth of the Gay Liberation Movement could be traced to the Stonewall Riot in New York in 1969 when occupants of a gay bar resisted a police raid. The event had a radicalizing effect on Homosexual Rights groups throughout the United States and Europe. The Gay Liberation Movement in the 1970s had two main goals: to resist persecution and discrimination against a sexual minority, and to encourage gay people to develop a pride in their sexual identities. It utilized two main strategies: "consciousness-raising," borrowed from Black and women's movements, and "coming out"—publicly affirming gay identity—which is unique to gay communities whose oppression partly lies in their social invisibility. Gay Liberation activities saw themselves as part of a more general move towards the liberalization of sexual attitudes in the 1960s, but in particular challenged the homophobic prejudices and repressive character of mainstream heterosexual society.

In the 1970s and the 1980s, gay and lesbian activities and theories used the term "heterosexism" to refer to the prevailing social organization of sexuality, which privileges and mandates heterosexuality so as to invalidate and suppress homosexual relations. In comparison with heterosexism, "homophobia"—the irrational fear or hatred of same-sex love—implies an individualized and pathological condition; "heterosexism" designates an unequal social and political power relation. Therefore, heterosexism has arguably proved the more useful theoretical term in lesbian and gay theories. It clearly owes a debt to the feminist concept of sexism: the unequal social organization of gender, and in this respect, has been of more importance to lesbian feminist theory than to gay theory which developed in overlapping but distinct ways.

A. Gay Theory and Criticism

Gay is a term that primarily refers to a homosexual person or the trait of being homosexual. The term was originally used to mean "carefree," "happy," or "bright and showy." The term's use as a reference to homosexuality may date as early as the late 19th century, but its use gradually increased in the 20th century. In modern English, *gay* has come to be used as an adjective, and as a noun, referring to the people, especially to gay males, and the practices and cultures associated with homosexuality. By the end of the 20th century, the word *gay* was recommended by major LGBT (Lesbian Gay Bisexual Transgender) groups and style guides to describe people attracted to members of the same sex.

At about the same time, a new, pejorative use became prevalent in some parts of the world. Among younger speakers, the word has a meaning ranging from derision (e.g., equivalent to *rubbish* or *stupid*) to a light-hearted mockery or ridicule (e.g., equivalent to weak, unmanly, or lame). In this use, the word rarely means "homosexual," as it is often used, for example, to refer to an inanimate object or abstract concept of which one disapproves. The extent to which these usages still retain connotations of homosexuality has been debated and harshly criticized.

The diversity of gay and bisexual research since the 1970s reflects the efforts to reclaim literary texts, cultural phenomena, and historical narratives that had remained hidden from critical attention. At the same time (largely as a product of Psychoanalysis and Feminism) there has been an explosion in the diversity of strategies for exploiting these materials. While there have been a number of attempts to provide explanatory models which posit defining moments in the history of sexuality this research generally concludes that past constructions of sexuality cannot be exhaustively understood, either in their own terms, or in ours. For many critics the past offers alien constructions of sexuality, in a contrasting relation to the present, rather than possible identifications or celebratory moments. A shared interest in recent gay and historical studies has been the construction of sexuality in a network of power relations, exercised both through the regulatory practices of church and state and the less overt yet manifold ways in which Western culture has circumscribed interpersonal relations.

Sigmund Freud and Michel Foucault have exerted main influences on gay theory. The first major influence upon gay theory is Sigmund Freud's theory of sexuality. Already in the 19th and early 20th century, detailed psychological case studies appeared to complicate and infinitely expand the range of sexualities. Karl Heinrich Ulrichs published twelve volumes on homosexuality between 1864 and 1879 (the term was first used by Benkert in 1869); Krafft-Ebing's *Psychopathia Sexualis* (in its 1903 edition) included 238 case histories. Such works were important for Freud in exploding the notion that heterosexuality was safely grounded in nature. In *Three Essays on the Theory of Sexuality* (1905), for instance, he noted that it was not a self-evident fact that men should find a sexual interest in women. Psychoanalytic theory therefore appeared to promise a new plurality of possible classifications. Yet in certain respects Freud's work proved to have a strictly normative effect in the work of his followers, whose goal appeared to return the patient to an integrated, healthy state, and purge the disorienting "illness" of homosexuality. Jeffrey Weeks's criticism of Freud (1985) focuses on the notion that desire cannot be reduced to primeval biological urges, beyond human control, nor can it be seen as a product of conscious willing and planning. It is somewhere ambiguously, elusively, in between, omnipotent but intangible, powerful but goalless. Insofar as desire is inherently unstable, the individual's procreative goal (or more specifically, genital sex) is threatened by perverse and transgressive forces. Freud had noted in *An Outline of Psychoanalysis* (1940) that sexual life was concerned primarily with obtaining pleasure from the body, often beyond the needs of reproduction. If this is the case, heterosexuality supports bourgeois ideologies to the extent that procreation mirrors production. Gay sex, in contrast, is desire deprived of this goal; it is the very negation of productive work.

The second major influence upon gay theory, which has returned some critics to a re-reading of Freud, has been Michel Foucault, who has inspired the study of the multiple operations of power and set the problematic of defining homosexuality within discourse and history. In *The History of Sexuality* (1976) Foucault saw late 19th-century homosexuality as characterized by a certain quality of sexual sensibility, a certain way of inverting the masculine and the feminine in oneself. Homosexuality appeared as one of the forms of sexuality when it was transposed from the practice of sodomy onto a kind of interior androgyny, a hermaphroditism of the soul. He concluded that the sodomite had been a temporary aberration; the homosexual was now a species. Foucault explored how sodomy was largely determined by civil or canonical codes as "a category of forbidden acts" which accordingly defined their perpetrator as no more than their judicial subject. In Foucault's opinion, the 19th century saw the emergence of the homosexual as a personage, a past, a case history, and a childhood... Nothing that went into his total composition was unaffected by his sexuality. This model has been broadly accepted, if not elaborated or sometimes disputed in its details. A general problem, however, lies in how Foucault theorized the transition from one mode to another. In Foucault's discontinuous profile, one model of same-sex relations is superseded by another, which may again be superseded by another. In each case the supposed model then drops out of the frame of analysis. Nonetheless, historians of sexuality have assembled models of shifting sexual categories across time influenced by, but more scholarly, and less rigid, or polemical than Foucault's own. The historian Randolph Trumbach, for instance, has been much more open than Foucault to the emergence of lesbianism in the 18th century, while Weeks Greenberg and Bray, though accepting the constructiveness of sexuality, have resisted the extreme position on the dating of the category of homosexuality which was characteristic of Foucault's work.

Foucault's influence upon gay studies extends beyond the above debates, however, to work done within the areas of New Historicism and Cultural Materialism. In the work of Jonathan Dollimore and Alan Sinfield, most noticeably in Great Britain, gay theory is part of a wider cultural poetics and cultural politics, focused within literary studies, and as such has affinities with the work of others pursuing a similar general project.

A number of categories have been mobilized in this criticism to discuss the inscription of homosexuality in texts and to reclaim aspects of gay life: "effeminacy," "drag," and "camp," for example, or the categories of "the homoerotic," "male bonding," or "homosociality" which have been used in the reading of non- or anti-gay texts. In this connection, the theory of "homophobia" has also given rise to the concepts of "panic" and of "internalized homophobia." Alan Sinfield, for example, showed how anti-effeminacy operated in "The Movement" writing of John Wain and Kingsley Amis (among others) and how effeminacy was used as a signifier of perversion. Yet he also demonstrated that the muscular, down-to-earth writing of "The Movement" was subverted in the poetry of Thom Gunn, who constructed figures of rough young men that shifted towards homoerotic identification. The construction of masculinities was explored further in the essay by Sinfield and Dollimore on *Henry V* and in Gregory Woods' work on Hemingway. Here Woods showed how writers who functioned as emblems of machismo need to be reassessed. What the struggle against effeminate eloquence in this writing expresses is the nagging anxiety which is the true condition (in both senses) of masculinity. The voice of heterosexual masculinity is to be compared with that of closed gay men, to the extent that it is terrified of indiscretion. To say too much might be to sound queer. In the related study, *Articulate Flesh* (1987), Woods explored the expression of homoeroticism in D. H. Lawrence, Hart Crane, W. H. Auden, Allen Ginsberg and Thom Gunn.

Gay criticism of this kind both borrows the techniques of cultural poetics and explores the relations between culture, history, and text in an increasingly politicized version of literary studies. Nicholas F. Radel, in his essay "Self as Other: The Politics of Identity in the Works of Edmund White," for example, argued that White's novels helped reveal a gay subject as it responds to political pressure from the culture at large. Far from being mere aesthetic products, these novels about gay life both confirm and interrogate their historical milieu and its construction of sexual orientation as gender difference. David Bergman's analysis of Baldwin's *Giovani's Room* (1956) serves to illustrate its deployment of "internalized homophobia." He sought to position Baldwin within a line he nowhere acknowledges—a line of both gay and African-American writers. Increasingly too, critics explored the relationship between nationalism, anti-imperialism and sexuality—in Parker et al., *Nationalism and Sexualities* (1992), for example, and Rudi C. Bleys' *The Geography of Perversion* (1996).

In Foucault's work, multiplying configurations of power are shown to be central to the production and control of sexuality. In developing this insight Jonathan Dollimore, in particular, explored the complex involvement of power with pleasure: pleasure and power do not cancel or turn back against one another, he wrote in *Sexual Dissidence* (1991), they seek out, overlap, and reinforce one another. They are linked together by complex mechanisms and devices of excitation and incitement. In this way, Dollimore effectively returned gay theory to Freud's concept of "polymorphous perversity"—the theory that the child enjoys multiple sexualities before it moves to the reductive primacy of genital sex. But Dollimore moved beyond Freud, and arguably beyond Foucault, remapping a politically subversive program for perversity. He argued that we should think in terms of the paradoxical perverse or the perverse dynamic which he claimed is a dynamic intrinsic to social process. Both Sinfield and Dollimore, and others working within a tradition of gay Cultural Materialist criticism, drew attention, in new ways, to the example of Oscar Wilde. In Wilde, Dollimore discovered a transgressive aesthetics: Wilde's experience of deviant desire... leads him not to escape the repressive ordering of society, but to a re-inscription within it, and an inversion of the binaries upon which that ordering depends; desire, and the transgressive aesthetic which it fashions, reacts against, disrupts, and displaces from within. Such a shift beyond binary oppositions marks the transition from gay to queer theory.

B. Lesbian Feminist Theory and Criticism

Lesbian Feminism is a cultural movement and critical perspective, most influential in the 1970s and early 1980s (primarily in North America and Western Europe), that encourages women to direct their energies toward other women rather than men, and often advocates lesbianism as the logical result of Feminism. Some key thinkers and activists are Charlotte Bunch, Rita Mae Brown, Adrienne Rich, Audre Lorde, Marilyn Frye, Mary Daly, Sheila Jeffreys, Barbara Smith, Pat Parker, Margaret Sloan-Hunter, Cheryl Clarke, Gloria Anzaldua, Cherrie Moraga, and Monique Wittig (although the latter is more commonly associated with the emergence of queer theory). Lesbian Feminist theory emerged as a response both to the heterosexism of mainstream culture and radical subcultures, and to the sexism of the male-dominated Gay Liberation Movement. Its focus is the interlocking structures of gender and sexual oppression. In particular, Lesbian Feminist Theory has consistently problematized heterosexuality as an institution central to the maintenance of patriarchy and women's oppression within it. Lesbian feminist theory, like Lesbian Feminism, is a diverse field which draws on a wide range of other theories and methods. While it cannot be reduced to a single model, several features stand out: a critique of "compulsory heterosexuality," an emphasis on "woman identification" and the creation of an alternative women's community. Whether taking a Black feminist, a radical feminist or a psychoanalytic approach, lesbian feminist theory foregrounds one or all of these elements.

The concept of "compulsory heterosexuality" was first articulated by Gayle Rubin (1975), and subsequently given wide circulation by Adrinene Rich in her essay "Compulsory Heterosexuality and Lesbian Existence" (1980). Unlike lesbian and gay sexuality, the concept of compulsory heterosexuality challenges the common sense view of heterosexuality as natural and therefore requiring no explanation. Rich argued that heterosexuality is a social institution supported by a range of powerful sanctions. The fact of lesbian existence, notwithstanding such sanctions, is evidence of a powerful current of woman-bounding which cannot be suppressed. Rich located the source of lesbianism in the fact that girl children are "of woman born" and have an original same-sex attachment to their mothers.

Monique Wittig put forward an analogous concept of "the straight mind" (1980) which viewed heterosexuality as an ideological construct. It is almost completely taken for granted yet institutes an obligatory social relationship between men and women. This concept, as an obvious principle, as a given prior to any science, "the straight mind," develops a totalizing interpretation of history, social reality, culture, language and all subjective phenomena at the same time. The discourses of heterosexuality work to oppress all those who attempt to conceive of themselves otherwise, particularly lesbians. In contrast to Rich, Wittig rejected the concept of "woman identification," arguing that it remains tied to the dualistic concept of gender which lesbians challenge. She claimed that in an important sense lesbians are not women, for what makes a woman is a specific social relation to a man and so "woman" acquires meaning only in heterosexual systems of thought and heterosexual economic systems.

Judith Butler is best known for her books *Gender Trouble: Feminism and the Subversion of Identity* (1990) and *Bodies That Matter: On the Discursive Limits of Sex* (1993), in which she challenged conventional notions of gender and developed her theory of gender performativity. This theory has had a major influence on feminist and queer scholarship. Butler drew on the work of both Wittig and Rich, used the term "heterosexual matrix" to designate that grid of cultural intelligibility through which bodies, genders, and desires are naturalized. Butler ceased to use the term in her later work but continued to argue for the subversion of sexual identities and for a distinction between sex, sexuality and gender in the social "performance" that constitutes them.

In their influential essays, such as "The Woman-identified Woman" (1973) in the collection of essays edited by Charlotte Bunch,[①] radical lesbians introduced the concepts of "woman identification" and "lesbian feminist community." Adrienne Rich (1980) further developed the concepts by depicting woman-bonding as an act of resistance to patriarchal power, and advanced the concept of "lesbian continuum" to describe a range—through each woman's life and throughout history—of woman-identified experience. Her definition encompasses not simply

① Charlotte Bunch, *Passionate Politics: Essays 1968–1986: Feminist Theory in Action*, New York: St. Martin's Press, 1986.

sexual experience, but all forms of "primary intensity" between and among women, including relationships of family, friendship and politics. Rich's own essay, "Jane Eyre: The Temptations of a Motherless Woman" (1976), perfectly illustrates the concepts of "lesbian continuum" and the related lesbian critical revisioning. It offers a lesbian reading of *Jane Eyre* which completely changes the focus from a heterosexual romance plot, to a narrative of loving female pedagogy in which Jane is nurtured and educated by a succession of female mother/mentors. Rich successfully demonstrated and denaturalized the ideological hegemony of heterosexuality in our reading and interpretive strategies.

Barbara Smith's essay "Towards a Black Feminist Criticism" (1986) adopts a critical model similar to Rich's. The French feminist Luce Irigaray explored an analogous concept of autonomous female sexuality in *This Sex Which Is Not One* (1985). She redefined women's sexuality as based on difference rather than sameness, arguing that it is multiple since a woman does not have a sex, she has at least two of them... and she has more than that. Her sexuality, always at least double, is in fact plural.

Irigaray further attempted to combine a psychoanalytic and political approach to lesbianism. In "When the Goods Get Together" she advanced the concept of homosexuality—punning on the signifiers of both maleness and sameness—to capture the dual nature of hetero-patriarchal culture. Homosexual discourse privileges male homosocial relations and a male sexuality of the same (whether hetero or homosexual). Her work links critiques of both gender and sexual power relations and in its anti-essentialism chimes with the political aims of Lesbian Feminism.

Some lesbian feminists, especially Black and Third World critics challenge the concept of "woman-identification." In 1981, Gloria Anzaldúa and Cherrie Moraga drew attention to the way the concept was used to mask power relations among women. Rejecting a universal model of identity, they created more flexible concepts of lesbian identity—such as Anzaldúa's concept of the new *mestiza* in 1987—able to encompass the connections between women of different cultures and ethnicities.

Representation—in both the political and the literary senses—is a key issue for lesbian criticism. In 1982 Margaret Cruikshank identified the crucial role literature has played in the development of lesbian criticism. In the twenty-five years since its emergence, lesbian literary criticism has developed from a largely polemical form of criticism calling for the acknowledgement of lesbian writers, readers and texts—and the definition of these—to a sophisticated and diverse body of politically informed theoretical work which aims to explore the multiple articulations of the sign "lesbian."

The early agenda for lesbian criticism was set by Virginia Woolf's analysis of the relationship between women and writing in *A Room of One's Own* (1929) which shows how literary power relations result in a textual effacement of relationships among women. It was not until Jane Rule's *Lesbian Images* (1975), however, that a critical text sought to delineate a lesbian literary tradition. Here Rule analyzed the life and work of a group of 20th-century lesbian writers including Gertrude Stein, Ivy Compton-Burnett, Maureen Duffy and May Sarton. Despite its focus on individual writers, Rule's text goes beyond a celebratory biographical approach and anticipates the multi-generic and intertextual style of much later lesbian literary criticism.

Lesbian literary criticism of the 1970s and early 1980s was concerned to identify a lesbian literary tradition and a lesbian literary aesthetic whether this was based on textual content, characters, themes, or the identification of the author as herself lesbian. This was aided by a number of reference works (Monique Wittig & Aandi Zeig, 1979; Monique Wittig & Aandi Zeig, 1979; Margaret Cruikshank, 1982) which continued to provide invaluable source materials for lesbian teachers, students and researchers. Work of this kind also performed the valuable "(re) discovery" of writers assumed to be heterosexual [Judith Fetterley's essay on Willa Cather (1990) is a later example], or, in Alison Hennigan's 1984 essay "What Is a Lesbian Novel?", identified a lesbian "sensibility" in a text's "necessarily oblique vision of the world." Related to this was the "encodement" approach advanced by Catharine Stimpson (1988) which analyzes the strategies of concealment (the use of an obscure idiom, gender and pronoun ambiguity, or a male pseudonym), or of internal censorship and silence necessarily employed by woman-identified writers in a homophobic and misogynistic culture. One example of this approach was Stimpson's analysis of the sexual codes, use of silence and experimentation with syntax in the writings of Gertrude Stein. Other critics used the approach to interpret the work of Angelina Weld Grimke, Emily Dickinson, H. D. and Willa Cather.

Given the historical difficulty of writing lesbian, however, as well as the changing definitions of the sign lesbian, lesbian critics progressively moved away from this search for a single lesbian identity or discourse. Mandy Merck (1985), for example, took issue with Hennegan's view that lesbians share a common perspective. What Hennegan called lesbian "sensibility," said Merck, can be found in works by other writers who don't identify as lesbian. She also questioned an emphasis, such as there is in Hennegan's "On Becoming a Lesbian Reader," on the importance of textual representations in the formation of readers' lesbian identities. A more radical approach, Merck argued, lies in the application of perverse readings which rely neither on the author's or text's concealment or discourse of sexual identity but on the queer perspective of the reader who subverts the dominant interpretive frameworks. Bonnie Zimmerman (1986), also, in her essay "What Has Never Been: An Overview of Lesbian Literary Criticism," offered more sophisticated model of lesbian textuality. Zimmerman cautioned against reductive and essentialist models of the lesbian text, and proposed the notion of lesbian "double vision" drawn from the dual perspectives of lesbians as members of mainstream and minority cultures simultaneously. In a later study, *The Safe Sea of Women* (1991), Zimmerman advanced a historically based definition of lesbian fiction, grounding this category in the cultural and historical contexts in which it is produced and read.

Rather than seek an autonomous lesbian tradition, distinctive aesthetic, lesbian author or reader, therefore, more recent lesbian criticism addressed the question of how texts internalize heterosexism and how lesbian literary strategies can subvert its norms. One such strategy is intertextuality. In an early essay, Elaine Marks (1979) argued that lesbian writing is fundamentally intertextual, and it drew on historical figures such as Sappho in the ranking of its discursive history and the production of "challenging counter images": lesbian texts "written exclusively by women for women, careless of male approval." More recently, some of the most exciting lesbian criticism was produced by bilingual and post-colonial/Third World lesbian writers who similarly foregrounded the intertextual, dialogic aspects of their texts. The Quebequoise writer, Nicole Brossard, and the Chicana writer, Cherrie Moraga, produced lyrical, polemical writings which interweave theory, politics and poetry. In *Amantes* (1980, translated as *Lovhers*, 1987), Brossard practiced "writing in the feminine" which like *écriture féminine* deconstructed the opposition body/text. Similarly, Moraga and Anzaldúa's concept of "theory in the flesh" (1981) elided the gap between the Chicana lesbian body and text.

Teresa de Lauretis (1993), in her article "Sexual Indifference and Lesbian Representation," also drew on French theory, using Irigara's concept of "hom(m)-osexuality" to discuss the invisibilizing of the lesbian body/text. Her essay subverts dominant interpretations of Radclyffe Hall's famous lesbian novel, *The Well of Loneliness*, by reading against the grain of sexology, and drawing out the text's "other" lesbianism. In common with lesbian and queer theory, de Lauretis plays on the distinction between sex/gender and sexuality, celebrating the diversity of lesbian writing, both critical and creative, and the ways in which lesbian writers "have sought variously to escape gender, deny it, transcend it, or perform it in excess, and to inscribe the erotic in cryptic, allegorical, realistic, camp, or other models of representation."

These various strategies and the resulting intersection of postmodern discourses and lesbian criticism have led to the textualization of lesbian identity whereby lesbianism is seen as a position from which to speak "otherwise" and thereby "queer" heterosexist discourse.

C. Queer Theory and Criticism

Queer theory is a way of thinking that dismantles traditional assumptions about gender and sexual identities. The field emerged from sexuality studies and women's studies. Queer theorists analyze gender and sexuality as socially and culturally constructed concepts. Italian feminist and film theorist Teresa de Lauretis coined the term "queer theory" for a conference she organized at the University of California, Santa Cruz in 1990 and a special issue of *Differences: A Journal of Feminist Cultural Studies* she edited based on that conference. Queer theory emerged in the early 1990s out of the fields of queer studies and women's studies in a field of post-structuralist critical theory. It includes both queer readings of texts and the theorization of "queerness" itself and focuses on mismatches between sex, gender and desire. Heavily influenced by the work of Lauren Berlant, Leo Bersani, Judith Butler, Lee Edelman, Jack Halberstam, David Halperin, José Esteban Muñoz, and Eve Kosofsky Sedgwick, queer theory builds both upon feminist challenges to the idea that gender is part of the essential self and upon gay/lesbian studies' close examination of the socially constructed nature of sexual acts and identities. Queerness has been associated most prominently with bisexual, lesbian and gay subjects, but its analytic framework also includes such topics as cross-dressing, intersex bodies and identities, gender ambiguity and gender-corrective surgery. Queer theory attempts to debunk stable (and correlated) sexes, genders, and sexualities. This attempt develops out of the specifically lesbian and gay reworking of the post-structuralist figuring of identity as a series of multiple and unstable positions. In order to place the "queer" into historical context, deconstructing contemporary arguments both for and against this latest terminology, queer theory examines the discourses of homosexuality developed in the last century.

Though built upon certain principles of Lesbian Feminism, queer theory is largely set opposed to Lesbian Feminism, tending to embrace whatever Lesbian Feminism was traditionally critical of, such as S&M (Sadism and Masochism), butch/femme identities and relationships, transgenderism and transsexuality, pornography, and prostitution. Queer theorists and Lesbian feminists have critiqued each other. To queer theorists, Lesbian Feminism has an essentialist understanding of gender that runs counter to their stated aims, and subsequently embraces gender fluidity, while to Lesbian Feminism, queer theory is implicitly male-oriented, and a recreation of the male-oriented Gay Liberation Front that Lesbian feminists initially sought refuge from. Actually, as queer theorists have countered and pointed out, the majority of the most prominent queer theorists are feminists, and many (including Judith Butler, Judith Halberstam, and Gayle Rubin) are lesbians.

As one of the figures and arguments influencing the transition from gay to queer theory that have been referred to above, Jeffrey Weeks (1985), while arguing that sexualities were historically constructed, saw them as none the less refusing to yield up a stable cognitive core, but only changing patterns in the organization of desire. Yet if this is true of homosexuality, surely heterosexuality too is also a recent construction and not a naturally grounded identity. As we have seen, the notion that sexual desire naturally and necessarily involves a gravitation towards a person of the opposite biological sex was already challenged by Freud. In a postmodern, post-colonial world in which the object of knowledge has itself become a problematic space, queer theory seeks further to question all such essentializing tendencies and binary thinking. Perverse particularities, as elusive, fragmented into local, are celebrated in all its deviant versions. Such "perversions" are mobilized in resistance to the bourgeois construction of self modeled upon a rigid, patriarchal heterosexuality which has exercised its hegemony for over two centuries.

Queer theory drew on Foucault, and in its inflection towards Cultural Materialism, on the work of Althusser and Raymond Williams in re-politicizing gay theory along these lines. Here between queer positions and more traditional Marxist approaches some tension emerged. Jeffrey Week thought that capitalist social relations have an effect on sexualities (as on many other matters), but a history of capitalism is not a history of sexuality (1985). In his own work, he demonstrated that power is not single and unitary but diverse, shifting and unstable, and hence open to resistance in a variety of ways. In consequence, his argument makes possible the formation of a "reverse discourse" (in Foucault's term) in which homosexuality began to speak on its own behalf, to demand that its legitimacy or "naturality" be acknowledged, often in the same vocabulary, using the same categories by which it was medically disqualified (1976). Theories and critics following the Marxist or post-Marxist tradition must negotiate the situation summarized by Raymond Williams in *Marxism and Literature* (1977) as one in which all or nearly all initiative and contributions, even when they take on manifestly alternative or oppositional forms, are in practice tied to the hegemonic. Queer theory would question the implication, apparent here and in Foucault's work, that alternative or oppositional meanings are fully appropriated by the state.

In the emergence of queer theory, Judith Butler and Eve Kosofsky Sedgewick were of special importance. Butler used the non-category of queer to disrupt not only the authority of the homosexual economy but also the attribution of identity *per se*. In "Imitation and Gender Insubordination" (1991), she called for a rejection of the essentialism of the heterosexual/homosexual binary opposition, and for the queering of heterosexist master narratives. Unlike Lesbian Feminism such as Wittig, she refused to identify lesbian as a positive oppositional term, arguing that it is the absence of a defined lesbian counter-identity that enables the postmodern lesbian to queer the master discourse, saying she would like to have it permanently unclear what precisely that sign signifies (1992). Queer theory thus proposes a disruption of identity which enacts agency in the performativity of becoming lesbian. Similarly, Eve Kosofsky Sedgwick also drew upon deconstructive postmodern theory but with a more evident political intent or implication. In her view, the supposed opposition between sex and gender seems only to delineate a problematical space rather than a crisp distinction (1991), sexuality has often been confused with sex, and categories such as race or class might themselves be important in the construction of sexuality. There is no privileged narrative of nation just because there is no single sexuality. Therefore, like nationalities, sexualities are completely formed by their differences, not by something innately grounding them. Like national boundaries, sexual ones are also not fixed though they may, for a period, serve to delineate a particular discursive space. Recent work in this area has shown how sexology and colonial anthropology were linked but that one nation's sexual classifications do not neatly equate with those of another. This has coincided with a move away from the black denunciation of homosexuality as something alien to black culture. At the same time, though the existence of cross-dressing and a homosexual rite of passage into manhood in other cultures have been sometimes exoticized and misunderstood, a critical reading of ethnographic literatures (such as that of Rudi C. Bleys, 1996) can provide a sense of the larger narratives involved in the construction of gay identities.

Eve Kosofsky Sedgwick also deployed the concept of "homosociality" as an interpretative tool to demonstrate "the usefulness of certain Marxist-feminist historical categories for literary criticism." In her *Between Men: English Literature and Male Homosocial Desires* (1985), she began to distance herself from determinate notions of patriarchy; male and female homosociality nonetheless have different historical shapes and they remain articulations and mechanisms of the enduring inequality of power between women and men. She acknowledged a debt to Feminism, but increasingly, in a move typical of the deconstructive tendencies of queer theory, considered the multiple constructiveness of sex, gender and sexuality. Her study of Shakespeare's Sonnets, Wycherley's *The Country Wife*, Tennyson, George Eliot and Dickens illustrates the paradoxically historicizing and de-historicizing tendencies of this kind of work. The book is also notable for its discussion of the Gothic as: Terrorism and Homosexual Panic. In particular (building on Freud) she explored the theory that paranoia is the psychosis that makes graphic the mechanisms of homophobia.

In queer theory's view, the traditional and prescriptive essentialist model of sexuality fail to do the conceptual work involved in the adequate description of how desires function and how sexualities are made. The range of critical terminologies, models and strategies confirms that it is no longer viable to think in terms of a single, coherent "sexuality" and has effected the transition from the "natural" homosexual individual to whom rights could be attached, to the disorienting notion that all sexualities are perverse, and can be reclaimed and celebrated as such. If gay or lesbian theory has often been defensively grounded in liberal rights, queer theory is a deeper philosophical challenge to the status quo, which at the same time aims to provide readings which at once subvert difference and celebrate Otherness.

Further Reading

Krijnen, Tonny & Sofie van Bauwel. *Gender and Media: Representing, Producing, Consuming*. New York: Routledge, 2015.

Salime, Zakia. *Between Feminism and Islam: Human Rights and Sharia Law in Morocco*. Minneapolis: University of Minnesota Press, 2011.

Smith, Anne-Marie. *Julia Kristeva: Speaking the Unspeakable*. London: Pluto Press, 1988.

Blechner, Mark J. *Sex Changes: Transformations in Society and Psychoanalysis*. New York: Taylor & Francis, 2009.

Ettinger, Bracha L. *The Matrixial Borderspace*. Minneapolis: University of Minnesota Press, 2006.

Gallop, Jane. *The Daughter's Seduction: Feminism and Psychoanalysis*. Ithaca: Cornell University Press, 1993.

Howe, Mica & Sarah A. *He Said, She Says*. Teaneck: Fairleigh Dickinson University Press, 2001.

Humm, Maggie. *Modernist Women and Visual Cultures*. New Brunswick: Rutgers University Press, 2003.

Cornietz, Nina. *Dangerous Women, Deadly Words*. Redwood: Stanford University Press, 1999.

Grebowicz, M. *Gender after Lyotard*. New York: SUNY Press, 2007.

Zohar, Ayelet. *Post Gender*. Cambridge: Cambridge Scholars Publishing, 2009.

Butler, Judith. *Bodies That Matter: On the Discursive Limits of Sex*. London: Taylor & Francis, 2011.

Bruno, Perreau. *Queer Theory: The French Response*. Redwood: Stanford University Press, 2016.

Bibliography

Cuddon, J. A. *A Dictionary of Literary Terms and Literary Theory*. 5th ed. Malden: Wiley-Blackwell, 2013.

Rice, Philip & Patricia Waugh. *Modern Literary Theory*. New York: Oxford University Press, 2002.

Bressler, Charles. *Literary Criticism: An Introduction to Theory and Practice*. Beijing: Higher Education Press, 2004.

Habib, Rafey. *A History of Literary Criticism: From Plato to the Present.* Oxford: Blackwell Publishing, 2005.

泰勒，温奎斯特. 后现代主义百科全书. 章燕，李自修，等译. 刘象愚，校. 长春：吉林人民出版社，2007.

王治河. 后现代主义辞典. 北京：中央编译出版社，2004.

张中载，王逢振，赵国新. 二十世纪西方文论选读. 北京：外语教学与研究出版社，2002.

朱刚. 二十世纪西方文艺批评理论. 上海：上海外语教育出版社，2001.

Selected Readings

Michel Foucault: "The Perverse Implantation"

A. Jagose: "Queer Theory, An Introduction"

M. Witting: "One Is Not Born a Woman"

J. Butler: *Gender Trouble*

Chapter Fourteen

Cultural Studies

Cultural Studies is a field of theoretically, politically, and empirically engaged cultural analysis that concentrates upon the political dynamics of contemporary culture, its historical foundations, defining traits, conflicts, and contingencies. Cultural Studies emerged in Britain in the late 1950s and subsequently spread internationally, notably to the United States and Australia. Originally identified with the Center for Contemporary Cultural Studies at the University of Birmingham (founded in1964) and with such scholars as Richard Hoggart, Stuart Hall, and Raymond Williams, Cultural Studies later became a well-established field in many academic institutions, and it has since had broad influence in sociology, anthropology, historiography, literary criticism, philosophy, and art criticism. Among its central concerns are the place of race or ethnicity, class, and gender in the production of cultural knowledge. A key concern for Cultural Studies' practitioners is the examination of the forces within and through which socially organized people conduct and participate in the construction of their everyday lives.

Cultural Studies combines a variety of politically engaged critical approaches including Semiotics, Marxism, Feminism, Ethnography, Post-structuralism, Post-colonialism, Postmodernism, Social Theory, Political Theory, History, Philosophy, Literary Theory, Critical Race Theory, Media Theory, Film/Video Studies, Communication Studies, Political Economy, Translation Studies, Museum Studies and Art History/Criticism to study cultural phenomena in various societies and historical periods. Cultural Studies seeks to understand how meaning is generated, disseminated, contested, bound up with systems of power and control, and produced from the social, political and economic spheres within a particular social formation or conjuncture. Important theories of cultural hegemony and agency have both influenced and been developed by the Cultural Studies Movement, as have many recent major communication theories and agendas, such as those that attempt to explain and analyze the cultural forces related to processes of globalization.

During the rise of neo-liberalism in Britain and the US, Cultural Studies both became a global movement, and attracted the attention of many conservative opponents both within and beyond universities for a variety of reasons. Some left-wing critics associated particularly with Marxist forms of political economy also attacked Cultural Studies for allegedly overstating the importance of cultural phenomena. While Cultural Studies continues to have its detractors, the field has become a kind of a worldwide movement that is to this day associated with a raft of scholarly associations and programs, annual international conferences, publications and students and practitioners from Bangalore to Santa Cruz. Somewhat distinct approaches to Cultural Studies have emerged in different national and regional contexts such as the United States, Canada, Australia, New Zealand, Italy, Latin America, Asia, and Africa.

The objects of Cultural Studies are numerous and complicated forms and phenomena of the contemporary cultures, especially the contemporary mass culture in the non-mainstream position as well as other cultures similarly in the marginal positions, such as women culture, meta-culture of the working class and the cultural experience and the identity of the ethnic minority. The "culture" in the Cultural Studies is no longer the cultural products and activities in the traditional sense but the multitudinous ways of everyday life. Today, in the classes of some American universities, what the literary professors take delight in talking about are English novelist Ian Fleming's popular novels *007*, soap operas and Madonna but not the famous works by Milton and Shakespeare usually looked upon as classics.

This marks a tendency towards breaking the narrow field of the literary study in the past and putting popular culture into the view of studies. Some professors in American universities even put forth the idea to replace the literary study with Cultural Studies.

A. The Development of Cultural Studies

The beginning of Cultural Studies as a field was when Richard Hoggart used the term in 1964 in founding the Birmingham (UK) Centre for Contemporary Cultural Studies or The Birmingham School. The Birmingham School at the University of Birmingham thus became the world's first institutional home of Cultural Studies. However, English Cultural Studies actually emerged from the womb of the cultural concept and literary criticism of Frank Raymond Leavis and Thomas Stearns Eliot. It came into being from two revolts—one was against the cultural elitism and the other was against the economic determinism. Cultural Studies established the characteristics of its own thought in their revolts. Leavis, in his two works of Cultural Studies, *The Mass Civilization and the Minority Culture* (1930) and *Culture and Environment* (1934), using literary analysis of close-reading type, interpreted the forms of the so-called "mass civilization," such as popular novels, broadcasting, movies, and advertisements, and called on the cultural elite to shoulder the heavy responsibility to educate the masses in order to save the depraved customs. In his famous pamphlet, *Notes Towards the Definition of Culture* (1948), Eliot acknowledged that culture was not limited to the knowledge spread by schools only. He defined culture as a way of life and extended the meaning of culture beyond literature and art. Their ideas and statements have inspired Cultural Studies from the reverse direction and provided theoretical starting point for the formation of the cultural ideas of Raymond Williams, founder of Cultural Studies. His works *Culture and Society: 1950–1780* (1958) and *The Long Revolution* (1961) almost synthesized Leavisism and Marxism.

Williams inherited from Leavis the cultural concept of totality and the analytic method of close-reading type. He criticized the cultural elitism that thought of "the mass civilization" as conflicting with "the minority culture." Meanwhile, he inherited from Marx the radical social criticism on the political, economic and cultural powers of the ruling class. *Culture and Society: 1780–1950* (1958), exploring how the notion of culture developed in the West, especially Great Britain, from the 18th to the 20th centuries, determined the task of cultural analysis and defined culture as all the ways of life and as the expression of "meanings and values." The task of cultural analysis was to clarify the meanings and values contained in a certain way of life. He opposed Leavis' restoring culture as the cultural concepts of the ideal classical works held by the cultural elite and did not approve the cultural concept regarding culture as the byproducts of history and the process of economic development. He saw culture as a self-sufficient field of study.

In *The Long Revolution*, the "long revolution" of the title is a revolution in culture, which Raymond Williams saw as having unfolded alongside the democratic revolution and the industrial revolution. Following on from *Culture and Society*, in this book, Williams led the way in recognizing the importance of the growth of the popular press, the growth of standard English, and the growth of the reading public in English-speaking culture and in Western culture as a whole. Williams concretely presented the device of cultural analysis. He thought that, when we analyze the culture of a period, we must examine the emotional structure universally existing in people's ideas. In this book, he analyzed the popular cultural forms and mechanisms in 19th-century England. In his practice of Cultural Studies in the 1960s and the 1970s, he compared the popular cultural forms, such as movie, TV, physical education, music, etc., with classical works, thinking that the two had instructive significance in understanding universal cultural experiences.

In addition, Williams' discussion of how culture is to be defined and analyzed has been of considerable importance in the development of Cultural Studies as an independent discipline.

Richard Hoggart's *The Uses of Literacy* (1957), examining the influence of mass media in the United Kingdom, has been described as a key influence in the history of English and media studies and in the founding of Cultural Studies. It is a powerful work of Cultural Studies. Hoggart did his utmost to advocate restoring and discussing the popular culture of the working class because Britain consistently thinks that the refined literature is culture and thus the culture of the working class loses its voice due to its being discriminated. Hoggart thought that culture is people's expression and we should allow the culture of the marginal communities (e.g. the working class) to restore its voice already disapproved. Marxist theory regards the mass culture as a thing that ideology imposes and studies it as an oppressive formation of ideology. The two cultures interact and influence each other and play the most important role in the development of Cultural Studies. In *The Uses of Literacy*, Hoggart continued to use the method of literary analysis of Leavis type and delineated the decaying course of the working class traditional culture. He used the research method of anthropology in narrating the working class culture in England in the 1930s, employed the method of practical criticism in analyzing all kinds of mass culture emerging after World War II, and showed his deep worries about the old-type working class culture which is corroded by the new-fashioned commercial culture.

1. Marxism, Feminism, Race and Culture

As noted above, Marxism has played an important originating role as being one of the first critiques of Culture and has hence been reflected in the history of Cultural Studies. The early Frankfurt School of Sociology were particularly influenced by Antonio Gramsci, and the members of the later Birmingham School were in the early 1970s influenced by the Structuralism of Louis Althusser. Cultural Studies has since branched out from Marxist readings of Sociology to more broad readings that involve race, gender, ideological and identity based readings of the composition of society, with Post-modernism and Post-structuralism furthering these readings into the artistic, psychological and philosophical realms. Culture also means deep consciousness according to social norms.

2. Gramsci and Hegemony

To understand the changing political circumstances of class, politics and culture in the United Kingdom, scholars at the Birmingham School turned to the work of Antonio Gramsci, an Italian thinker, writer and communist party leader of the 1910s, 1920s and 1930s. Gramsci had been concerned with similar issues: Why would Italian laborers and peasants vote for fascists? What strategic approach is necessary to mobilize popular support in more progressive directions? Gramsci modified classical Marxism, and argued that culture must be understood as a key site of political and social struggle. In his view, capitalists used not only brute force (police, prisons, repression, military) to maintain control, but also penetrated the everyday culture of working people in a variety of ways in their efforts to win popular "consent." It is important to recognize that for Gramsci, historical leadership, or "hegemony," involves the formation of alliances between class factions, and struggles within the cultural realm of everyday common sense. Hegemony was always, for Gramsci, an interminable, unstable and contested process.

In the work of Hall, Hebdige and McRobbie, popular culture came to the fore... What Gramsci gave to this was the importance of consent and culture. If the fundamental Marxists saw power in terms of class-versus-class, then Gramsci gave us a question of *class alliance*. The rise of Cultural Studies itself was based on the decline of the prominence of fundamental class-versus-class politics. The theory of hegemony was of central importance to the development of British Cultural Studies. It facilitated analysis of the ways subordinate groups actively resisted and responded to political and economic domination. The subordinate groups did not need to be seen merely as the passive dupes of the dominant class and its ideology.

3. Structure and Agency

The development of hegemony theory in Cultural Studies was in some ways consonant with work in other fields exploring agency, a theoretical concept that insists on the active, critical capacities of subordinated peoples (e.g. the working classes, colonized peoples, women). As Stuart Hall famously argued in his 1981 essay, "Notes on Deconstructing 'the Popular'," ordinary people are not cultural dopes. Insistence on accounting for the agency of subordinated peoples runs counter to the work of traditional structuralists. Some analysts have however been critical of some work in Cultural Studies that they feel overstates the significance of or even romanticizes some forms of popular cultural agency.

Cultural Studies often concerns itself with agency at the level of the practices of everyday life, and approaches such research from a standpoint of radical contextualism. In other words, Cultural Studies rejects universal accounts of cultural practices, meanings, and identities.

Judith Butler, an American feminist theorist whose work is often associated with Cultural Studies, wrote that the move from a structuralist account in which capital is understood to structure social relations in relatively homologous ways to a view of hegemony in which power relations are subject to repetition, convergence and rearticulation brought the question of temporality into the thinking of structure. It has marked a shift from a form of Althusserian theory that takes structural totalities as theoretical objects to one in which the insights into the contingent possibility of structure inaugurate a renewed conception of hegemony as bound up with the contingent sites and strategies of the rearticulation of power.

4. Globalization

In recent decades, as capitalist culture has spread throughout the world via contemporary forms of globalization, Cultural Studies has generated important analyses of local sites and practices of negotiation with and resistance to Western hegemony.

5. Cultural Consumption

Cultural Studies criticizes the traditional view of the passive consumer, particularly by underlining the different ways people *read*, receive and interpret cultural texts, or appropriate other kinds of cultural products, or otherwise participate in the production and circulation of meanings. On this view, a consumer can appropriate, actively rework or challenge the meanings circulated through cultural texts. In some of its variants, then, Cultural Studies has thus shifted the analytical focus from (traditional understandings of) production to consumption, which is nevertheless understood as a form of production (of meanings, of identities, etc.) in its own right. Stuart Hall, John Fiske, and others have been influential in these developments.

A special 2008 issue of the field's flagship journal, *Cultural Studies*, examined "Anti-Consumerism" from a variety of Cultural Studies angles. As Jeremy Gilbert noted in his contribution to this issue, Cultural Studies must grapple with the fact that we now live in an era when, throughout the capitalist world, the overriding aim of government economic policy is to maintain consumer spending levels. This is an era when "consumer confidence" is treated as the key indicator and cause of economic effectiveness.

B. Objects of Cultural Studies

In the 1970s, the objects of Cultural Studies were mainly the youth subculture and media and had gained some achievements. Under the inspiration of the theories of Gramsci and Althusser, Cultural Studies revealed the mechanism at large with which culture forms social consciousness and tries to unearth the relation of cultural power between the marginal community and the dominant class in the society. The dominant class put its advantage of cultural hegemony to good use and interpreted the social meaning that tallies with its own benefits as the "common meaning" approved by the whole society. The subordinated communities resisted this practice to different extents. Proceeding from the angle of defending their own benefits, they formed their own understanding of social phenomena. The important works of youth subculture study emerging in this period were the following three important books. Firstly, *Subculture: The Meaning of Style* (1979) by Dick Hebdige, drawing from Marxist theorists, literary critics, French structuralists, and American sociologists, presents a model for analyzing youth subcultures; while arguing that each subculture undergoes the same trajectory, outlines the individual style differences of specific subcultures, such as Teddy boys, mods, rockers, skinheads, and punks, and emphasizes the historical, class, race, and socioeconomic conditions that surrounded the formation of each subculture. Secondly, *Resistance Through Rituals* (1926) by Stuart Hall/Tony Jefferson, shows resistance with a more open-plan sense of ritual, here conceived as the multiple, elaborate, tangible and/or subtle cycles of communication and interaction in which artists and cultural producers are frequently moving. Thirdly, *Learning to Work* (1977) by Paul E. Willis, is a provocative and troubling account of how education links culture and class in the reproduction of social hierarchy, etc. The general tendency of these works is stressing mankind's creative and responsive ability to the oppressive social environment and praising their resisting spirit. In these works, though their rebellious behavior departing from the classics and rebelling against the orthodoxy, usually only symbolic and unable to shake the existing social foundation at all, the youth subculture is described as a cultural force to resist the ideology of the middle class occupying the leading position.

Media studies deals with the content, history, and effects of various media; in particular, the mass media. Media studies may draw on traditions from both the social sciences and the humanities, but mostly from its core disciplines of mass communication, communication sciences, and communication studies. Researchers may also develop and employ theories and methods from disciplines including Cultural Studies, rhetoric (including digital rhetoric), philosophy, literary theory, psychology, political science, political economy, economics, sociology, anthropology, social theory, art history and criticism, film theory, feminist theory, and information theory. Media studies in this period of the 1970s stressed the decisive role of structure in the communication process and the audience's reception of the media controlled by ideology, the relation between the subordinate and the dominant, and hegemony. In short, people's dynamic role was limited by the unbalanced power relation. In the same period, the more famous works of media studies dealt with the topics such as the audience of the national news report, family TV, the crossroads: the drama of TV serials, the crisis of watching and controlling, etc. Races were also put into the view of Cultural Studies. *The Empire's Counterattack: The Races and Racism in Britain in the 1970s* (1982), collectively compiled by the Center for Contemporary Cultural Studies, discusses the relation between racism and the social crisis in Britain in the 1970s. The deep concern of Cultural Studies about women problems and racial problems was the reflection of the huge and grand Feminist Movement and the Human Rights Movement in the same period in the Cultural Studies.

C. Modes of Cultural Studies

1. The Concept of "Text"

Cultural Studies, drawing upon and developing semiotics, uses the concept of *text* to designate not only written language, but also television programs, films, photographs, fashion, hairstyles, and so forth; the texts of Cultural Studies comprise all the meaningful artifacts of culture. Such concept of text was worked out by Juri Lotman together with his colleagues from Tartu-Moscow School. Similarly, the field widens the concept of "culture." "Culture," for a Cultural Studies researcher, includes not only traditional high culture (the culture of ruling social groups), but also everyday meanings and practices, which have, as noted above, become a central focus of Cultural Studies. Cultural Studies even approaches sites and spaces of everyday life, such as pubs, living rooms, gardens and beaches, as "texts."

Jeff Lewis brought together much of the discussion on text and textual analysis in his studies on media, culture and cultural politics. According to Lewis, "textual studies" is the most complex and difficult heuristic method, requiring both powerful interceptive skills and a subtle conception of politics and context. Lewis' own mode of textual analysis views all phenomena as potential "text" when set within a given knowledge system. Texts can only bear meaning that can be "interpreted," therefore, as they present within a given knowledge system. This knowledge system imbues the text with meaning. The task of the cultural analyst, therefore, is to engage with both the knowledge system and the text, and observe and analyze the ways the two interact with one another—and with other knowledge systems, including the one being deployed by the analyst himself or herself. This engagement represents the critical dimensions of the analysis, its capacity to illuminate the hierarchies within and surrounding the given text and its discourses.

Richard Hoggart's *The Uses of Literacy* provides research modes and important enlightenment for the early (the early 1960s and the 1970s) Cultural Studies. It insists on the legality and the organic totality of the working class culture and thinks that under the circumstances the mass culture invades in a large scale and the working class is quite able to create their own forms of popular culture and independently choose the cultural products provided by the mass culture. E.

P. Thompson's *The Making of the English Working Class* discusses the class consciousness of the working class and the process of the culture's forming in the early Industrial Revolution, emphatically looking on the formation of the English working class's consciousness from the angle of culture instead of the angle of economy.

Directly propelled by Williams and Hoggart, the Center for Contemporary Cultural Studies of the Birmingham University was established in 1964, which marked the beginning of institutionalization of Cultural Studies. In general opinions, the research work of the Center represented the achievements and directions of English Cultural Studies. Generally speaking, in the 1960s, the Center emphatically studied the working class culture; in the 1970s, it attached importance to the study of the medium culture and the youth meta-culture; in the 1980s, it paid close attention to the study of races and sexes. Taking a sweeping view of the development course of Cultural Studies, people generally think that there are two research modes that dominate the critical practice of the Center: culturalism and Structuralism. These two modes represent respectively two development periods of Cultural Studies.

Mode of culturalism stresses man's dynamic role, values, and experiences and it has important function in people's comprehensively understanding the society from the angles of sociology and historical science. The above-mentioned works by Williams, Hoggart, Thompson and others are the embodiment of this mode of Cultural Studies; the work of Cultural Studies in the 1960s initiated this mode and *The Popular Arts* (1964) by Stuart Hall *et al* is a representative work following this mode. In the late 1960s the European Structuralism and the Western Marxism represented by Althusser and Gramsci began to exert important influence upon Cultural Studies that correspondingly entered the period of the mode of Structuralism.

Mode of Structuralism emphasizes social conditions' limitation to man's initiative role and has strong coloring of anti-humanism. Contrary to the mode of culturalism, the mode of Structuralism does not regard culture as the objective experience of a social community but sees culture as the place to generate and comprehend meaning... the area to play a decisive and propelling role in constructing, experiencing, and interpreting the social reality. An important idea in Gramsci's theory of "hegemonism" is that he regarded the area of culture and ideology as the area where the ruling class and the ruled class in the society conflict with each other when they construct the social meaning. In Althusser's ideological theory, culture or ideology is not only the manifestation of human experiences but also the premise and basis of consciousness and subjectivity and it is just through culture or ideology that the social reality is constructed, produced, and interpreted. The shortcoming of the mode of Structuralism lies in that it has strong coloring of determinism and over-desalinates man's subjective and dynamic role.

2. Joint Relation Net in Cultural Studies

Fredric Jameson, an American literary critic and Marxist political theorist, is best known for his analysis of contemporary cultural trends. He described postmodernism as the spatialization of culture under the pressure of organized capitalism. Jameson's best-known books include *Postmodernism, or, The Cultural Logic of Late Capitalism* (1991), *The Political Unconscious* (1981), and *Marxism and Form* (1971). In his essay "On 'Cultural Studies'" (1993), Jameson pointed out that it is best to comprehend Cultural Studies as a special way of discussing the social universal problems instead of the field belonging to a small number of people or a specialized field. Therefore, Cultural Studies should welcome hybridized "identity," disseminate and analyze new complicated structures. Jameson advocated replacing the concept of the single writer with the concept of the joint relation net. In his opinion, in Cultural Studies, there is not any true individual text, and the objects of its study are all kinds of joint relations. If there is no motivational tension that tries hard to combine, lead, and coordinate all kinds of identities, responsibilities, and states, it is not possible for truly meaningful and very effective works and ideas to appear. The tension here also refers to the tension between text and society, superstructure, and foundation, or it is culture's changing position from the social reality to the imaginary world. Therefore, people should regard the tensions caused by all kinds of influences and promises of many kinds of ideologies as quite different tensions. That which forms the connotation of a thought is the act to respond to these tensions but neither to the analysis to draw a conclusion nor a big united plan created by excluding contradictions and suppressing the operation of many kinds of ideology. The tension among the "identities" of all kinds of communities forms another important aspect of Cultural Studies.

Fredric Jameson held that any community cannot possess only one culture; culture is a community's externalization of the atmosphere that it finds when it contacts and observes another community or the strange aspect of that community. In other words, culture is a thought of the Other, that is, the things like faith or religion is projected into a stranger's mind. Though people really often talk about their own culture, religion, faith or some other things, any of these things is not possessed only by one community. Therefore, people must regard culture as a tool or a medium with which the relation between communities can realize and that we must reveal culture as a concept of the Other or we will not be able to comprehend this kind of relation formed in history. Between communities there is a variety of differences in culture. In cultural exchange, one community's borrowing another community's culture is its acceptance of and respect for another community. In the practice of Cultural Studies, Jameson emphasized that there are three levels for interpretation. The first level is the political one, that is, all texts (including the social text) are to be interpreted as symbols or allegories. The second one is social, which means that the object of our attention is turned to communities and to the ideology contained in the text. The third is the level of human production and it is the most important level among the three.

The existence of different modes of production leads to counterwork, and the contradiction between communities forms the focus of political, social and historical life, for instance, colonialism led by capitalism in the period of imperialism, and post-colonialism caused by the late capitalism at the present, etc. *Postmodernism, or, The Cultural Logic of Late Capitalism* is a 1991 book by Fredric Jameson, in which Jameson offered a critique of modernism and postmodernism from a Marxist perspective, just by starting with the mode of production that Jameson himself interpreted the cultural logic of postmodernism or the late capitalism.

Further Reading

Du Gay, Paul, Anders Koed Madsen, Stuart Hall, Keith Negus, Hugh Mackay & Linda Janes. *Doing Cultural Studies: The Story of the Sony Walkman.* London & Thousand Oaks: Sage in association with The Open University, 1997.

During, Simon. *The Cultural Studies Reader.* 3rd ed. London: Routledge, 2007.

Edgar, Andrew & Peter Sedgwick. *Cultural Theory: The Key Concepts*. 2nd ed. New York: Routledge, 2005.

Hall, Stuart. *Culture, Media, Language: Working Papers in Cultural Studies*, 1972–1979. London: Routledge, 1980.

Hall, Stuart. Cultural Studies: Two Paradigms. *Media, Culture, and Society*, 1980, 2(1): 57–72.

Hall, Stuart. Race, Culture, and Communications: Looking Backward and Forward at Cultural Studies. *Rethinking Marxism,* 1992, 5 (1): 10–18.

Hoggart, Richard. *The Uses of Literacy: Aspects of Working Class Life*. London: Chatto and Windus, 1957.

Johnson, Richard. What Is Cultural Studies Anyway? *Social Text,* 1986–1987, 16: 38–80.

Johnson, Richard. Multiplying Methods: From Pluralism to Combination//Practice of Cultural Studies. London/Thousand Oaks: SAGE, 2004: 26–43.

Lash, Scott. Power After Hegemony: Cultural Studies in Mutation? *Theory*, *Culture & Society*. 2007, 24 (3): 55–78.

Lewis, Jeff. *Cultural Studies*: *The Basics.* 2nd ed. London: Sage, 2008.

Longhurst, Brian, Greg Smith, Gaynor Bagnall, Garry Crawford & Michael Ogborn. *Introducing*

Cultural Studies. 2nd ed. London: Routledge, 2008.

Miller, Toby. *A Companion to Cultural Studies*. Malden: Blackwell Publishers, 2006.

Pollock, Griselda. *Generations and Geographies: Critical Theories and Critical Practices in Feminism and the Visual Arts*. London: Routledge, 1996.

Pollock, Griselda. *Psychoanalysis and the Image*. Boston and Oxford: Blackwell, 2006.

Smith, Paul. Looking Backwards and Forwards at Cultural Studies//Ed. Toby Miller. *A Companion to Cultural Studies*. Malden: Blackwell Publishers, 2006: 331–340.

Williams, Raymond. *Keywords: A Vocabulary of Culture and Society*. Rev. ed. New York: Oxford University Press, 1985.

——. *Culture and Society:* 1780–1950. New York: Harper & Row, 1966.

Bibliography

Cuddon, J. A. *A Dictionary of Literary Terms and Literary Theory*. 5th ed. Malden: Wiley-Blackwell, 2013.

Rice, Philip & Patricia Waugh eds. *Modern Literary Theory*. New York: Oxford University Press, 2002.

Bressler, Charles. *Literary Criticism: An Introduction to Theory and Practice*. Beijing: Higher Education Press, 2004.

Habib, M. A. R.. *A History of Literary Criticism: From Plato to the Present.* Oxford: Blackwell Publishing, 2005.

泰勒，温奎斯特. 后现代主义百科全书. 章燕，李自修，等译. 刘象愚，校. 长春：吉林人民出版社，2007.

王治河. 后现代主义辞典. 北京：中央编译出版社，2004.

王守仁，朱刚，姚成贺 . 英美文学批评史 . 南京：南京大学出版社，2021.

张中载，王逢振，赵国新. 二十世纪西方文论选读. 北京：外语教学与研究出版社，2002.

朱刚. 二十世纪西方文艺批评理论. 上海：上海外语教育出版社，2001.

Selected Readings

Raymond Williams: “Base and Superstructure in Marxist Cultural Theory”

Dick Hebdige: “From Culture to Hegemony”

Chapter Fifteen

Postmodern Ecological Literary Criticism

Postmodern Ecological Literary Criticism, often shortened as Eco-criticism, is the study of literature and the environment from an interdisciplinary point of view, where literature scholars analyze texts that illustrate environmental concerns and examine the various ways literature treats the subject of nature. Some eco-critics brainstorm possible solutions to the correction of the contemporary environmental situation, though not all eco-critics agree on the purpose, methodology, or scope of eco-criticism. In the United States, Eco-criticism is often associated with the Association for the Study of Literature and Environment (ASLE), which hosts biennial meetings for scholars who deal with environmental matters in literature. ASLE publishes a journal—*Interdisciplinary Studies in Literature and Environment* (*ISLE*)—in which current international scholarship can be found.

Eco-criticism is an intentionally broad approach that is known by a number of other designations, including "green (cultural) studies," "eco-poetics," and "environmental literary criticism," and is often informed by other fields such as ecology, sustainable design, biopolitics, environmental history, environmentalism, and social ecology, among others.

A. Ecological Literature

Ecological literature mainly refers to those works that sensitively reveal the ecological crisis in the modern world, criticize the values of anthropocentrism, and reflect the modern civilization that leads to ecological crisis. Ecological literature does not regard man as the center of the natural world and opposes the idea that takes human interest as the absolute measure to judge the values of nature. Writers of ecological literature are deeply aware of the evil consequences of ecological calamities and the warnings of innumerable ecological crises for the future. They think that, only by taking the holistic interest of the whole ecosystem of the world (including nature and spirit) as the ultimate premise and the highest value of human future, can human beings effectively and all-roundly eliminate the ecological crisis that threatens the existence of human beings, and accordingly, obtain the earth that readjusts itself in favor of the long-term or ultimate interest of human beings and in which human beings exist harmoniously. In the realm of ecological literature, there are works of ecological literature in a general sense and that in a narrow sense. The works of ecological literature in a general sense are those traditional literary works having consciousness of ecological culture. Though they do not directly put forward the key word "ecology" and even do not push the aftermaths of ecological crisis to the startling extent, this sort of works do contain the consciousness of harmonious life that man and nature mingle with each other and the deep criticism of the modern civilization that causes distance and opposition between man and nature. The works of ecological literature in a narrow sense are those whose writers have sharp-cut stand of ecological culture, reflect the relationship between man and nature in advance-guard position, confront modern ecological crisis and utter their own critical voice.

What ecological literature sends out is the human spiritual appeal for "residing poetically." Its central dimensionality is to grasp the relationship between man and nature generating with each other and examine how nature impacts man's existence and spirit. The writing of ecological literature pays attention to deep thought of ecological philosophy, deepens aesthetic experiences of ecological culture, achieves correct judgments of values, and explores man's new ways of apperceiving to regain the sense of "homestead." The formation of the works of ecological literature is concerned with nature-centrism, the harmony between man and nature, man's cultivation of ecological humanities, the possibilities to go out of the ecological crisis of the whole globe under the guidance of the narrative text, and reshaping of man's soul in the text's reflection of values. The reading of ecological literature will promote people's inherent spiritual worldview to morally and poetically live in the natural matrix, have the sense of crisis—the personal experience of the damaged situation of nature and the plight of the earth, attain proper ecological thinking and the sense of homestead, evoke their moral character to love life, and resume the inherent harmony between human society and nature. While reading literary works, we can have newer understanding of the complex mechanism adjusting the interaction between man and environment revealed in the text. The literary studies with the consciousness of environment provide a more extensive and deeper chance for us to read literary works with new sensitivity to the sound of nature. The key of the writing and reading of ecological literature is readjusting the central thinking pattern of the self-unscrupulousness, continually stepping forward to the worldview of eco-centrism, and obtaining the right aesthetic perception of the notion of the whole globe including the forms of nonhuman life and the physical environment.

The particularity of ecological literature lies in that it is an expression in the literary form showing that man and nature, after walking out of a vicious circle of confronting—conquering—retaliating, express their appeal to replace themselves in the correct positions. Many works of ecological literature forecast man's future of tribulation and the possibilities to walk out of the plight, bring forth the "perspective" that man and nature re-mingle into one in the warning of ecological culture in advance, and do their best to return to nature in order to escape the ecological disasters and the destruction of man in the future. Therefore, instead of describing the sense of quietness of man and nature in the natural scenes, ecological literature gives unprecedented prominence to man's grave plight in reality, offers aesthetic solutions to the plight which threatens the existence of human beings, goes beyond the thinking of the concrete problems and directly enters the deep concern of wisdom, wakens people's inherent sensibility of the moral relationship between man and the natural world, looks for the new way to go back to the harmonious world in which man and nature get along well with each other, and explores the new ethics of man and nature benefiting to each other in the development of man and nature.

B. Postmodern Ecological Literary Criticism

As an important way of literary criticism, Postmodern Ecological Literary Criticism enters ecological problems. On the one hand, it wants to solve the problem of the deep relationship between literature and the natural environment and on the other hand, it pays attention to the inherent relation between literature and social ecology, cultural ecology and spiritual ecology. Postmodern Ecological Literary Criticism pays attention to how a text displays or evokes man's nature of loving life which focuses itself in the inherent tendency of man in the course of life or something like the course of life, and inspires our imagination of the relation between us and the non-human natural world and our sensitivity for it. After the religious faith has brought the sense of security, modern anxiety, postmodern fragments and chaos, writers begin exploring the new way for man to return himself to the world, the new way to develop a cautious and benefiting-to-each-other ethics between man and nature. Therefore, an important drive force of Postmodern

Ecological Literary Criticism is to define, open and discuss the earnest request shown in literary forms. By using the views of modern ecology, Postmodern Ecological Literary Criticism examines the relationship between literature and nature, literature and society, and literature and man's spiritual state. At the same time, by using the narrative techniques of literary imagination, Postmodern Ecological Literary Criticism reflects ecological culture, gropes for man's poetical state of existence, and considers the relation between man-nature-art and criticism—the reflection of the relation of conquering and retaliating between man and nature, the confirming of the humanistic principles of Postmodern Ecological Literary Criticism, the deduction of the problem of modern subject-centrism, and the new construction of plural values. Finally, Postmodern Ecological Literary Criticism promotes all the members of the human world to bring up their deeper cultivation of ecological humanities.

There are six basic characteristics of Postmodern Ecological Literary Criticism:

1) Postmodern Ecological Literary Criticism mainly studies the problems of natural ecology and spiritual ecology, does its best to present the complicated tendency of man and natural world in the works, and grasps the relationship between literature and the natural environment interacting and involving each other. The frequency of Postmodern Ecological Literary Criticism used in literary criticism has been increased and extended in large scale so that ecological criticism has become an important term of literary theories included into dictionaries of terms of Western critical theories.

2) Postmodern Ecological Literary Criticism can also reinterpret traditional literary classics, unscrambling the covered cultural meaning and the aesthetic meaning of ecology, and reestablishing the poetic aesthetic relationship between man and himself, man and the Other, man and society, man and nature, and man and the earth.

3) Postmodern Ecological Literary Criticism keeps the "politically right" position in the problem of man's subjectivity in artistic creation—that is, it cannot hold the stand of anthropocentrism, nor the stand of absolutely nature-centrism, claiming man to change from self-awareness to ecological consciousness. The relationship between man and the earth is that they rely on each other in their coexistence and they die together if one of them is ruined. Man is no longer the dominator of nature but rather a member of the species of the earth, living and dying together with the other members in the natural world.

4) Postmodern Ecological Literary Criticism links literary studies to life science, does research of literature and nature from the two domains, and pays attention to entering the literary world from the angles of the development of human society and the change of ecological environment, and accordingly Postmodern Ecological Literary Criticism is characterized by trans-

disciplinary study. Postmodern Ecological Literary Criticism is the literary reflection after man has met ecological disasters, the artists' redefinition of man's position on the earth, and the re-liquidation of abuses of Western modernity.

5) When it views the phenomena of ecological culture, Postmodern Ecological Literary Criticism inherits the ideology of Green Revolution, stresses that literary creation should not deviate from literary spirit and literary discourse and that it should do its best to develop discourse narrative from the levels of literary forms and artistic techniques, and embodies the spirit of ecological culture through the formal beauty of the writing of "literariness."

6) The contents of Postmodern Ecological Literary Criticism require examining man's existent state in the past and in the future from the double field of vision of life essence and the earth. This angle of view links the literary study having merged into formalism with the survival problem of the earth full of all sorts of crises. Literature can hence abandon the word play of formalism, pull itself together from all sorts of discourses of literary criticism of language deconstruction, and resurvey the meaning of "man's" life and the ecological meaning of the "world."

As a whole, Postmodern Ecological Literary Criticism takes the relationship between literature and the natural environment as the domain of its own study. On the one hand, it must study "literariness," and on the other hand, it must touch the problem of "ecology." This synthesis of "literariness" and "ecology" is different from other literary criticism or literary theories. Postmodern Ecological Literary Criticism is full of hope for the human future, continually calls for the poetic and optimistic attitude toward existence, and spurns "despair for the future," and thereby shows the idiosyncrasy of optimistic spirit of Postmodern Ecological Literary Criticism.

C. Three Main Theories of Postmodern Ecological Literary Criticism

In order to solve the increasingly austere environmental crisis, deep ecology points out that the fundamental causes of environmental crisis lies in anthropocentrism in the existing culture of man. Deep ecology has established two principles: Self-realization and Biocentric Equality. Social ecology stoutly determines the roots of ecological crisis in the relation that man rules man. The ruling over nature is the product of man's ruling over man in human society. Social ecology thinks that man as a product of an endless natural evolution should belong in nature and make for an ecological society—a combination of non-hierarchical social system with perception. The tenet of Ecological Feminism (or Eco-feminism) lies in revealing the close relation between the ruling over nature and the ruling over women, opposing all sorts of forms of rule and oppression, taking opposing oppression, liberating women and solving ecological crisis together as the aim of its own struggle.

1. Deep Ecology

In 1973 in his essay, "The Shallow and the Deep, Long-range Ecology Movements: A Summary," Arne Naess definitely brought forward the notion of deep ecology. In Naess' opinion, the shallow ecology and the deep ecology are two entirely different ecological ideas in essence and the two ecologies have their different philosophical positions. The shallow ecology claims to protect environment and improve the relation between man and nature on the premise of not affecting man's interest, taking man's interest as the starting point and end-result of environment protection. The basis of its idea is anthropocentrism. Deep ecology regards the whole biosphere as an ecological holistic system and thinks that all the things in the system interrelate and interact with each other and that man is only a part of this system and absolutely not the center of it. The basis of its idea is ecological holism.

Deep ecology rejects the notions of Enlightenment, which separate man from nature, regard nature as the object of man's conquest and the Other, set up a binary hierarchical system between man and nature, and determines the relation between the two as that between master and slave. Deep ecology opposes this binary thought and thinks that man, animals and plants coexist in an equal space and closely relate to each other, and that the change of any one will affect the other two. Naess points out that the "depth" of deep ecology means "to ask closely the deep questions of 'why' and 'how.'" On the basis of endless questioning, deep ecology has discovered that man's environmental crisis lies not only in the superficial causes of population, economy, technique, etc., but also in the causes of the existing cultural mechanism and behavioral pattern of man, the binary hierarchical system and anthropocentrism in the system of philosophy. In this respect, the "depth" of deep ecology means a new non-binary thought, that is, the monistic holism. This holism thinks that everything in the world has its inherent values, has the right to exist and thrive; and that those practices of anthropocentrism not only harm the existence of other life bodies but also result in the alienation of man himself. The relationship between man and everything on earth should be harmonious coexistence, which is "live and let live" but not the intense confrontation with each other. In this respect, deep ecology and Post-structuralism have the same purports, both denying the values or the meaning center of separation and isolation, both abolishing the organizational body in which the center decides all and replacing it with a web structure stressing universal relations.

Eight Principles of Deep Ecology

On the basis of criticizing traditional anthropocentrism, deep ecology has established its own notion of ecological holism and instituted a sort of new criteria of existence that Naess calls Ecosophy, at the same time exposing negative influence brought by science. Deep ecology emphasizes using the ecological criteria to guide people's behavior and therefore more displays itself as a sort of ethical appeal, a sort of wisdom of existence or life.

On the basis of plural theories, deep ecology has summed up eight principles:

1) The existence and flourishing of human beings and non-human beings on the earth have their own values (synonyms: inherent values, connatural values). These values have nothing to do with the serviceability of non-human beings to human beings and the purposes of human beings.

2) The abundance and variety of the forms of life help to realize these values and the abundance and variety of the forms of life itself has values.

3) Man has no right to reduce these abundance and variety of the forms of life unless he needs to meet his basic requirements.

4) The thriving of man's life and culture needs to reduce the amount of population and the flourishing of life of non-human beings also needs to reduce the amount of population.

5) The contemporary human beings interfere too much in the world of non-human beings and this situation is rapidly deteriorating.

6) We must alter the existing policies. These policies are harmful to the basic configuration of economy, technology and ideology and the result of alteration will be greatly different from the present situation.

7) The change of ideology will be embodied in the judgment of life quality (stressing the intrinsic value of life) but not in the persistence of higher and higher standard of living. Human beings will deeply realize the difference between big quantity and high quality.

8) Those who support the above points of view are amenable to directly or indirectly actualize the necessary alteration.

On the basis of criticizing the dualism insisting that man and nature are opposite to each other, deep ecology has established the idea of monism insisting on ecological holism, carrying out this holism to the end and persisting in the high consistency of man's body and soul, action and understanding. In this respect, deep ecology is a sort of idea of monism persisting in ecological holism, which deviates from Western individualism but is more close to eastern holistic notion of "unity of heaven and man."

Two Supreme Principles of Deep Ecology

The idea of ecological holism is especially embodied in the two supreme principles of deep ecology indicated by Naess: Self-realization and eco-centric equalitarianism. The Self in Self-realization of deep ecology is composed with the capitalized letter S. It is the transcendental self, a sort of "great self," not the non-capitalized "self." The non-capitalized "self" in the Western tradition is a sort of detached self. It regards self as a specific and single person but not as an individual closely related to all sorts of factors; on the other hand, it often relates to *id*, emphasizing personal desire, pursuing hedonist satisfaction, and impetrating personal narrow salvage for this life or future life. Deep ecology thinks that this sort of narrow self makes man a victim for social fashion, and causes him to lose the chance of exploring his own special spirit and become an alienated being. The Self-realization in ecological sense is the full exhibition of man's potential, the state in which man becomes a genuine man. This sort of Self must be realized in the relationship between man and human community, between man and mother earth community. Only when people break away from the state of being detached and isolated "small self" and are able to closely hang together with the others, or break away from his family and friends and join the whole humanity, can the spirituality, which only human beings have, grow and develop, and will the Self gradually expand, surpass the whole humanity, and reach the whole identity including the natural world. Man is not an individual detached from nature but a part of nature. Self-realization means the realization of life potentials. Its process can be summarized as the idea that "nobody could be saved unless everybody is saved." Everybody here includes not only me or the single person but also the whole humanity, whales, gray bears, the whole ecological system in the rain forest, rivers and mountains, animalcules in the earth, etc.

Self-realization contains in it the principle of eco-centric equalitarianism because the process of Self-realization is a process in which self continually extends its identity with nature. The premise for Self-realization is just equality of all lives and esteem for all lives. Therefore, the harm done by man to the other parts of the natural world is the harm to himself. The abundance and variety of species in the natural world is the basis for stability and healthy development of ecological system. All existences are valuable to ecological system. All life bodies have their inherent purposes and have equal positions without distinction of ranks in the ecological system. Thereby, man does not have any prerogative to be superior to other species, neither being nobler nor being lowlier than other species. To see from this respect, the principle of eco-centric equalitarianism actually includes a basic principle of life: man's life should least but not most affect other species and the earth. That also is, man should live a kind of life with simple substance and rich spirit. Deep ecology does make deep reflection on the high substance demand advocated by capitalist modernity, thinks that the advertisement covering anywhere anytime in the industrial society constructs a wrong consciousness thinking that happiness is the greatest abundance of substance, which makes people's desire for substance continually swell as a result that capitalism unlimitedly expands production and catches more profit and consequently leads to the further intensified plunder and exploitation of nature. As a matter of fact, man's essential demand of substance is much simpler than people usually imagine. Man's extremely great desire for substance envelops man's spiritual direction, and makes man a slave of substance and unable to reach Self-realization. At the same time criticizing modern infinitely inflated desire for substance, deep ecology has established a new principle of life, that is, the life with "simple means but rich result" stated briefly by Naess.

2. Social Ecology

Social ecology is ecological science of human society, that is, science that works over the interrelation and interaction between human society and its environment (including the natural environment and the social environment), and it is an ecological theory that examines ecological problems from the social angle. The purpose to study the problem of social ecology is to reduce a variety of actions that are adverse and even harmful and that have already happened or will happen to the ecological environment of human society, which human beings themselves rely on to exist and develop, and accordingly consciously establish and maintain step by step ecological balance in favor of man's existence and development. Social ecologists think that the essence of ecological crisis is the problem of social philosophy and political philosophy, and its essential root is not the traditional metaphysics nor the misplay of ethics but the abuse of the pattern of social life. The notion that man rules over nature directly roots in the actuality that man rules over man. It is just the oppressive social structure, in which man rules over man, derives and strengthens the thinking patterns and the life patterns corresponding to all ruling forms (including the rule of man over nature). Thus, social ecology claims that we must abolish the oppressive system of society or else we cannot radically solve the ecological crisis. Through studying the relationship between individuals and the patterns of the social organizations in which they live, social ecology explores to establish the developmental patterns of the future society with healthy ecology and the equal relationship between man and nature on the basis of social equity.

Basic Viewpoints of Social Ecology

In order to eliminate the ecological crisis in the world and save the earth today, according to different theories, people provide different ways: family planning, green science and technology, limited production, reasonable consumption, constructing ecological culture, etc. However, these methods are only limited in the direction of man's practice and activities to change the natural world, and have failed to criticize and reflect the society itself from the overall height of the whole human society. Population, science and technology, culture, economy, production, and consumption are all component elements of the society itself. No matter how they develop and operate, they all are affected and controlled by the notion of social existence itself. Modern human society takes pursuing opulence of substance and extravagance as the ultimate aim of its existence, and conquers and plunders the natural world through its component elements of "will for power"—production, consumption, science and technology, culture, etc. It contains the essential rupture from the natural world and the inherent intension to oppose and destroy nature. Modern human society prescribes the society as a pure human society that has essentially broken up with the natural world and at the same time stipulates the anti-nature essence of the human society. That which suffers from the ecological crisis is not the natural world itself but also includes man himself. Consequently, only through deeply knowing the human society itself from the angle of social ecology, can we radically remove the ecological crisis.

Insisting on Organic Holism of Ecological System

American social ecology, represented by Murray Bookchin, insists on the worldview of organic holism of ecological system, criticizes and opposes the ideology of dualism that considers man has broken up with nature and has held the dominant position since the industrial civilization. At the same time, social ecology thinks that human beings should not only belong in nature but they are products of the lengthy evolution of nature. Judging by appearance, if there was no natural quality which was formed in large numbers of years, though they have brains and walk with their feet, and accordingly they set free their hands and use their hands to make tools and take food, human beings' non-natural activities, such as the development of science and technology, the formation of inconstant social system, the formation of the communication forms with high degree of signs, the formation of aesthetic sensitivity, the establishment of cities and towns, etc., all are impossible. In many respects, the notable characteristics of human beings are the amplification of nonhuman characteristics that have passed through the evolution for a long period of years.

Bookchin thinks that human beings root in their history of biological evolution, which we call "the first nature," but they have formed their own special human social nature, which we may call "the second nature." Man's second nature is far from being "non-natural," but obviously the creature of the first nature from the evolution of the organic world. From social ecology, we understand that nature and the society interrelate with each other through entering an evolution of nature and the nature includes the first (biological) nature and the second (human) nature. The biological nature and the human nature share the potential of evolution that will realize greater subjectivity and adaptability. The second nature is a way of human beings as the highly intellective quadrumana that have the ability of adaptation to live in the natural world. In other words, human beings create circumstances that are most fit for the way of their existence. In this respect, the circumstances are accordant with the biological physical circumstances—the economic community—that each animal creates and adapts itself to with its own ability and in which each animal must live. Therefore, human beings emerging from the process of organic evolution have begun, by right of their purely biological force and the force needed for survival, a development of social evolution, which deeply contains the process of their organic evolution. On account of the intellect, the power of communication, the ability of organization of institution that nature endows them and the relative freedom from their instinctive behavior, human beings, like non-human lives, bring their biological capacity into full play to re-create circumstances. Now, this sort of capacity makes it possible for them to undertake social development.

Human Beings Must Give up the Idea to Rule and Conquer Nature

In Bookchin's opinion, civilization cannot but inevitably compete with nature and human beings obtain simple things that they need for their survival from biological circumstances. Actually, civilization characterized by rationalism and techniques is regarded as a new destruction of nature. Excluding the natural world out of the social essence and the inner structure of human society metaphorically means two notions of basic values in the modern society. One is the construction of the master-slave relationship between human society and nature. In this structure of relation, human society is in the absolute position of master and the natural world in the absolute position of slave. That which man legislates for nature is the immanent logic of this structure of relation. The other is human society's mental state of technological functionalism toward natural world as well as the value idea of modern instrumentalism breeding out of this mental state.

Due to the appearance of hierarchy and human rule, people have planted the seed of faith that nature exists not only as a detached world but also as a world that is organized in hierarchy and could be controlled by man. Here, we must stress that the idea to rule nature mainly roots in man's ruling over man and in the construction that natural world becomes a hierarchical chain of existence. The idea to rule nature has a history as age-old as the history of the idea of hierarchy. Only in modern ecological activities, the society of elite had destroyed many places in the basin of Mediterranean Sea and the beautiful rivers and mountains in other parts of the world. This point sufficiently proves that the hierarchical society and the class society began rebuilding and plundering this planet early before the appearance of the linear rationalism of modern science and the industrial society. No doubt, the second nature did not create a Garden of Eden in the process in which it stably absorbed and damaged the first nature. It frequently plunders many nice, creative and vigorous things in the biological world just as it destroys human life per se in the actions such as causing wars to make deaths, carrying out genocide and slaughter, and implementing ruthless oppression. Social ecologists pay attention not only to the fact that the damage done by the society of elite to the natural world exceeded that to human beings but also to the fact that the fate of human life and the fate of non-human world stand together through thick and thin. In order to realize the harmony between society and nature in the ecological system, human society must give up the idea to rule and conquer nature and establish an ecological system in which the relationship between society and nature is harmonious.

Knowing the Destructiveness of Capitalism

Bookchin deeply criticizes the destructiveness of everlasting expanding of capitalism to the social ecology. He pointed out that just like the hierarchical and class structures that tend to obtain a sort of their own drive and infiltrate it into most of the society, human markets also begin to acquire a sort of their own life and expand its area outside of their limited field and come into the depth of the far-flung continent. Transaction no longer mainly provides means needed within measure but it has overthrown the limitations imposed upon it through guilds or moral and religious restrictions. It not only encourages science and technology but also becomes the producer of necessities, many of which are completely worthless. It also greatly promotes consumption, science and technology. The industrial capitalists in the modern world have created intensely competitive markets that encourage industrial expansion and the business forces that it endows, and move on in the manner as if development is purpose per se. What social ecology emphasizes is that modern capitalism has nothing to do with morality in structure and therefore it is not influenced by any moral requests. Modern markets have their own rules. The direction that they follow does not rely on ethical elements but rather on the mindless rules of supply and demand, which means development or death, eating off or being eaten off. The society based on "development or death" as its rule over every aspect certainly has a destructive impact on ecology. If they want to survive, enterprisers must always expand, foster media to promote mindless consumption, and increase commodity purchase regardless of whether these commodities are needed. Modern technology does not rely on its own force to destroy this planet; it fosters a phenomenon—continually expanded markets: the hierarchical and class elaboration has formed a sort of distributive system based on exchange not on complementarity and mutual help.

Basic Propositions of Social Ecology to Construct an Ecological Society

About human cooperation and its origin, the view of ecological society admits that human beings as animals are organized according to the biological principles, thereby they live together with their same species, care for and cherish their same species in a wide and extensive and freely defined social community. These human characteristics are regarded not only as natural characteristics of human beings but also as components of human nature per se. As a matter of fact, they are inseparable from the evolution of human subjectivity and individuality. These characteristics are not only treated as the mechanism of survival or social characteristics but also as the component materials of the structure of ecological society. This presupposition can provide basis for reconstructing an ecological society.

Social ecology not only appeals to moral regeneration, what is more important, it calls on social reconstruction along the ecological course. Though it always pays attention to spiritual change, social ecology seeks to correct the ecological abuse imposed upon the natural world by society through discussing subjective and objective roots of the notions such as "ruling over nature." To speak more exactly, it challenges the entire ruling system, pursues eliminating the hierarchical and class mansion that imposes itself upon human beings, and defines non-human and human nature. In order to replace the existing hierarchical and class system, social ecology brings forward a society, built on the basis of helping each other, caring for each other, and the social values of public ownership, that claims equality. Social ecology relies on the following few interrelated preconditions:

1) Human beings are a part of the nature but have their special social consciousness.

2) Environmental crisis is the result of the structures of hierarchical power located in the heart of our society.

3) The damages that these structures of power have done to human beings are at least as much as those that they have done to environment.

4) Through establishing society on the basis of the principles of social ecology, the relationship between us and nature will be changed.

5) These principles of social ecology claim equality and are based on helping each other, caring for each other and the social values of public ownership.

6) This sort of change will be realized through complete collective actions and cooperative social movements.

Ecological society is the essential unification of human society and the natural world as well as the dialectical unification of the relationship between man and man and the relationship between man and nature. The inherent purpose of the development of ecological society is to make the existence of the natural world no longer outside of society, to make the existence and development of ecological society no longer the pure pursuit of realizing man's own interest, and to maintain the harmonious and evolutionary relationship between man and nature without fail.

3. Eco-feminist Criticism

The term, Eco-feminism, was put forward for the first time by French woman scholar Francoise d'Eaubonne in her work *Feminism or Death* in 1974. Her purpose was to appeal to women to join up and launch an ecological revolution to save the earth. In her book, d'Eaubonne binds ecological ideas and feminist ideas together, revealing that there is an important and natural relation between nature and women. From then on, Eco-feminism as a philosophical thought full of vital force and vigor began to gradually diffuse and spread in the West and has been increasingly developed and become grander and grander along with the grandness of environmental protection movement and the rise of green revolution. Its advocates say that paternalistic/capitalistic society has led to a harmful split between nature and culture. Early Eco-feminists propagated that the split can only be healed by the feminine instinct for nurture and holistic knowledge of nature's processes. Modern Eco-feminism, or feminist Eco-criticism, eschews such essentialism and instead focuses more on intersectional questions, such as how the nature-culture split enables the oppression of female and nonhuman bodies. It is also an activist and academic movement that sees critical connections between the exploitation of nature and the domination over women both caused by men.

The tenet of Eco-feminism consists of revealing that in the field of human thoughts and the structure of society there is a close relation between ruling women and ruling nature, opposing all sorts of dominion and oppression, and taking opposing oppression, liberating women, and solving ecological crisis together as its own aim of struggle.

Eco-feminism can be divided approximately into Cultural Eco-feminism represented by American scholar Susan Griffin, Spiritual Eco-feminism whose representative is American scholar Charlene Spretnak (1946–), Social Eco-feminism represented by American scholars Karen J. Warren and Carolyn Merchant, and Socialist Eco-feminism whose representative is Indian scholar Vandana Shiva and German scholar Maria Mies. The former two emphasize the relation between women and nature, Social Eco-feminism attempts to weaken the relation between women and nature, and Socialist Eco-feminists think that both enhancing and weakening the relation between women and nature cannot benefit women. Eco-feminism must equally look on men and women because each person is "natural" and "cultural" as well. Though there are differences between schools, their theoretical propositions have more to communicate with each other.

Theoretical Propositions of Eco-feminism

Eco-feminist scholar Karen J. Warren put forward the following viewpoints. There is a close relation between the oppression of women and the oppression of nature. The understanding of the essence of the relation helps fully understand the oppression that women and nature suffer from. The theory and practice must depend on the angle of ecological view. The resolution of ecological problems must rely on the angle of feminist view. These viewpoints have become the basic common understanding of eco-feminists.

After she examined the relation between man's ruling over women and human beings' ruling over nature, Warren pointedly indicated that they both rooted in the worldview and ideology of "patriarchy," revealing that the theoretical basis of "patriarchy" to enslave women and nature is a sort of "framework of oppressive notion." The framework of oppressive notion has three key characters: 1) the values of dual opposition; 2) the values of hierarchical thinking; 3) the logic of ruling. In this framework of notion, all things are divided into two opposite sides. One of them holds higher values and position and the other is endowed with lower values and position. In terms of the ruling logic, the side with higher values and position has the legitimate right of ruling over the other side. In the culture of patriarchy, the logic of ruling used to justify enslaving women and nature is based on the following points of logical reasoning: 1) Human beings are able to consciously change their own social life but plants and rocks have no such ability; 2) No matter what, if only they are able to consciously change their own society, human beings are morally superior to those that are short of such ability; 3) Therefore, human beings are morally superior to plants and rocks; 4) For any X and Y, if X is morally superior to Y, X's ruling over Y could be morally justified; 5) Accordingly, human beings' ruling over plants and rocks is morally justified.

In a similar way, in the culture of patriarchy, men's ruling over women follows the same logic: 1) Women are affirmed as belonging in the domain of nature and substance, and men in the realm of mankind and spirit; 2) The colony affirmed as belonging in the domain of nature and substance is lower than the colony in the realm of mankind and spirit; 3) Therefore, women are lower than men; 4) For any X and Y, if X is superior to Y, Y should be subject to X; 5) Men's ruling over women is justified.

Eco-feminist Val Plumwood has further studied the logical structure of oppressive dualism, pointing out that it is the tradition of rationalism formed since ancient Greece that sustains the framework of notion of Western patriarchy and finally leads to the dimidiate manliness's colonization of womanliness.

The aims of Eco-feminism are to deconstruct all oppressive frameworks of notion, to oppose all sorts of forms of dominion and oppression, and to reconstruct more feasible forms of society and politics. Eco-feminism takes opposing oppression, liberating women, and solving ecological crisis along with all the Others as its own aims of struggle and does its best to realize the common development of women and nature and the continuable development of all human beings.

Eco-feminism is one of the schools of postmodern criticism. It challenges, deconstructs, and criticizes logos-centrism, which shows itself in two aspects: in the aspect of relation between man and nature, eco-feminism criticizes and deconstructs androcentrism; in the aspect of the relation between power and order, eco-feminism criticizes and deconstructs Phallocentrism.

While casting back the history of androcentrism, eco-feminist Marie Richmond Abbott indicated that since the patriarchal society was founded, men conquer nature and also introduce the metaphor of conquering nature into the discourse system of conquering women. Women are related to the natural world represented by their bodies, considered low-grade and in the subordinate position. Women represent desire of bodies and the earth dominated by men. Men represent spirit, thought and soul. Just because they are linked to earthborn bodies and desire, women are at the same time deemed to be unclean, impure, and wicked. Through dichotomy of soul/body, spirit/nature, men/women, men comprehend women as objects of dominating, taming, civilizing, and purifying. Through their debasing bodies, nature and women, men have acquired the right to suppress the force of women.

As a rising theory of Cultural Criticism, Eco-feminist Criticism is a sort of ethical criticism in essence. In recent years, Eco-feminism has had new development. Some environmentalists and social critics paying attention to ecological problems think that anthropocentrism is the root of thought that leads to the crisis of ecology. But Eco-feminist critics think that “anthropo” in anthropocentrism should not indicate “all people” but only include “men” especially “white men.” Women, colored ethnic group, working class, the poor and backward countries of the Third World, and other weak and small nations are all direct victims of patriarchal culture that leads to ecological crisis. Therefore, the root of ecological crisis should be androcentrism but not broad anthropocentrism.

Further Reading

Abram, David. *The Spell of the Sensuous: Perception and Language in a More-than-Human World*. New York: Pantheon, 1996.

Alex, Rayson K., S. Susan Deborah & Sachindev P. S. *Culture and Media: Ecocritical Explorations*. Cambridge: Cambridge Scholars Publishing, 2014.

Barry, Peter. Ecocriticism // *Beginning Theory: An Introduction to Literary and Cultural Theory*.

3rd ed. Manchester: Manchester University Press, 2009.

Buell, Lawrence. *The Environmental Imagination: Thoreau, Nature Writing, and the Formation of American Culture*. Cambridge: Harvard University Press, 1995.

Bilbro, Jeffrey. *Loving God's Wildness: The Christian Roots of Ecological Ethics in American Literature*. Tuscaloosa: University of Alabama Press, 2015.

Buell, Lawrence. *Writing for an Endangered World: Literature, Culture, and Environment in the U.S. and Beyond*. Cambridge: Harvard University Press, 2001.

Coupe, Laurence. *The Green Studies Reader: From Romanticism to Ecocriticism*. London: Routledge, 2000.

Frederick, Suresh. *Contemporary Contemplations on Ecoliterature*. New Delhi: Authorpress, 2012.

Garrard, Greg. *Ecocriticism*. New York: Routledge, 2004.

Garrard, Greg. *The Oxford Handbook of Ecocriticism*. Oxford: Oxford University Press, 2014.

Glotfelty, Cheryll & Harold Fromm. *The Ecocriticism Reader: Landmarks in Literary Ecology*. Athens: University of Georgia, 1996.

Heise, Ursula K. Greening English: Recent Introductions to Ecocriticism. *Contemporary Literature* 47. 2, 2006: 289–298.

Kroeber, Karl. *Ecological Literary Criticism: Romantic Imagining and the Biology of Mind*. New York: Columbia University Press, 1994.

Lindholdt, Paul. *Explorations in Ecocriticism: Advocacy, Bioregionalism, and Visual Design*. Lanham: Lexington Books, 2015.

Marx, Leo. *The Machine in the Garden: Technology and the Pastoral Ideal in America*. Oxford: Oxford University Press, 1964.

McKusick, James C. *Green Writing: Romanticism and Ecology*. New York: St. Martin's, 2000.

Meeker, Joseph W. *The Comedy of Survival: Studies in Literary Ecology*. New York: Scribner's, 1972.

Moore, Bryan L. *Ecology and Literature: Ecocentric Personification from Antiquity to the Twenty-first Century*. New York: Palgrave Macmillan, 2008.

Morton, Timothy. *The Ecological Thought*. Cambridge: Harvard University Press, 2012.

Nichols, Ashton. *Beyond Romantic Ecocriticism: Toward Urbanatural Roosting*. New York: Palgrave Macmillan, 2011.

Nicolson, Marjorie Hope. *Mountain Gloom and Mountain Glory: The Development of the Aesthetics of the Infinite*. Seattle: University of Washington Press, 1959.

Phillips, Dana. *The Truth of Ecology: Nature, Culture, and Literature in America*. Oxford: Oxford University Press, 2003.

Rueckert, William. Literature and Ecology: An Experiment in Ecocriticism. *Iowa Review* 9. 1,

1978: 71–86.
Slovic, Scott. *Seeking Awareness in American Nature Writing: Henry Thoreau, Annie Dillard, Edward Abbey, Wendell Berry, Barry Lopez.* Salt Lake: University of Utah Press, 1992.
Williams, Raymond. *The Country and the City.* London: Chatto and Windus, 1973.
Zapf, Hubert. Literary Ecology and the Ethics of Texts. *New Literary History* 39. 4, 2008: 847–868.

Bibliography

Cuddon, J. A. *A Dictionary of Literary Terms and Literary Theory*. 5th ed. Malden: Wiley-Blackwell, 2013.
Rice, Philip & Patricia Waugh. *Modern Literary Theory*. New York: Oxford University Press, 2002.
Bressler, Charles. *Literary Criticism: An Introduction to Theory and Practice*. Beijing: Higher Education Press, 2004.
胡志红 . 西方生态批评史 . 北京：人民出版社，2015.
泰勒，温奎斯特. 后现代主义百科全书. 章燕，李自修，等译. 刘象愚，校. 长春：吉林人民出版社，2007.
王治河. 后现代主义辞典. 北京：中央编译出版社，2004.
王守仁，朱刚，姚成贺 . 英美文学批评史 . 南京：南京大学出版社，2021.
张中载，王逢振，赵国新. 二十世纪西方文论选读. 北京：外语教学与研究出版社，2002.
朱刚. 二十世纪西方文艺批评理论. 上海：上海外语教育出版社，2001.

Selected Readings

Arne Naess: “The Shallow and the Deep, Long-range Ecology Movements: A Summary”

Murray Bookchin: *The Ecology of Freedom: The Emergence and Dissolution of Hierarchy* (a part of a chapter)

Karen J. Warren: “Introduction to Ecofeminism”

Chapter Sixteen

Ecological Postmodernism

Generally speaking, Ecological Postmodernism is closely related with Eco-criticism. It is the postmodern turn of Eco-criticism. Furthermore, it is the newest development of Eco-criticism in the new historic condition. In fact, it derives from Eco-criticism. Some critics saw the connection between the Eco-criticism and Postmodernism. They work to explore their characteristics in common. In the long exploration, they found that it is possible to combine these two theories.

When the spring tide of deconstruction gradually ebbed in the 1980s, Charlene Spretnak, American famous thinker of postmodernism and theorist of Ecological Feminism, put forward and constructed the new theory of Ecological Postmodernism which Spretnak often called "Ecological Postmodernism," "constructive postmodernism" or "reconstructive postmodernism." Spretnak was an activist of American feminist movement and green movement, an active advocator and an initiator of Ecological Feminism and Ecological Postmodernism. So far she has participated in organizing and masterminding 5 international conferences on Ecological Postmodernism. Her work in the fields of Spirituality, Cultural History, Feminism and other social criticisms and ecological thoughts (Green Politics, Eco-feminist Movement, Eco-philosophy) etc. has been internationally recognized. Through her work in the second half of the 1970s and in the earlier 1980s, she has become one of the founders of female spiritual movement. Her first monograph *Lost Goddess of Early Greece: A Collection of Pre-Hellenic Myths* (1978) is the first reconstruction of the Olympic myths. In 1982, Spretnak edited an anthology entitled *The Politics of Women's Spirituality*, in which she put forward a framework for understanding the female spiritual movement that had naturally generated. This anthology is divided into three parts: the first part discusses the history of resuming female spirit; the second part deals with the growth of individual spirit; the third part expounds the political activism that was encouraged by spiritual practice. In 1991, she wrote the book *States of Grace: The Recovery of Meaning in the Postmodern Age* which explains the four great spiritual traditions and the relativity of their solutions of modern crises. The four great traditions discussed in the book are Buddhism, American indigenous spirit, the contemporary renaissance of female spirit, and the religious group of Abraham (Judaism, Christianity, and Islam). *Boston Globe* highly praised this work, thinking that Spretnak has outstanding genius to span a bridge between knowledge and the "real" world. Besides these works, Spretnak also wrote and published three works dealing with ecological politics and ecological philosophy. She wrote in collaboration with Fritjof Capra the book *Green Politics: The Global Promise* (1984), which became the catalyzer of the formation of German Green Party Movement. In 1986, her speech at the Annual Meeting of E. F. Choumacher Academy in U.S. A. was published with the title *The Spiritual Dimension of Green Politics*. Her work *The Resurgence of the Real: Body, Nature, and Place in a Hypermodern World* (1997), with its original view, critical insight, and purified writing, was praised as an important masterpiece and a beacon of thoughts and called one of the best works of the year by *The Los Angeles Times*. Being different from other postmodernist works, *The Resurgence of the Real* not only discloses all sorts of phenomena that take man and logos as centers and analyzes the modern ideology behind them, but also pays attention to the resisting movements that people launched against the background that modern worldview dominated everything under the sun. In her next work, *Missing Mary: The Queen of Heaven and Her Re-Emergence in the Modern Church* (2004), Spretnak challenged the great depreciation of the position and meaning of Virgin Mary that had been modernized in Roman Catholicism in more than 40 years in the past. Roman Catholicism largely denied the dimensions of the symbolic meaning of Virgin Mary, cosmism, and mysticism. When explaining several social forces at the joint between religion and modernity, Spretnak not only explained but also promoted the coming round of grass roots with the contemporary spirituality of Virgin Mary. In 2011, she published *Relational Reality: New Discoveries of Interrelatedness That Are Transforming the Modern World*. In this new work, she emphasized the importance of interrelatedness in the modern life. Besides, she published a mass of articles, lectures, and interviews. These works and articles not only directly impelled the development of green political movements, but also just in these articles and works Spretnak brought forward her own thoughts of "Ecological Postmodernism" and accordingly made great contributions to the development of postmodernism.

A. Thoughts of Ecological Postmodernism

In its origin of thoughts, Ecological Postmodernism put forward by Spretnak was consistent with "non-deconstructionist forms of postmodernism" by David Griffin, Richard Falk, Charles Jencks, and the others, and closely related to constructive postmodernism so that it could be considered an important component part of constructive postmodernism. Ecological Postmodernism spurns modernity because "in many deep meanings modernity had not realized the better life that it promised."① Modernity has not brought with it a "peaceful world" nor a "free world" as it promised but with many problems. For example, the United States today is not only faced with the exterior crises of modernity (such as the destruction of the natural world, nuclear threat, and the sacrifice of the Third World) but also with the internal crises of modernity (such as the destruction of ideals, the loss of meaning, etc.). In this situation, "The drive to look for another way of survival hatches Ecological Postmodernism," and "we are forced to look for a new way or a way that has been already discovered to understand nature and our relation with nature."②

While analyzing the crises of modernity, Spretnak described their exterior forms as: 1) supposition of economic man; 2) industrialism; 3) objectivism; 4) rationalism; 5) worldview of mechanism, scienticism; 6) standardization; 7) bureaucratic politics and centralization; 8) anthropocentrism; 9) being opposite to nature and despising countrymen; 10) compartmentation, getting away from religions, and the reducing of the background of cosmism; 11) being extremely male. Among these forms, the supposition of economic man is one of the most central suppositions of modernity. It is just based on this supposition that nature is regarded as dirt-cheap and it is only the "resource"③ to be exploited for the Gross National Product. It is also based on this supposition that the meaning of man's life is identified with the struggle with nature. Spretnak thought that this worldview of modernity has engendered huge negative influence on the development of human society. The hurt to the real is one of its main negative influences. In the book *The Resurgence of the Real*, she concretely analyzed the harm that modernity does to the three aspects of the real—body, nature and place. Spretnak pointed out that "Modern life promised freedom from the vagaries of the body, the limits of nature, and the local ties to

①② Charlene Spretnak, *States of Grace: The Recovery of Meaning in the Postmodern Age*, San Francisco: Harper San Francisco, 1991, p. 12.

③ Charlene Spretnak, *Postmodern Directions in Spirituality*; Wang Zhihe, "Spretnak and Her Ecological Postmodernism," *Foreign Social Science*, 1997: 6, p. 50.

place."[①] In terms of modern worldview, "The body came to be seen as a biological machine, the natural world as a mere externality in modern economies, and the sense of a place as a primitive precursor to cosmopolitan sophistication."[②] Day after day, people are deeply poisoned by this worldview. Ecological Postmodernism thinks that "body" is "the unified bodymind," "nature" is "our physical context from which our bodies are not separate," and "place" is "the bioregion, the physical site of community and personal unfolding."[③]

In economy, politics and education, technology plays an important role in creating hypermodern conditions. Therefore, the criticism of technology (including the technology in the information times) also becomes a component part of Ecological Postmodernism. Spretnak thought, "The purpose and design of every new technology reflect our culture. In recent years, we have seen that technical innovation carries forth modern values into the hypermodern forms."[④] In judging the technique in the information times, it will not do that only by narrow-sensed "efficiency" that can be estimated in quantity, which will ignore its complicated and systematic influence. Take TV for example. Though TV provides amusement, it performs the function of business and orientation: it diffuses modern values. It conciliates values and desires by screening other views. Spretnak criticized modern people's blind optimism to technology. She indicated, "Those of us socialized in modern societies generally maintain an irrationally uncritical attitude toward new technologies,"[⑤] the result of which is that people are willingly to become testees of all sorts of techniques. The reason why people believe in new techniques is that the faith that modernity keeps in technical innovation like the faith in progress is found everywhere in people's thoughts. Therefore, if we want to explode the blind faith in technology, we must radically reflect modernity.

For Spretnak, "Our age is *hypermodern*"[⑥] because modern worldviews and modernity are still very commercioganic, and the conditions of modernity are driven by the large-scale development of technology and the whole global economy. "'Cyberspace' is hardly *post*modern,"[⑦] because it is so unreal, non-embedded and divorced from background. On the contrary, the computer era can be said to be the most modern. Spretnak definitely pointed out, "A truly postmodern choice would, starting from body, nature and place, struggle with the modern

①② Charlene Spretnak, *The Resurgence of the Real: Body, Nature, and Place in a Hypermodern World*, New York: Addison-Wesley Publishing Company, Inc., 1997, p. 2.

③ Ibid., p. 4.

④⑤ Ibid., p. 124.

⑥⑦ Ibid., p. 222.

ideology. It would be a grounded, deeply ecological, and spiritual postmodernism."[①] If they want to break away from modern crises, people must seek a new thinking and discover a new way. Postmodernism (regardless of constructive postmodernism or deconstructive postmodernism) is just a breakthrough to modernity and the result of seeking the new thinking.

Though the "deconstructive postmodernism" represented by Jacques Derrida and Ecological Postmodernism by Spretnak are both breakthrough to modernity, there is an important difference between Ecological Postmodernism and deconstructive postmodernism. The philosophical core of deconstructive postmodernism is the rejection to the "Real." To deconstructive postmodernism, there is no so-called stable, changeless, and universal real, oneness is the result of rule and oppression, and the temporary success of specific rhetoric strategy and all the structures of knowledge are invented. An unacknowledged will to power lies concealed within the claim to truth. The quest for the Real conceals most Western philosophers' desire, which is to master the world once and for all.[②] Deconstructive postmodernism stressed that in human experiences there is only the "social construction" of concepts (such as language, knowledge system, and culture) and that we could not know nature or our bodies outside of the cultural structure that we have accepted, that is, we would deny that human beings could approach to the real. In Spretnak's opinion, deconstructive postmodernism is right to negate absolute truth, but its denial to truth *per se* is not different from the case of "throwing out the baby with the bathwater."[③] It is obvious that criticizing and denying deconstructive postmodernism becomes an important theoretical content of Ecological Postmodernism.

Spretnak criticized deconstructive postmodernists in that they had cited the works by Jacques Derrida, Michel Foucault, Jean-Francois Lyotard, and others for so many years but they have never mentioned the existence of the part of anti-foundationalism in Western philosophy since the Greeks, the loss of faith in scientific positivism in the late 19th century, the capricious viewpoint of Nietzsche, the integrated "language games" illuminated by Wittgenstein, the sociology of knowledge, and the various political critiques of rationalist, patriarchal, racist framings of reality that were put forth by grassroots movement of the 1960s.[④] What is more important, "deconstructive postmodernism is still confined in the patriarchal hedge of modernity."[⑤] Spretnak

---

① Charlene Spretnak, *The Resurgence of the Real: Body, Nature, and Place in a Hypermodern World*, New York: Addison-Wesley Publishing Company, Inc., 1997, p. 223.

② Ibid., p. 65.

③ Ibid., p. 66.

④ Ibid., p. 67.

⑤ Wang Zhihe, "Spretnak and Her Ecological Postmodernism," *Foreign Social Science*, 1997: 6, p. 51.

pointed out, "Deconstructive postmodernism continues the project of patriarchy to distrust and debase the body through regarding the body as a feelingless container full of power's encroaching and a trustless and double-dealing collaborator."① In practice, deconstructive postmodernism has accepted the humanism of Renaissance and the meta-narrative of scientific revolution. This meta-narrative deviates from the greater actuality so that it apotheosizes man and accordingly anthropocentrism has been generated. Not only that, because it is deeply influenced by economic determinism, deconstructive postmodernism regards economic terms (such as "libido economics" and "social production") as right ways to describe everything.

In terms of the views of Ecological Postmodernism, deconstructive postmodernism is actually "modern" because the education that deconstructive postmodernists have received is all the while scientistic-humanist. In the social circumstance in which they are, this worldview in dominant position disregards the right and presence of nature and has never challenged the dual oppositions set up by modernity between man and nature, body and spirit, self and the Others. This is why deconstructive postmodernists do not criticize all sorts of ideas that distort truth (such as regarding truth as an entity that is independent of us in its existence), instead they oppose people to pursue truths, do not attack Hegelian absolute system, do not criticize Plato-type stable and invariable and anti-ecological actuality. Spretnak definitely pointed out that modernity places human beings in a glass box on the summit of nature, insists on the radical opposition between man and nature, and separates human stories from greater community of the earth; the true postmodernists should spurn this sort of opposition, should open the box and replace human beings back to the greater background, that is, to the earth, the universe and into the divine whole. In other words, the true essence of postmodernism should be "ecological."②

However, in the attention to ecology, Ecological Postmodernism is different from all kinds of environmentalisms, also different from the ecology in broad sense (because the latter is short of understanding the modern crises historically, politically and philosophically). Ecological Postmodernism is a sort of ontology, a brand-new way of thinking, which helps to radically change modern men's way of thinking. Ecological Postmodernism thinks, "not only all beings are related in tow through the chain of universe but all beings are inherently composed with their relationship

① Charlene Spretnak, *States of Grace: The Recovery of Meaning in the Postmodern Age*, San Franciso: Harper San Franciso, 1991, p. 150.

② Wang Zhihe, "Spretnak and Her Ecological Postmodernism," *Foreign Social Science*, 1997: 6, p. 52.

to the others."[①] Spretnak indicated, "Foremost, 'Ecological Postmodernism' changes the essential gestalt. Instead of perceiving ourselves as social 'atoms' colliding and combining with other abstract 'atoms' in a human society that uses and projects concepts onto its background matter (nature), we perceive an unbroken continuity of cosmos/Earth/continent/nation/bioregion/community/neighborhood/family/person. These are the extended boundaries of the self. The cosmos is our field, our foundation, and our existence. Moreover, we finally slough off the modern obsession with escaping from nature and realize that all human behavior is derivative of the Earth community, not the other ways around. As Thomas Berry, a geologist, reminds us, the Earth is the great economy, the great educationist, the great healer, the great organizer, the great artist and the storyteller, the great experimentalist, and the great blend of cosmic novelty and continuity. Our institutions and actions can fit well or badly into that larger context, our extended sense of being. Ecological Postmodernism, then, replaces groundlessness with groundedness, supplanting freedom *from* nature with freedom *in* nature. This orientation acknowledges the enormous role of social construction of concepts in shaping human experiences, but it also acknowledges our constitutive embeddedness in subtle bodily, ecological, and cosmological *processes*."[②]

The scientific basis of Ecological Postmodernism is postmodern science. Postmodern physics has discovered the distant but profound interrelation of nature. All these help to change the worldview of modern science. Spretnak's Ecological Postmodernism is on-limits. It is open to all cultural heritages of human beings, that is, it is open not only to modernism but also to deconstructive postmodernism. She definitely points out that Ecological Postmodernism refuses to become a sort of stuffy "foundationalism" of ecocentrism, but wants to become "a creative orientation." Scientists holding holism, philosophers insisting on processes, artists of vision and deconstructive postmodernists are all objects of its dialogs. It pays special attention to drawing nutrition from the traditional wisdoms of some nations, including the cultural tradition of Buddhism, the cultural tradition of American aborigines, the spiritual tradition of Goddess, the tradition of Judaism, the tradition of Chinese culture, etc. The wisdoms in these traditional cultures make man's spirit (soul) change from restlessness to inherent balance, from enfeebling banishment to embracing the earth community, from denying body to affecting ecology, and from being indifferent to the Others to actively caring for the Others. Spretnak thought that these

① Charlene Spretnak, *States of Grace: The Recovery of Meaning in the Postmodern Age*, San Francisco: Harper San Franciso, 1991, p. 20.

② Ibid., pp. 72–73.

wisdoms help us develop new ways of boosting differences, subjectivity and our relation to the earth community.①

Ecological Postmodernism tells us that what the abandonment of determinate modern worldview will bring to people should not be feeling lost and despair but a sort of liberation. "Instead of being indifferent manipulators, we now begin to understand ourselves as participators in the universe."② Spretnak's Ecological Postmodernism takes resuming man's groundwork in the universe, resuming the meaning of life, and making people get back into groups as its aims of struggle in its initial stages. Spretnak clear-headedly knew that modern worldview has already been so deeply immersed in people's thoughts that it is not an easy thing to transform it. This will be resisted by those whose thoughts have been intruded into by modern worldview not only inwardly but also soulfully. "When they heard the criticism on the negative effects of modernity, they would think it was the criticism on all that we perceive (all that they said)."③ Besides, modern people persist in thinking that progress has carried us into an era that is better than any time in the past. If we stay in this course, we will continue to be far from harm and adversity. It turns out that other choices are considered hazardous and fearful. Therefore, if we want to radically change modern worldview, we must have the key points in mind and set about from the unimportant issues, especially start with education and with children. In the setup of curriculum, we must carry out ecological consciousnesses such as "interdependency," "continuity," "partnership," "flexibility," "diversity," etc. into it. We will have a thorough reform in schoolbooks full of anthropocentrism, male-centrism, Europe-centrism, economic determinism.④

Spretnak's Ecological Postmodernism was a fresh troop in the postmodernist camp. It is also the new development of postmodernism in the contemporary era. Where she was different from Derrida, Foucault (male philosophers, thinkers), and Griffin (male scientist), Spretnak was a green politician, feminist, and a female as well. Her Ecological Postmodernism not only made people wake up to the inherent relation between Feminism, Ecologicalism (the Green Movement), Eco-feminism, and Postmodernism but also made us discern the rich diversity and

① Wang Zhihe, "Spretnak and Her Ecological Postmodernism," *Foreign Social Science*, 1997: 6, pp. 52–53.

② Charlene Spretnak, *The Resurgence of the Real*; Wang Zhihe, "Spretnak and Her Ecological Postmodernism," *Foreign Social Science*, 1997: 6, p. 53.

③ Charlene Spretnak, *States of Grace: The Recovery of Meaning in the Postmodern Age*, San Franciso: Harper San Franciso, 1991, p. 32.

④ Wang Zhihe, "Spretnak and Her Ecological Postmodernism," *Foreign Social Science*, 1997: 6, pp. 49–53.

immanent generativity of postmodernism.[①] Spretnak thought that whether you accept Ecological Postmodernism is not important (you might also call it "reconstructive postmodernism" or "constructive postmodernism"), what is important is that a new angle of view different not only from Western modern thinking but also from the negation of this modern thinking (deconstructive postmodernism) has appeared. Spretnak made a table (see Table 16–1), which distinctly shows the differences between Ecological Postmodernism and modernism and deconstructionist postmodernism.

Table 16–1 Differences Between Modernism, Deconstructionist Postmodernism, and Ecological Postmodernism

Modernism	Deconstructionist Postmodernism	Ecological Postmodernism
Meta-narrative: salvation, progress	None (They are all power plays.)	The cosmological unfolding
Truth mode: objectivism	Extreme relativism	Experimentalism
World=a collection of objects	An aggregate of fragments	A community of subjects
Reality=fixed order	Social construction	Dynamic relationship
Sense of self: socially engineered	Fragmented	Processual
Primary truth: the universal	The particular	The particular-in-context
Grounding: mechanist universe	None (total groundlessness)	Cosmological processes
Nature as opponent	Nature as a wronged object	Nature as a subject
Control over the body	Erasure of the body (It is all social construction.)	Trust in the body
Science: reductionist	It's only a narrative!	Complexity
Economics: corporate	Postcapitalist	Community-based
Political focus: nation-state	The local	A community of communities of communities
Sense of the Divine: God the Father	"Gesturing toward the sublime"	Creativity in the cosmos, ultimate mystery
Key metaphors: mechanics, law	Economics ("libidinal economy"), signs/coding	Ecology

Source: Charlene Spretnak, *The Resurgence of the Real: Body, Nature, and Place in a Hypermodern World*, New York: Addison-Wesley Publishing Company, Inc., 1997, p. 73.

Ecological Postmodernism is not only a protest against the modern worldviews but also an open practice, a practice that explores the new ways of cognition and the new ways of existence. In her book, *The Spiritual Dimension of Green Politics*, Spretnak invited people to participate in deliberating the main values of the green movement so as to make problems poignant and to translate viewpoints into practical and effective political actions. In the book she brings forward

① Wang Zhihe, "Spretnak and Her Ecological Postmodernism," *Foreign Social Science*, 1997: 6, p. 54.

for discussion ten great core values of the green movement: ecological wisdom, grassroots democracy, personal and social responsibility, nonviolence, decentralization, community-based economics, post-patriarchal values, respect for diversity, global responsibility and future focus.① She called on people's active participation, encouraged people to receive the challenges of reality and "create new possibilities."②

B. Propositions of Ecological Postmodernism

1. Establishing an Ecological Society

Ecological Postmodernism warns people that the ecological crisis of the world today is continually deteriorating and forms a threat to man's existence. People must wake up as early as possible to the urgency of solving the ecological crisis, change their concepts, walk along a road that man gets along well with nature, and make great efforts to construct an ecological society. What Ecological Postmodernism represented by Spretnak "most worries about is not the ecological status nowadays but the change of the worldviews of human beings. When human beings can discard their old views of nature and philosophy that they had in the past and turn to a brand-new worldview is the chief problem that must be solved urgently."③ Ecological Postmodernism expounds, from the angles of view of the wholeness and system, a sort of worldview of "the Real" that the ecological society must require, and puts forward a series of suppositions on the construction of an ecological society.

Ecological postmodernists claim that people should not regard economic factors as the social core focus and the driving force to manipulate and control everything in the society, and spurn the practice to alienate man into an economic man. Spretnak refuted globalization. The ecological society that she conceived is based on the construction of community because only the society that is established with all sorts of relations as bonds is a society that human beings need indeed. She said, "The economy in an ecological society is understood to serve community, and serve creating genuine wealth. That is human community's restoration,

① Charlene Spretnak, *The Spiritual Dimension of Green Politics*, Santa Fe: Bear & Company, Inc., 1986, pp. 77–82.

② Charlene Spretnak, *States of Grace: The Recovery of Meaning in the Postmodern Age*, San Franciso: Harper San Franciso, 1991, p. 10.

③ Xie Zhongqi, Zhu Shudi and Zhang Yun, "Construction of Ecological Society in the Context of Postmodernism—A Comment on Spretnak's Thought of Ecological Society," *Studies in Dialectics of Nature*, Volume 24, 2008: 11, p. 85.

cultivation, and prosperity embedded in the healthy ecological system."① In her opinion, "The economy in an ecological society exists in serving the community and it will activate and consummate the relation existing in the community. It is all like this whether it is in cities, towns or rural areas."② The ultimate aim of the economy in the ecological society is to improve everybody's index of happiness in the community. People no longer make money for money's sake but pay more attention to the close bonds of association with relatives, friends, and nature. The ultimate aim of economy functions as the ultimate decisive force of social development, yet measuring the function of the increase of economy depends on whether the increase of economy is propitious to environmental protection, whether it is in favor of deepening the relation between man and man, and whether it is contributive to form a space of systematization and wholeness in the community. The economy of an ecological society should overcome the malpractice of being far from industrialization by setting up a suit of complete and green provision mechanism, for example, establishing an ecotype base for producing and sending non-staple foodstuffs such as vegetables, and fruits.

2. Establishing the Ideology of the Ecological Society

Being contrary to modernity advocating dual opposition, Ecological Postmodernism proposes to make the thoughts of the theories of social system and social holism go deep into the hearts of people in the ecological society, and to gradually replace the dual opposition with a sort of real worldview. Spretnak thought that "Every manifestation of universe life in the Earth community emerges into being in its own way, but none does so in isolation. Animate or inanimate, our relatives are all around us, lighting the night sky, rushing through a river bed, thrusting upward through Earth's crust."③ The basis of the ideology of the ecological society is a tight and firm chain which consists of universe, earth, continent, nation, bioregion, community, neighborhood, family, relatives, and the surrounding life circumstance, etc. "If people did not pay attention to the existing situation of soil, water, and air and even thought that they were unimportant, this materialism is strange materialism. The wrong consciousness of ideology is

---

① Charlene Spretnak, "Significance of Ecological Postmodernism to Chinese Modernization," Zhang Nini trans., *Marxism and Reality*, 2007: 2, p. 62.

② Charlene Spretnak, "China: Ecological Postmodernism Is Imperative," Xie Zhongqi, Zhu Shudi and Zhang Yun, "Construction of Ecological Society in the Context of Postmodernism—A Comment on Spretnak's Thought of Ecological Society," *Studies in Dialectics of Nature*, Volume 24, 2008: 11, pp. 85–89.

③ Charlene Spretnak, *The Resurgence of the Real: Body, Nature, and Place in a Hypermodern World*, New York: Addison-Wesley Publishing Company, Inc., 1997, p. 183.

destroying us and our ecological system. The urgent task of the modern society is to cast off the distortion of economism, which is at present driving the trains of thoughts of almost all governments. We must understand that the aim of economic activity is to improve people's life in all relations (including the relation between man and nature)."① The people of the ecological society regard themselves as a part of the family, the community, the nation, the Earth, and the universe, having inherent relations with other animals, plants, and animalcules around them. While designing for the natural environment, people are designing for their better life. Man is no longer the only subject in the world, we live on the Earth, and we must rely on the Earth that our survival depends on, so that we must care for and love the people and other animate or inanimate objects around us. The current studies indicate, "The health status of those who often willingly help other people is better than someone else; those who often trim garden or hobnob with nature much less fall ill; the old people who live in the family and the circle of friends less suffer from dementia."②

3. Constituting the Government of the Ecological Society

In the ecological society, what politicians do should also be a sort of green politics. The government no longer measures the success and failure of its own work with economic indicators but makes great efforts to promote the development of the community's economy, cultural construction, and ecological green democratic politics. The government ought to more hear the opinions of grassroots organizations and specialty teams, and take ecological construction as its direction, and manage well the relations between man and man, man and society, people and government, man and nature because the government's harmonizing function is propitious to promoting all sorts of relationship to develop toward closer contact. Spretnak emphasized the functions of grassroots organizations, grassroots democracy, and grassroots movement to promote the government to serve the ecological economy and the ecological community even better. She said, "The pressure of ecologicalization of economy (and all systems) comes mainly from grassroots movement, grassroots organizations and grassroots democracy. In Europe, especially in Germany and Scandinavia, the grassroots' request to 'go toward green' has been impelling the establishment of laws, statutes, and the prompting mechanisms for several decades."③ It is

① Spretnak, "China: Ecological Postmodernism Is Imperative," pp. 86–87.

② Spretnak, "China: Ecological Postmodernism Is Imperative," p. 87.

③ Charlene Spretnak, "China: Ecological Postmodernism Is Imperative," Xie Zhongqi, Zhu Shudi and Zhang Yun, "Construction of Ecological Society in the Context of Postmodernism—A Comment on Spretnak's Thought of Ecological Society," *Studies in Dialectics of Nature*, Volume 24, 2008: 11, p. 87.

often when the government has not yet changed its concepts of ecology that some individuals have already perceived the changes of the circumstances around them. They have perceived that they live in the circumstances whose ecology is increasingly deteriorating and such a perception is gradually diffusing. When many individuals have had such perceptions, there have appeared green associations. Pursuing the improvement of the life circumstance around them, these individuals and associations are likely to require the government to take some actions through all sorts of movements.

In the process of constructing her theory of Ecological Postmodernism, Spretnak, holding the hope to change the world, has overcome the Western traditional mechanical worldview, criticized and corrected the deconstructive postmodernist negating-all worldview, and put forward a brand-new, determinate, "real" ecological postmodernist worldview. This worldview can be taken as one of the foundation stones for developing ecological civilization, ecological culture, and ecological economy, guiding the construction of ecological society and establishing the really happy life with all sorts of relations as bonds.

Further Reading

Albanese, Catherine. *Nature Religion in America*. Chicago: University of Chicago Press, 1990.

Griffin, David Ray. *Whitehead's Radically Different Postmodern Philosophy*. New York: State University of New York Press, 2007.

Interviewed by Derrick Jensen in *Listening to the Land: Nature, Culture, and Eros*. San Francisco: Sierra Club Books, 1995.

Interviewed for "Behind the Cult of Mary," *Women of the Bible*, a Special Collector's Edition Published by *US News & World Report*, January/February 2006.

Kassman, Kenn. *Envisioning Utopia: The U.S. Green Movement and the Politics of Radical Social Change*. New York: Praeger Publishers, 1997.

Moon, Michael. *Green Ideology and Its Relation to Modernity, Studies in Human Ecology*. Lund: Lund Studies in Human Ecology, 2008.

Spretnak, Charlene. *Lost Goddesses of Early Greece: A Collection of Pre-Hellenic Myths*. Boston: Beacon Press, 1978, 1981.

——. *The Politics of Women's Spirituality: Essays by Founding Mothers of the Movement*. New York: Anchor/Doubleday, 1981.

——. Fritjof Capra. *Green Politics: The Global Promise* New York: E. P. Dutton, 1984.

——. *The Spiritual Dimension of Green Politics.* Santa Fe: Bear & Co., 1986.

——. *States of Grace: The Recovery of Meaning in the Postmodern Age.* San Francisco: Harper San Francisco, 1991.

——. *The Resurgence of the Real: Body, Nature, and Place in a Hypermodern World.* New York: Routledge, 1997.

——. *Missing Mary: The Queen of Heaven and Her Re-Emergence in the Modern Church.* New York: Palgrave Macmillan, 2004.

——. *Relational Reality: New Discoveries of Interrelatedness That Are Translating the Modern World.* Topsham: Green Horizon Books, 2011.

——. *The Spiritual Dynamic in Modern Art: Art History Reconsidered, 1800 to the Present.* London: Palgrave Macmillan, 2014.

Vardey, Lucinda. *God in All Worlds: An Anthology of Contemporary Spiritual Writing.* New York: Random House, 1995.

Wang Zhihe. Spretnak and Ecological Postmodernism. *Journal of Social Sciences Abroad*, 1997 (6): 50–56.

Bibliography

Cuddon, J. A. *A Dictionary of Literary Terms and Literary Theory*. 5th ed. Malden: Wiley-Blackwell, 2013.

Rice, Philip & Patricia Waugh. *Modern Literary Theory*. New York: Oxford University Press, 2002.

Bressler, Charles. *Literary Criticism: An Introduction to Theory and Practice*. Beijing: Higher Education Press, 2004.

泰勒，温奎斯特. 后现代主义百科全书. 章燕，李自修，等译. 刘象愚，校. 长春：吉林人民出版社，2007.

王治河. 后现代主义辞典. 北京：中央编译出版社，2004.

张中载，王逢振，赵国新. 二十世纪西方文论选读. 北京：外语教学与研究出版社，2002.

朱刚. 二十世纪西方文艺批评理论. 上海：上海外语教育出版社，2001.

Selected Readings

Charlene Spretnak: *The Resurgence of the Real: Body, Nature, and the Place* (a part of a chapter)

Charlene Spretnak: *States of Grace: The Recovery of Meaning in the Postmodern Age* (a part of a chapter)

Charlene Spretnak: *Relational Reality: New Discoveries of Interrelatedness That Are Transforming the Modern World* (a part of a chapter)

Chapter Seventeen

Postmodern Ethical Literary Criticism

Ethics is a sub-discipline of philosophy. It is the theory about moral problems, the doctrine to study the coming-into-being, development, essence, evaluation, and function of morality as well as the law of moral education and moral cultivation. As the object of ethical study, morality is the code of conduct of virtues and vices, and the sum total of its corresponding psychological consciousness and actions and activities in all interest relationships of survival and development of society and nature. Ethic and morality are the two most basic concepts of ethics that are interrelated and to some extent differ from each other as well. Their interrelation mainly manifests itself in that both embody and express the objective requirements of human spiritual life and social development and progress, both are a special spiritual life and the standard of value that people keep up and estimate according to social opinion, traditional habit, and inner belief. The difference between them is that ethics usually indicates specific social relations including the "human relations according to feudal ethics" between man and man, the thought relation and value system on the basis of interest relation between individual and society. However, morality usually indicates social moral rule and personal moral trait and it is unification of social rules and personal quality. Morality comes into being and exists in the complicated human social life, appears to be a special social ideology, a special social value relation, and a special mode of spiritual life. As a moral philosophy, ethics not only constructs in theory the category system in which the view of truth and axiology of ethics and morality are united but also promotes in practice the social harmony and the all-round development of human beings by using the ways and means of ethics and morality.[①] Ethics is closely related to social life, changes along with the social changes, thus can effectively carries out its mission to guide the all-round development of human beings and to promote the social harmony by using the ways and means of ethics and morality. As a special social ideology in the postmodern times, postmodern Western ethics calls on paying true attention to the value and meaning of the existence and development of postmodern human beings, deconstructs and criticizes modernity and modern Western ethics, reestablishes the value system of postmodern social morality, reconstructs the moral relation that self respects the Other (including nature), emphasizes that self must shoulder the absolute responsibility for the Other, and gives and is giving play to distinctly important role in guiding the behavior of human beings and human community, promoting the harmony of the whole society and even the whole international society, and pursuing the comprehensive sustainable development of economy, society and environment. It is from the angle of view of postmodern Western ethics that Postmodern Ethical Literary Criticism interprets the texts of postmodernist literature, reveals "the accepted and approved ethic relations and the moral order formed on the basis of these relations and a variety of norms to keep up with these relations as well" in the postmodern times (or the times of post-industrial society, late capitalism, globalization) represented by postmodernist literary texts through fictional characters and society, uncovers the postmodern "changes of ethic relations, moral order, and all kinds of problems triggered by them and the different consequences brought about by them"[②] that the texts of postmodernist literature represent, and provides postmodern ethic edification and moral experiences for the progress of postmodern human civilization. Moreover, Postmodern Ethical Literary Criticism also studies the postmodern ethical narrative forms of carnivalization and intertextuality used to represent the postmodern ethical thoughts, and the themes of postmodern ethical concerns about the society.

A. Core Thought of Postmodern Western Ethics

Postmodern Western ethics has been gradually formed in the context of postmodernist culture. Postmodernism emerged in due form at the end of the 1950s and the early 1960s, and formed the momentum of grasping one's heart and dazzling one's eyes, and frightening the whole thought circle. Postmodernism is deconstruction, criticism and subversion of modernity. Modernity stresses reason, democracy, and freedom, and praises highly the progress of modern

① Dou Yanguo, *Principles of Ethics*, Beijing: China Social Sciences Press, 2010, p. 2.

② See also Nie Zhenzhao, *Introduction to Literary Ethical Criticism*, Beijing: Peking University Press, 2014, p. 13.

science and technology, equality, and philanthropism. But everything that modernity has actually brought up makes people doubt about its original belief. Postmodernists think that modernity is no longer a liberation power; on the contrary, it is the origin of enslavement, oppression, and repression. Postmodernism rejects all theories of modernity, regards all kinds of concepts of modernity as logos-centrism, foundationalism, essentialism, covers all things narrated by meta-narrative without discrimination, and has destroyed them all. Postmodernists have abandoned all kinds of authorities, centers, foundations, and essences in regard to modernity, and dispelled legality of all codes (or statute books). The philosophical basis of modernism was pursuing a present metaphysics, an eternal truth, and ontology and epistemology of ultimate value. Postmodernism opposes not only the idea that man has congenital mirror essence (that is, man is the subject knowing and understanding the being of all beings) but also the discourse that the world has identity, consistence, integrality, and centrality, and objects to not only grading among different disciplines but also seeking a first discipline.[①] Postmodernism opposes using a single and changeless logic, formula, principle, and a universal law to explain and rule the world, but proposes transformation and innovation, emphasizes openness and pluralism, admits differences, and respects the Other. Postmodern plurality is the essence of all knowledge areas and all aspects of social life. The direct conclusion of the principle of pluralism is that postmodernism opposes any attempt for unification. Postmodern thought actively maintains diversity and richness of things, and resolutely opposes any wild ambition for hegemony trying to impose one's own choice on other people, and submit alien things to one's own will; it (the principle of pluralism) respects and admits all choices about social conceptions, modes of life, and cultural types.[②] The basic concepts of postmodernism to dispel authority and center, admit difference, respect the other, and propose thorough pluralism are the ideological foundation of postmodern Western ethics.

1. Critical Transcendence of Modernity and Modern Western Ethics

In his book, *Postmodern Ethics* (1993), Zygmunt Bauman (1925–2017), professor of the sociology of the University of Leeds of England, earlier used the two concepts of "postmodern ethic" and "postmodern morality."[③] In Bauman's opinion, modernity pursues universality, analyzes and estimates things, and determines what is true, by using a universally consistent plan

① See also Zhang Guoqing, *Center and Margin*. Beijing: China Social Sciences Press, 1998, p. 45.

② See also Chen Shidan, "On the Existence of Postmodernist Fiction," *Foreign Literatures*, 2005: 4, pp. 26–27.

③ Zygmunt Bauman, *Postmodern Ethics*, trans. Zhang Chenggang, Nanjing: Jiangsu People's Publishing House, 2003, p. 1.

which it considers absolutely right by itself. Modernity repels, refuses and denies differences, and makes all the Others illegal. Rejecting differences is the essence of modern politics, modern knowledge, and modern life. Modern knowledge rejects heresy, ambiguity, cognitive contradiction, and contingency; modern practice also excludes and overwhelms all different things by using a definite universality.① Modernism makes originally nonexistent metaphysical things present, imposes them on people, and thus makes itself possible by means of impossible truth, pure art and universality of human nature. Modernity's pursuit and emphasis of unification, integrality, and monism result in inflation of universalism, absolutism, monism, and centralism.

Modern Western ethics, takes modernity as its core idea, criticizes and negates feudal hierarchy and the values of feudal hierarchy, propagates such values as freedom, equality, philanthropism, democracy, human rights, etc., and has constructed the value system of modern capitalist morality. It takes establishing and consolidating the reasonable grounds of morality of capitalist system as its main purpose, has provided powerful theoretical support for the development of capitalism of the Western countries, and has thus powerfully promoted the development of Western capitalism. However, because of the essence of exploitation and private interests of capitalism, the governments of capitalist countries cannot solve the inherent contradictions of the oppressor and the oppressed, the exploiter and the exploited, between capitalists and the working class, the unconquerable inner contradictions in the capitalist system itself, and the contradiction between the unprecedentedly accumulated material wealth and the gap between the rich and the poor increasingly enlarged, but can just allow them to develop like that. In the course of its insane expansion of capitalism often breaks out economic crisis that brings about enormous harm to the working class people. In the course of using the progress of modern science and technology to propel industrialization to develop rapidly, human beings are alienated to be parts of the big machine of capitalism and can be replaced any time, which leads amounts of workers to be out of work into poverty, and lose man's dignity and values. Western capitalist countries develop economy at the cost of plundering and destroying nature, in the result of giving rise to resource exhaustion, climate warming, and making human society caught in ecological crisis. In brief, the value system of capitalist morality constructed by modern Western ethics has failed to provide infallible guarantee of rationality for capitalist development, also failed to provide Westerners with the ideal moral order that they expected.② All these make people in deep trouble at the end of the 20th century and at the beginning of the 21st century, and

① See also Zhou Xian, "Bauman, Zygmunt," *A Dictionary of Postmodernism*, ed. Wang Zhihe, Beijing: Central Compilation & Translation Press, 2005, p. 24.

② See also Xiang Yuqiao, *A Study of Postmodern Western Ethics*, Beijing: China Social Sciences Press, 2011, pp. 33–34.

they begin to reconsider the value system of capitalist morality and in the course of querying, criticizing, and negating this system postmodern Western ethics has been formed.

Postmodern Western ethics takes post-modernity as its core notion. Post-modernity means a powerful change impulsion and an initiative spirit. It wants to abolish modernity's maintenance of authority, center, and hierarchy, emphasizes recognizing differences and esteeming the Other, and proposes pluralism and containment, and it is criticism, negation and subversion of modernity. As "a morality without ethical norm,"① through the ideology and practice spirit of carrying forward innovation, post-modernity tries to overcome the limitation and deficiency of modernity, change and transcend modernity or modern spirit in order to establish the reasonable postmodern social order and postmodern spirit that admit differences, respect the Other (including nature), and propose pluralism and containment. Postmodernity advocates replacing enlightening reason (namely, the reason of high instrumentalization) made widely known by modernity with such new rational forms as "intersubjectivity," "public reason," etc.,② appeals to truly paying close attention to the value and meaning of survival and development of human beings, and pursues overall and sustainable development of society and environment. Since the end of the 20th century, in the contexts that all kinds of Western cultural theories intensely contended with each other, such concepts and terms as "postmodern ethics," "postmodern morality," etc. have risen in response to the proper time and conditions. Postmodern ethics with post-modernity as its core notion abandons dualistic and supernatural modern spirit, changes the values of individualism and nationalism, no longer lets human beings attach to machine, and no longer lets social, moral, aesthetic and ecological considerations submit to economic interest, having become critical transcendence of modernity and modern Western ethics.③

2. Reconstruction of the Value System of Postmodern Western Morality

Postmodern Western ethics deems that, because capitalist political system and economic system are not established on the basis of reasonable and just concept of shouldering the absolute responsibility for the Other, that is, for the wide working class, capitalist society is inundated with social, political and economic inequality. Because in capitalist society, people in the power class do not follow Habermas' dialogue ethics and Bakhtin's dialogue theory, and have no moral consciousness of eliminating authority, center and ranks, and consequently people's moral life is

① Zygmunt Bauman, *Postmodern Ethics*, trans. Zhang Chenggang, Nanjing: Jiangsu People's Publishing House, 2003, p. 36.

② Xiang Yuqiao, *A Study of Postmodern Western Ethics*, Beijing: China Social Sciences Press, 2011, p. 27.

③ See also Xiang Yuqiao, *A Study of Postmodern Western Ethics*, Beijing: China Social Sciences Press, 2011, pp. 27–28.

filled with ethical arguments. Because deeply influenced by existentialist idea that Others are Hell and Materialism in modern capitalist society, people do not understand the ethical meaning of life. Because in the capitalist countries certain people and organizations are wild about the values of nationalism and racialism, racial discrimination and ethnic conflicts frequently occur, regional wars constantly appear, and in the history even broke out two world wars in which human beings killed each other. Because in the process of industrialization there exist the economic men (the subjects that carry out economic activities in complete pursuit for material interest as purpose) in the capitalist society, nature has suffered a lot from merciless predatory exploitation and destruction, which leads to many species' extinction and resource exhaustion, and human beings faced with ecological crisis. In a word, "all the problems that Western countries come up against in the process of developing capitalism are all derived from the value system of capitalist morality demonstrated by modern Western ethics."① At the same time deconstructing the rational foundation of modern ethics, some famous philosophers such as Jacques Derrida, Emmanuel Levinas (1906–1995) and others have established a theory of postmodern ethics that can reestablish the value system of postmodern Western morality.

(1) Derrida's Deconstruction of Modernity's Metaphysics

Jacques Derrida (1930–2004), French postmodernist philosopher, queried, criticized, and disintegrated all kinds of final conclusions of knowledge and the basis of enlightenment thought, opposed modernity's eternal center, origin, present metaphysics, dualistic thought, and phonecentrism that takes itself as center and rejects alien culture (that is, the concept which thinks that there is difference between spoken language and writing symbols, and puts the entire privilege on the side of spoken language, and which is a present metaphysics), and actively participated in postmodernist criticism and negation of the values of enlightenment's Logos (reason and essence), etc. Derrida thought that metaphysics takes Logos or the presence of phonetics as center that governs traditional ways of thought, daily language, ethics and morals, value judgment, etc. The present meaning of metaphysics originates from Logos. This shows that there is a self-closed structure that takes Logos as center (and in which any element is controlled by purpose and origin), and its most basic element is antagonism between the signifier and the signified. Derrida pointed out that in the formation of structure "... there was no center, that the center could not be thought in the form of a present thing, that the center had no natural site, that it was not a fixed locus but a function, a sort of non-locus in which an infinite number of

① Xiang Yuqiao, *A Study of Postmodern Western Ethics*, Beijing: China Social Sciences Press, 2011, p. 35.

sign substitutions came into play."[1] A sign is not the close combination of the signifier with the signified, a sign cannot represent the thing that it signifies and can produce the present signified: a sign about a sort of thing is bound to mean the absence of that thing (and to only defer the presence of the signified).

A symbol is always a movement of "differentiating" in synchronic time and "delaying" in diachronic time the meaning of the signified. The *différance* (Derrida's coinage, meaning to differ and delay)[2] of characters makes dissemination of meaning like seeding as "sowing a little here, sowing a little there,"[3] continually revolting center and origin by distributing the obtained disorderliness and incompleteness, and refusing to form any new heartland. The incompleteness of signs caused by *différance* makes it forever turning into a group of traces referring to other signs. Traces point to differentiating and delaying, always delay meaning, and make the activity of questing textual meaning become a movement of the text's self-centrifuging and self-deconstructing. In this case, the text always points to the textual group outside of the text and always moves towards indeterminacy in differentiating and delaying meaning and in suggesting traces. Derrida regards this mechanism of movement of meaning's self-deconstruction as supplement. Supplement rises out of the void of being, and is the evidence of incompleteness of being. Its cardinal direction is completely denying the source of being and the myth of metaphysical absolute truth. Derrida's deconstruction lies in analyzing the illusory of Logos' central privilege of "signifying" and its privilege of the transcendental "signified" (concept). Along with the disintegration of center and the disintegration of the opposite limit between the signifier and the signified, the total basis of metaphysics has collapsed. Obviously, Derrida's pursuit is to liberate all stipulated traditional norms, liberate philosophy, literature, ethics and religion, and in a word, liberate culture, erase original norms, and rewrite new characters.[4]

(2) Derrida's Construction of the Awareness of the Messiah, Righteousness, and the Spirit of Fraternal Love

After his deconstruction of modernity, in his works since the initial stage of the 1990s,

① Jacques Derrida, "Structure, Signs, and Plays in Humanist Discourse," Selected Readings in 20th Century Western Critical Theory, eds. Zhang Zhongzai, Wang Fengzhen and Zhao Guoxin, Beijing: Foreign Language Teaching and Research Press, 2002, p. 320.

② Jacques Derrida, *Position*, Chicago: Chicago University Press, 1981, p. 27.

③ Jacques Derrida, *Dissemination*, Chicago: Chicago University Press, 1981, p. 32.

④ Shang Jie, "Derrida, Jacques," Dictionary of Postmodernism, ed. Wang Zhihe, Beijing: Central Compilation & Translation Press, 2005, pp. 80–82.

Derrida put forward the unvarying ultimate value such as the awareness of the Messiah, righteousness, and the spirit of fraternal love, with which he constructed postmodern Western cultural ethics.

a. Derrida's Awareness of the Messiah: Shouldering the Unconditional Responsibility for the Other

History proves that modern Western politics and political themes have not only failed to turn ideal values such as freedom, equality, philanthropism, democracy, human rights, etc. into reality, but on the contrary, brought about chaos, absurdity, suffering and evils to the people in reality. In such a reverse age, Derrida wanted to heal the world, "continue the history which is said to have been 'ended' and the values that have been 'dead,'" drive away "the 'democracy' that has claimed to bring the whole world into its domination—a sort of totalitarian discourse having anti-totalitarian face," and recall "the souls of 'difference' and 'the Other.'"① In his book, *Specters of Marx* (1994), Derrida put forward the notion of Spirit of the Messiah. Messiah is the Savior that the Jews anxiously look forward to and persistently expect. But here in Derrida's opinion, Messiah is "the absolutely different Other," who exists in foreign lands, keeps at calling and hoping for attention, demands us to make responses to him and shoulder absolute responsibility for him, which is "the spirit of Messiah without Savior."② Derrida's "the spirit of Messiah without Savior" is exactly an expectation, an open heart, kept for "the Other" that is upcoming, and it is an unconditional responsibility shouldered for the Other. The future "Other" will be "the final arrival of righteousness."③

b. Derrida's Concept of Righteousness: An Absolute Responsibility for the Other and an Idea Pointing to Infinite

On the basis of the spirit of Messiah, Derrida put forward the concept of righteousness that cannot be deconstructed. Righteousness means conflict, and that the self's shouldering unconditional responsibility for the Other without expecting anything in return. Therefore, this is self's unsymmetrical responsibility relation to the Other. This righteousness is immeasurable and it goes beyond all measures and tends to the infinite and the future. Righteousness can be defined as an unreducible responsibility for the Other, a gift given to the Other without requiring return and without exchanges, and an idea pointing to infinite.④

① Hu Jihua, *The Ethical Cultural Turn in Postmodern Context*, Beijing: Jinghua Publishing House, 2005, pp. 102–103.

② See also Derrida's *Specters of Marx*: *The State of the Debt*, *The Work of Mourning & the New International*, trans. He Yi, Beijing: China Renmin University Press, 1999, pp. 85–86.

③ See also Hu Jihua, *The Ethical Cultural Turn in Postmodern Context*, Beijing: Jinghua Publishing House, 2005, p. 110.

④ Ibid, pp. 111–112.

Derrida made explicit differentiation between righteousness and law: righteousness is an absolute responsibility for the Other and an idea pointing to infinite; law is a mysterious authority system established on the basis of man-made violence. As a construction, law can be deconstructed; as an "unsymmetrical responsibility," righteousness is an impossible and paradoxical experience and it cannot be deconstructed. Deconstruction always begins from pursuit of the Other and his language, and shoulders infinite responsibility for the Other. Therefore, righteousness cannot be deconstructed, and deconstruction is righteousness.① In Derrida's opinion, law is full of violence, and violence always exists in language. "Law's mythological violence requests sacrifice," when resulting in bleeding, it carries out extinction of pure life according to its own preference, and sadness of life and sorriness of nature are both of the bloody fate caused by this law's mythological violence; the sacred violence, contrary to law's mythological violence, carries out violence to life in order to protect and defend the benefit of life as Derrida pointed out that "the sacred violence accepts sacrifice and takes on sacrifice,"② "it is the sacred violence that deconstructs law," and it includes "all decisiveness, all spiritual strength that exercises sovereignty, all the strength that destroys law and deconstructs law."③

Thus, history becomes antagonistic to myth and points to sacredness, and sacredness becomes a promise that cannot be deconstructed. Sacredness has a sacred dimensionality, and it motivates madness of deconstruction: the madness of deconstruction of all violence, all mysterious authorities (including Western center, White supremacy, and the superiority of mankind), and all sacrifice structures that do not conform to the concept (ultimate value) of infinite righteousness. Derrida equated righteousness to deconstruction, aimed at abolishing all efforts to understand righteousness from reason, and got ready for the coming of Messiah and righteousness.④

c. Derrida's Expected Friendly Affection and Future Democracy

In his book, *The Politics of Friendship* (1997), on the basis of calling the Messiah spirit and establishing righteousness, Derrida put forward mankind's nice values and ideals: expected fraternal love and future democracy. Derrida deconstructed and criticized Aristotle's question,

① See also Jacques Derrida, "Force of Law: the Mystical Foundation of Authority," *Deconstruction and the Possibility of Justice*, eds. Drucilla Cornnel, Michael Rosenfield and David Gray Carson, trans. Mary Quaintance, London: Routledge, 1992, pp. 12–13.

② Jacques Derrida, "Force of Law: the Mystical Foundation of Authority," *Deconstruction and the Possibility of Justice*, p. 53.

③ Hu Jihua, *The Ethical Cultural Turn in Postmodern Context*, Beijing: Jinghua Publishing House, 2005, p. 113.

④ Ibid., pp. 113–115.

"What is friendly affection?" and his traditional definition of friendly affection: "Fraternal love is the same soul living in two human bodies," and pointed out that this is the typical metaphysical asking and answering. Fraternal love is regarded as the "identity" of two existences, the relation of being-with-each-other between two limited individuals. This thought of "fraternal love" of Aristotle's attributes the "Other" to identity, "homogenizes heterogeneity," implements it into thinking about "fraternal love," and makes "friends" quantitative, and thus "fraternal love changes from the true love relation of being-with-each-other into a hegemony relation."① This sort of fundamental convention formed under the influence of Western metaphysical tradition is deeply rooted in language and has distorted the political thought of Western tradition but is deemed as natural, lawful and legitimate. Derrida points out that all values and ideals of human life such as "righteousness" and "goodness," "fraternal love" and "true love," "virtues" and "sympathy," "inculpating" and "punishment," etc. set by ethics and political discourse are established with an empty reference of "maybe," and a forever commitment that can never be realized.② Actually, there aren't any "democracy" and "fraternal love" that can be generally feasible across classes, and they are purely illusion imposed by language. In Western history, the classics about "fraternal love" foreclose women. This sort of myth about "philanthropism" does not have in the least any legitimacy and this kind of "philanthropism" contains deep inequality, dissymmetry, and nonreciprocal relation.③ Derrida defined the relation among people as "the irrelevant relation," "the community without community," which means to highlight deeply respecting "the Other" and "differences," respecting "the specificity" of "differences" and "the Other," and emphasizes that self must make an answer to the Other and shoulder absolute responsibility for the Other. Therefore, people's responsibility for the Other becomes more fontal, more fundamental, and more unconditional.④ On the basis of self's absolute sense of responsibility for the Other, Derrida and Emmanuel Levinas established together the possibility of "the minimal ethical community." This sort of ethical community is negation of all communities such as the community of a nation, of a country, of a culture, of a language, even the community of human beings, and it is a commitment to recognizing differences and respecting the Other. After all secret personal relationships have been made public, fraternal love has become an expectation of the sense of the sacred for the Other.⑤

---

① Hu Jihua, *The Ethical Cultural Turn in Postmodern Context*, Beijing: Jinghua Publishing House, 2005, p. 118.

② Jacques Derrida, *The Politics of Friendship*, trans. G. Collins, New York & London: Verso, 1997, p. 79.

③ Hu Jihua, *The Ethical Cultural Turn in Postmodern Context*, Beijing: Jinghua Publishing House, 2005, pp. 121–123.

④ See also Jacques Derrida, *The Politics of Friendship*, trans. G. Collins, New York & London: Verso, 1997, p. 250.

⑤ See also Hu Jihua, *The Ethical Cultural Turn in Postmodern Context*, Beijing: Jinghua Publishing House, 2005, pp. 127–128.

Derrida pointed out that the democracy in the Western capitalist society today is also a dictatorial system developed by the durably distorted political discourse formed under the Western metaphysical tradition, "like totalitarianism and anti-humanism, it is also a flower blooming on the same root trunk of metaphysics."① In his *The Politics of Friendship*, Derrida clearly pointed out, "Without esteem for the individual differences that can't be cut down, there is not democracy, but if there is no 'community of friends,' no most people's calculation, and no entirely equal subjects that can be identified with, can be stabilized, and can be represented, there is not likely to be democracy."② That is to say, without subjects that esteem and equally treat the Other, there is no democracy. On account of the distorting function of Western metaphysics, the true democracy does not actually appear. Hence, Derrida put forward the concept of "future democracy." "Future democracy" indicates that at present democracy is not present, and it only exists in the promise for the values and ideals of good life in the construction of open experiences. "Future democracy" is unconditional esteem for individuality, unconditional embodiment of equality among "unknown subjects," and unconditional compatibility for the Other. It is an open promise, and open Messiah. The self that shoulders unconditional responsibility for the future comer (the Other) does not require his return nor require him to have any contractual relationship with any kind of territory power, regardless of whether this contract is of family, of nation-state, of territory-consanguinity, of language or of human beings.③ Derrida's "minimal ethical community" and "promise for future democracy" provide people with wonderful ideals that deserve expectation and pursuit in the life of human beings. In Derrida's opinion, "It is only under the absolute imperative to shoulder unconditional responsibility for the Other that talking about philanthropism, friendship, equality and future democracy is meaningful. In other words, it is only the 'fraternal love' in the minimal ethical community which is not an empty promise,"④ that is, it is only under the circumstances that self admits differences, esteems the Other, and shoulders absolute responsibility for the Other, that philanthropism, friendship, equality and democracy can be realized, and it is only in the minimal ethical community that the true fraternal love can come true.

3. Reconstruction of the Moral Relationship Between "Self" and "the Other"

The relationship between self and "the Other" refers to both the relationship between

① See also Hu Jihua, *The Ethical Cultural Turn in Postmodern Context*, Beijing: Jinghua Publishing House, 2005, p. 118.

② Jacques Derrida, *The Politics of Friendship*, trans. Collins G., New York & London: Verso, 1997, p. 22.

③ See also Derrida's *Specters of Marx: The State of the Debt, The Work of Mourning & the New International*, trans. He Yi, Beijing: China Renmin University Press, 1999, pp. 93–94.

④ Hu Jihua, *The Ethical Cultural Turn in Postmodern Context*, Beijing: Jinghua Publishing House, 2005, p. 128.

subjectivity and objectivity and the relationship between subjects. The relationship between subjectivity and objectivity is exactly the relationship between the "self" that can become subject and "the Other" that can't become subject. "The self that can become subject" is precisely the self in Descartes' famous statement: "I think therefore I am" while "the Other" "that can't become subject" includes "nature" that contains individual human bodies. "The relationship between subjects" refers to a problem how a subject distinguishes himself from other subjects and how a subject treats other subjects. It seems that the relationship between "self" and "the Other" involves not only self and the Other, self and society, but also self and nature. "Self" and "the Other" not only distinguish from each other but also interrelate each other① and depend on each other. To the problem how to know and treat the relationship between "self" and "the Other," modern Western ethics and postmodern Western ethics put up completely different attitudes: modern Western ethics takes self as the center, rejects, scorns, and negates the Other, while postmodern Western ethics acknowledges differences, respects the Other, and shoulders absolute responsibility for the Other.

(1) Self Esteems the Other and Shoulders "Absolute Responsibility" for the Other

Concerning the relationship between "self" and "the Other," modern Western ethics insists on subjectivism or the centrism of subjectivity. As a philosophical mode or way of thinking, subjectivism is a dualism that distinguishes "subjectivity" from "Otherness"; as a philosophical belief, subjectivism asserts that only the subject that has subjectivity can know and understand the existence of all the existents; as a concept of moral values, it reflects this subject of self's emotional attitudes such as rejecting, scorning, even denying the "Other" and "Otherness." Postmodern Western ethics thinks that the theoretical subjectivism of ethics will inevitably aggravate the antagonism between "self" and "the Other" in the realistic moral life and fundamentally result in the absurdity of human existence.② Therefore, postmodern Western ethics advocates abandoning subjectivism or the centrism of subjectivity and reconstructing the ethics for the Other.

Postmodern Western ethicists advocate reestablishing the firm moral relationship between self and the Other in which self respects the Other (including nature), and constructing the self for the Other, that is to say, constructing "the humanism of the Other" that Emmanuel Levinas

① See also Xiang Yuqiao, *A Study of Postmodern Western Ethics*, Beijing: China Social Sciences Press, 2011, p. 36.
② Xiang Yuqiao, *A Study of Postmodern Western Ethics*, Beijing: China Social Sciences Press, 2011, p. 37.

contends to construct.[①] Levinas' ethics is postmodern ethics moved by open strategy, which makes self walk out of subject's own subjectivity and become a subject that transcends self. Levinas thinks that human nature and subjectivity are the responsibility for the Other.[②] The Other here refers to "the Other" in the moral community, and "Otherness" indicates the "Otherness" or heterogeneity, relative to moral subjectivism that has moral values, and the relationship between self and the Other which is a moral relationship that self esteems the Other and shoulders absolute responsibility for the Other.[③]

(2) Levinas' Humanism for the Other

Postmodern philosopher Emmanuel Levinas thought that "the Other" is unique, absolutely dissimilar, and it continually breaks with identity and melts different identity. The ethical value of "the Other" lies in that "the Other" is a face, a speech behavior, and it calls for love, and earnestly implores responses, and self's responsibility for the Other is to make an answer to the Other's speech. The Other, through the face, conveys a commandment: self must make responses to the Other's speeches, that is, shoulder absolute responsibility for the Other. In a word, the Other and self form a relationship of origin and what the Other evokes is self's infinite and absolute responsibility for the Other. Levinas' "Other" is diversity, peculiarity, and the individual that enjoys sacred dignity. Obeying "the Other" is unconditionally esteeming these unique individuals that are full of dignity, regarding obeying the Other as glory and freedom, and shouldering absolute responsibility for the Other. This is "ethics for the Other,"[④] a new humanism: the humanism for the Other.

In Levinas' opinion, the relationship between self and the Other has become a transcendental relationship. As soon as it is established, this relationship means the beginning of ethical significance. This ethical relationship between "the I" and the Other contains the (the Other's) ethical calling to "the I," "the I" hears the command from the Other, which compels "the I" to be "for the Other." The command precedes freedom, goes beyond essence, and emerges as source of sources, as basis of bases.[⑤] The meaning that Levinas gives to ethics is precisely the

---

①② Zygmunt Bauman, *Postmodern Ethics*, trans. Zhang Chenggang, Nanjing: Jiangsu People's Publishing House, 2003, p. 99.

③ See also Xiang Yuqiao, *A Study of Postmodern Western Ethics*, Beijing: China Social Sciences Press, 2011, p. 38.

④ See also Hu Jihua, *The Ethical Cultural Turn in Postmodern Context*, Beijing: Jinghua Publishing House, 2005, pp. 57–58.

⑤ See also Du Xiaozhen, "Levinas, Emmanuel," *A Dictionary of Postmodernism*, ed. Wang Zhihe, Beijing: Central Compilation & Translation Press, 2005, p. 421.

humanism for the Other or "the ethics for the Other," calling on that self must see the Other with his face, must esteem the Other that he meets face to face, and shoulder absolute responsibility for the Other. The correlation with the Other is exactly righteousness![①] At the same time calling responsibility, friendliness, and self's shouldering absolute responsibility for the Other, Levinas' postmodern ethics also rethinks and criticizes concentration of power and violence.

4. Reconstruction of the Moral Relationship Between Self and Nature

The relationship between "self" and "the Other" refers not only to the relationship between self and the Other, the relationship between self and society, but also to the relationship between self and nature, that is, the relationship between the human society governed by modernity and nature. Modern Western ethics insists on the values of anthropocentrism (a variant of the centrism of subjectivity), makes man opposite to nature, and regards nature as "the Other." It thinks that man can make legislation for nature, that mankind must conquer, govern, and control nature for mankind's own existence and for the development of society and economy, and therefore emphasizes rationality and legality of mankind's conquering nature. Consequently, nature has become the object of man's enslaving and oppressing. Ecological ethics, as one of the important sub-disciplines of postmodern Western applied ethics, discloses modern Western ethics' neglect of ecological morality, fundamentally negates the moral and rational basis of man's conquering nature, calls on that every human individual should cultivate the virtue to respect, love, and protect nature, and thus extends man's moral concern from interpersonal relationship to the relationship between man and nature. Ecological ethics thinks that natural existing things are not the force of alienation to human beings but man's companions and stresses harmonious coexistence and sustainable development of self, society and nature, which should be the moral values owned by the whole human community.[②] Therefore, man and human society should highly esteem nature and shoulder absolute responsibility for nature. The thinkers of Ecological Postmodernism, social ecology, deep ecology analyze modern crisis and ecological crisis, seriously criticize modernity—the source of ecological crisis, and in the meantime put forward postmodern active and instructive ecological ethical propositions to reconstruct the moral relationship that self respects nature and reconstruct the ecological human society.

① See also Emmanuel Levinas. *Ethics and Infinity*, *Conversations with Philippe Nemo*, trans. Richard A. Cohen, Pittsburgh, Pennsylvania: Duquesne University Press, 1985, p. 90.

② See also Xiang Yuqiao, *A Study of Postmodern Western Ethics*, Beijing: China Social Sciences Press, 2011, p. 38.

(1) The Ecological Ethical Propositions of Ecological Postmodernism

Charlene Spretnak, theorist and thinker of Ecological Postmodernism, has deeply analyzed the crisis of modernity, criticized and corrected the deconstructive postmodernist worldview that negates all, put forward a brand-new, determinate and "true" worldview of Ecological Postmodernism, and advocated constructing an ecological human society that harmoniously coexists with nature and can develop sustainably. Spretnak pointed out that "Economic Person Assumption" is one of modernity's core concepts and it is a subject that takes entirely pursuing material benefits as purpose in their conducting economic activities so that it is regarded as an economic existence. On the basis of this concept, nature is deemed as a worthless "resource" that is exploited only for Gross National Product and the meaning of life is equated to struggling against nature.[①] Anthropocentrism, another core concept of modernity, thinks that mankind is the central phenomenon in nature. This concept regards mankind as master and nature as slave so that, according to this concept, mankind rules nature and nature serves mankind.[②] Spretnak clearly pointed out, "True postmodernists ought to reject this antagonism, ought to... anew put mankind back to the greater background, that is, to the earth, universe, the sacred whole.... The true postmodernism should be ecological."[③]

In her book, *The Spiritual Dimension of Green Politics* (1986), Spretnak translated viewpoints into practical and effective political activities, put forward ten great core values of Green Political Movement such as Ecological Wisdom, Grassroots Democracy, Responsibilities of Individuals and Society, Nonviolence, Decentralization, Economics Taking Communities as Its Basis, the Values of Post-patriarchy, Respecting Diversity, Global Responsibility, and Future Development, and invited people to participate in the discussion of them.[④] She called on people to actively take part in the green political movement, meet face to face the challenge of reality, confront the ecological crisis caused by modernity, and "create new possibility."[⑤] Ecological Postmodernism raises the following propositions:

---

① See also Charlene Spretnak, *Postmodern Directions in Spirituality*, Wang Zhihe, "Spretnak and Her Ecological Postmodernism," *Foreign Social Science*, 1997: 6, p. 50.

② See also Charlene Spretnak, *The Resurgence of the Real: Body, Nature, and Place in a Hypermodern World*, trans. Zhang Nini, Beijing: Central Compilation & Translation Press, 2001, pp. 274–277.

③ See also Wang Zhihe, "Spretnak and Her Ecological Postmodernism," *Foreign Social Science*, 1997: 6, p. 52.

④ See also Charlene Spretnak, *The Spiritual Dimension of Green Politics*, Santa Fe, New Mexico: Bear & Company, Inc., 1986, pp. 77–82.

⑤ Charlene Spretnak, *States of Grace: The Recovery of Meaning in the Postmodern Age*, San Franciso: Harper San Franciso, 1991, p. 10.

a. Constructing an Ecological Society

Ecological Postmodernism puts forward a series of propositions to construct an ecological society. Its basic viewpoints include that we should not regard economic factors as the core focuses and driving power of the society to manipulate everything of the society, reject the idea to alienate man to be "an economic person"; refute globalization and think that ecological society is based on community construction because it is only the society established with various kinds of relations as ties is the society that mankind truly needs; "the economy of an ecological society exists only in serving the community and it will activate and perfect the relations existing in communities,"① its ultimate goal is to increase everybody's happiness index in a community, and people no longer make money for making money but pay more attention to their close tie relation with their kinsfolk, friends, and nature; the ultimate goal of economy is the ultimate decisive force of social development, while measuring the function of economic increase is to see whether this kind of economic increase avails to protection of environment, whether avails to deepening the relation between man and man, whether avails to forming a space of systematization and integration in a community.

b. Constructing an Ideology of Ecological Society

Spretnak thought that "In the Earth community, the form of every universe life comes to the world in its own way but none of them comes here in isolation. Regardless of whether the things in the universe are animate or inanimate, they are all our relatives and exist around us."② The basis of the ecological social ideology is a tight chain, which is made up with universe, the earth, mainland, nation, biota, community, neighbor, family, relatives, friends, surroundings around, etc. Spretnak stressed that "If we do not pay attention to the existing state of soil, water and air, even think that they are insignificant, this kind of materialism is strange materialism.... We must realize that the purpose of economic activities is to improve people's life in all relationships (including the relationship between man and nature)."③

c. Establishing an Ecological Postmodern Government

Spretnak advocated establishing an ecological postmodern government and explicitly

---

① Charlene Spretnak, "China: Ecological Postmodernism Has to Be Followed," Xie Zhongqi, Zhu Shudi, Zhang Yun, "The Construction of Ecological Society in the Context of Postmodernism—A Comment on Spretnak's Ideas About Ecological Society," *Study of Natural Dialectics*, Volume 24, 2008: 11, pp. 86–87.

② Charlene Spretnak, *The Resurgence of the Real: Body, Nature, and Place in a Hypermodern World*, trans. Zhang Nini, Beijing: Central Compilation & Translation Press, 2001, p. 223.

③ Charlene Spretnak, "China: Ecological Postmodernism Has to Be Followed," Xie Zhongqi, Zhu Shudi, Zhang Yun, "The Construction of Ecological Society in the Context of Postmodernism—A Comment on Spretnak's Ideas about Ecological Society," *Study of Natural Dialectics*, Volume 24, 2008: 11, pp. 86–87.

stipulated: the objectives of public administration are "to provide opportunities for green economy, green education and green politics;"① this government no longer uses economic indicators to measure the gain and loss of its own work but strives to promote community economy, cultural construction and the development of ecological green democratic politics, often listens to the opinions of grassroots organizations and professional groups, handles properly the relationships between man and man, man and society, man and government, man and nature in the direction for ecological construction, and gives play to the coordinating function to the benefit of promoting all kinds of relationships to develop toward the direction of close connection. Spretnak particularly emphasized that grassroots organizations, grassroots democracy, and grassroots movements are bound to give fundamental play to promoting governments to serve ecological economy and ecological community well.

As one of the basic theories of the development of ecological civilization, ecological culture, and ecological economy, the philosophy of Ecological Postmodernism can be used to direct economic construction, political construction, cultural construction, social construction, and the construction of ecological civilization in an ecological society, and accordingly create truly happy life with all kinds of relationships as ties.

(2) The Ecological Ethical Propositions of Social Ecology

As one of the theories of postmodern ecology, Social Ecology is the ecological science to study the mutual relation and mutual effect between human society and its environment (including natural environment and social environment). It makes investigations of ecological problems from a social perspective, explores building the development pattern of the future society with ecological health, and advocates establishing the equal relationship between man and nature on the basis of social justice. Murray Bookchin (1961–2006), American social ecologist, thought that the intrinsic root of ecological crisis is not the fault of traditional metaphysics and ethics but is the problem of social philosophy and political philosophy, the malpractice of social life pattern, that "the concept that mankind dominates nature directly originates from the reality that man rules man,"② and that it is just the oppressive social structure that man rules man that derives and

① Charlene Spretnak, "China: Ecological Postmodernism Has to Be Followed," Xie Zhongqi, Zhu Shudi, Zhang Yun, "The Construction of Ecological Society in the Context of Postmodernism—A Comment on Spretnak's Ideas about Ecological Society," *Study of Natural Dialectics*, Volume 24, 2008: 11, p. 87.

② Murray Bookchin, *Post Scarcity Anarchism*, from Wikipedia, the Free Encyclopedia, *Post-Scarcity Anarchism* was written by Murray Bookchin and first published in 1971 by Ramparts Press, http: //en. wikipedia. org/wiki/ Murray_Bookchin, February 22, 2009, p. 6.

intensifies all forms of domination (including man's domination of nature), the corresponding way of thinking and mode of life. Therefore, in order to fundamentally solve the ecological crisis, firstly, we must break the oppressive system of society. Secondly, through studying and reestablishing the relationship between individuals and the patterns of social organizations in which they live, we must explore establishing the development pattern of the future society with ecological health, and set up the equal relationship between man and nature on the basis of social justice.① Social Ecology presents the following main ideas:

a. Man Is a Product of Long Natural Evolution

In his works and other treatises such as *The Ecology of Freedom*: *The Emergence and Dissolution of Hierarchy* (1982), etc., Murray Bookchin proposed and insisted organic integrity worldview, thought that human beings not only belong to nature but are also the products of lengthy natural evolution, criticized and opposed the dualistic ideology that advocates separation of man and nature. This dualistic ideology has taken up dominant position since industrial civilization. Bookchin thought, "Nature is ultimately a social evolutionary process which advances gradually from inanimate things to animate things though in this process it may appear a sort of differentiation."② The inhuman nature can be regarded as "the first nature," and correspondingly, the man-made social nature is called "the second nature." Man's second nature is far from being "unnatural" while it is obviously the creature of the first nature of organic evolution. Nature and society interknit each other through entering a natural evolution and that nature includes two differentiations: the first nature—biological nature, the second nature—human nature. Human nature and biological nature share a sort of evolution potency to realize greater subjectivity and adaptation. The second nature (human nature) is a mode in which human beings as primates that have adaptive capacity and high intelligence live in nature, that is, a kind of environment created by human beings and best fit their existing way. In this respect, this kind of environment created by the second nature is consistent with the biophysical environment—the economic community that every animal creates by relying on its own capacity and adapts to and in which it must live.③ Therefore, human beings emerging from the process of organic evolution,

① See also Chen Shidan, "Social Ecology: Move Towards an Ecological Society," *Journal of Henan Normal University*, 2010: 2, p. 57.

② Murray Bookchin, *The Ecology of Freedom: The Emergence and Dissolution of Hierarchy*, trans. Huan Qingzhi, Jinan: Shandong University Press, 2008, p. 10.

③ See also Murray Bookchin, *Post Scarcity Anarchism*, from Wikipedia, the Free Encyclopedia, *Post-Scarcity Anarchism* was written by Murray Bookchin and first published in 1971 by Ramparts Press, http: //en.wikipedia.org/wiki/Murray_Bookchin, February 22, 2009, p. 6.

by virtue of their purely biological power that they need for existence, has begun a kind of development of social evolution that deeply contain the process of their organic evolution. By means of the intelligence that nature gives them, communicative power, the capability of system organization, and the relative freedom coming from their instinctive behavior, like non-human life, they give full play to their biological capability and recreate their environment. Now, this kind of capability makes them possible to work on social development.

b. The Idea That Man Governs Nature Roots in the Idea That Man Rules Man

In Bookchin's opinion, since the appearance of class society and human rule, people grew the seeds of belief that nature not only exists as a world apart but it is also organized in hierarchy and can be controlled. In this way, the idea that man rules man becomes the main cause of the idea that man dominates nature, and makes nature become a construction of hierarchical existence chain.[①] The idea that human society is hierarchical and the idea that man rules nature have similar long history. Only the fact that only in modern eco-activities has human society destroyed beautiful rivers and mountains of Mediterranean Basin and many other places on the Earth suffices to show that the hierarchical, oppressive class society in which man rules man began plundering and destroying the Earth early before the appearance of the "linear" reason of modern science and "industrial society." However, the second nature (human nature) fails to create an infinitely happy Garden of Eden in the process of its steadily absorbing and damaging the first nature (biological nature). Just like it destroying human life by itself in its behavior such as constantly launching wars that makes deaths, genocide, and ruthless oppression, the second nature frequently plunders many nice, creative and great-hearted things in the biological world. Social Ecology seriously points out the fact that the fate of human beings and the fate of non-human world go through thick and thin together. Social Ecology insists on organic integrality of ecological system, calls on human society to give up necessarily the idea of ruling and conquering nature and establish an ecological system in which the relationship between human society and nature is harmonious.

c. The Mad and Always Infinitely Extending Capitalism Destroys Social Ecology

Social Ecology thinks that the crisis of social ecology roots in the mad and always infinitely extending capitalism. In Bookchin's words, "Until organized social relations broke up into market relations, was this planet of the Earth turned into the resource to be developed. In modern capitalist system, this time-honored tendency has got exasperate development. On account of

① See also Murray Bookchin, *Post Scarcity Anarchism*, from Wikipedia, the Free Encyclopedia, *Post-Scarcity Anarchism* was written by Murray Bookchin and first published in 1971 by Ramparts Press, http: //en.wikipedia.org/wiki/Murray_Bookchin, February 22, 2009, p. 6.

its intrinsic nature of competition, the bourgeois society not only makes man struggle with man but also makes human mass struggle with nature. Just like man who has been changed into commodity, every respect of nature has been also changed into commodity, having become a kind of resource that can be wantonly manufactured, bought and sold.... Market's plundering human spirit and capital's plundering the Earth run in parallel simultaneously."① In the capitalist system, the market of fierce competition created by modern industrial capitalists encourages industrial infinite extension and the commerce power that it endows. Both of them are running madly in the manner that development is exactly the end-in-self, and the predatory exploitation of nature has likewise been going on without choking.

Social Ecology calls on moral regeneration and social reconstruction along ecological line. In order to replace the existing hierarchical and class system, Social Ecology puts forward an ecological human society which is established on the basis of mutual aid, mutual care, and the social values of public ownership and in which everyone is equal, mankind concerns and loves nature, and harmoniously coexists with nature—to realize the instinct unity of human society and nature, and the instinct unity of the relationship between man and man and the relationship between man and nature.②

(3) The Ecological Ethical Proposition of Deep Ecology

In their book, *Dialectic of Enlightenment* (1947), M. Max Horkheimer (1895–1973) and Theodor W. Adorno (1903–1969) of Frankfurt School thought that science and reason initiated by Enlightenment put man in the position of an absolute subject ruling all things on earth, regarded nature only as resource and material available to be used, which has consequently caused man's perpetual objectification and enslavement of nature. Man's persistently and unscrupulously plundering of and treading on nature have, as a result, given rise to the global environmental crisis. Therefore, in the meantime bringing about civilization and progress, enlightenment has also caused extreme oppression to nature and accordingly moved toward the wrong side, made "the thoroughly enlightened world enveloped in a disaster incurred by victory."③ Arne Naess (1912–

① Murray Bookchin, *Post Scarcity Anarchism*, from Wikipedia, the Free Encyclopedia, *Post-Scarcity Anarchism* was written by Murray Bookchin and first published in 1971 by Ramparts Press, http: //en. wikipedia. org/wiki/Murray_Bookchin, February 22, 2009, pp. 24–25.

② See also Chen Shidan, "Social Ecology: Move Towards an Ecological Society," *Journal of Henan Normal University*, 2010: 2, p. 61.

③ M. Max Horkheimer and Theodor W. Adorno, *Dialectic of Enlightenment*, trans. Qu Jingdong and Cao Weidong, Shanghai: Shanghai Renmin Press, 2006, p. 1.

2009), Norway philosopher, put forward the thought of Deep Ecology in the 1970s and provided a way of eliminating the antagonism between man and nature and solving the environmental crisis.

a. Opposing Dualistic Hierarchy and Insisting on Monistic Holistic View

The idea of enlightenment separates man and nature, establishes a dualistic hierarchy between man and nature, determines man and nature as master and slave, and regards nature as the object that man conquers and the Other. Deep Ecology rejects the idea of enlightenment, opposes this kind of dualistic thinking, and thinks that man, animals and plants all equally co-exist harmoniously in a same space, they are related to each other, and either party's change will affect the other party's existence. Naess pointed out that the "depth" of Deep Ecology means to "question closely those questions such as 'why' and 'how' that other people do not question."① Deep Ecology discovers that what has caused today's environmental crisis is not merely population, economy, technique, etc. but are mainly the cultural mechanism, behavioral pattern and the dualistic hierarchy in the philosophical system and anthropocentrism. The "depth" of Deep Ecology even more lies in its proposition of a new non-dualistic thought, that is, of a monistic holistic view. According to this holistic view, all things on the earth, that make up the world, are equal, all things have their own intrinsic values, and all things have their rights to exist and flourish. Anthropocentrism has not only jeopardized the existence of life entities but also resulted in the alienation of man himself, and made man become crime culprit who deracinates a myriad of animals, plants and many other species. Deep Ecology negates the isolated values or the center for meaning of separation of man and nature in the traditional significance, abolishes the structural body in which the center controls everything, and replaces it with a net structure that emphasizes the universal relation between man and all other species. In this net structure, any one of these species should not be lacked, and any one net knob that becomes loose or falls out will affect the existence of other net knobs and even the entire net structure.②

b. Ethical Appeal: The Theoretical Core and the Program of Action of Deep Ecology

On the basis of criticizing anthropocentrism, Deep Ecology has established its own concept of ecological holism; at the same time exposing the negative effect that science has brought about, it has formulated a sort of new survival rules to be used to direct people's behavior. Naess called this kind of survival rule as Ecosophy. "'Sophy' comes from 'Sophia,' the root of Greek language,

---

① Stephan Bodian, "Simple in Means, Rich in Ends: An Interview with Arne Naess," *Deep Ecology for the Twenty-first Century*, ed. George Sessions, Boston & London: Shambhalla, 1995, p. 27.

② See also Li Jinyun, "Deep Ecology: One Type of Enlightenment Dialectics in the Post-structural Times," *Journal of Henan Normal University*, 2010: 2, p. 62.

meaning 'wisdom,' and it is related to ethics, norm, and practice. Therefore, Ecosophy or Deep Ecology means the change from science to wisdom."① Hence, Deep Ecology is, in effect, a sort of ethical appeal, a kind of survival (or life) wisdom. This is centrally embodied in the structure chart of Deep Ecology constituted by Naess. On the basis of discussing pure diversification of Deep Ecology, Naess has summarized eight basic principles as follows:

1) Human and non-human existence and flourishing have their own values (intrinsic values). These values have nothing to do with non-human usefulness to human beings as well as to human purposes.

2) The richness and varieties of life forms contribute to realization of these values, and the richness and varieties of life forms themselves have values.

3) Unless meeting basic needs, human beings have no rights to reduce the richness and varieties of life forms.

4) The prosperity of human life and culture needs lowering population and the prosperity of nonhuman life also needs reducing population.

5) Contemporary human beings excessively intervene in nonhuman world and this situation is being deteriorated.

6) We must change the current policies. These policies are affecting economy, techniques and the basic structure of ideology, and the consequence of change will be greatly different from the current circumstances.

7) The change of ideology will be mainly embodied in evaluating the quality of life (laying emphasis on the inherent value of life), rather than in insisting higher and higher living standard. Human beings will deeply realize the difference between large quantity and high quality.

8) The people who support the viewpoints above have an obligation to directly or indirectly implement necessary change.②

These eight principles have become the theoretical core and the program of action of Deep Ecology, which is generally accepted by the people who hold different philosophical and religious standpoints. On the basis of criticizing the antagonism between man and nature, Deep Ecology has established the monism of ecological unity, carries through the monism, and insists that man's

---

① Stephan Bodian, "Simple in Means, Rich in Ends: An Interview with Arne Naess," *Deep Ecology for the Twenty-first Century*, ed. George Sessions, Boston & London: Shambhalla, 1995, p. 27.

② Bill Devall and George Sessions, *Deep Ecology*, Li Jinyun, "Deep Ecology: One Type of Enlightenment Dialectics in the Post-structural Times," *Journal of Henan Normal University*, 2010: 2, p. 63.

body and spirit, action and cognition are highly consistent.[①]

Postmodern Western ecological ethics is one of postmodern applied ethics. It has broken the long history of Western traditional normative ethics that sums up morality completely as interpersonal morality, advocates to extend man's moral concern from human society to inhuman natural existing things or natural environment, and consequently establishes a stable moral relationship between man and nature that man respects nature, and thus ecological morality has become the ethical theory that studies the moral relationship between man and nature. The Ecological morality appeals to that man and nature should co-exist harmoniously and co-flourish, cooperate in progress, and opposes mankind's mode of production and mode of life which calculates, exploits, and pillages nature. Postmodern Western ecological ethics has successfully put forward and demonstrated the ecological moral principles that can be generally accepted such as environmentally friendly principle, resource saving principle, ecological equality principle, principle of sustainable development, etc., and has raised man's moral life to a new boundary and a new level.[②]

B. Main Concerns of Postmodern Ethical Literary Criticism

Postmodern Ethical Literary Criticism, from the perspective of postmodern Western ethics, analyzes the texts of postmodernist literature, discusses the themes of the postmodern ethical thoughts and the postmodern ethical concerns about postmodern human experiences represented in postmodernist works by postmodernist writers by using postmodern ethical narrative.

In the discussion of themes, Postmodern Ethical Literary Criticism thinks that postmodernist writers generally express the following postmodern ethical ideological views in their works: deconstructing metaphysics of modernity, deconstructing authority, wiping off the center, reconstructing the system of postmodern moral values, emphasizing pluralism of subjects, deeply respecting "differences" and "the Other," and reconstructing the moral relationship that "self" esteems "the Other," establishing the viewpoint of righteousness that self shoulders infinite absolute responsibility for the Other, establishing humanism for the Other, constructing minimal ethical community, calling responsibility, friendliness, and rethinking and criticizing concentration of power and violence. Postmodern Ethical Literary Criticism reconstructs the moral relationship that self respects nature, insisting on the Ethics of Ecological Postmodernism, emphasizing

① See also Li Jinyun, "Deep Ecology: One Type of Enlightenment Dialectics in the Post-structural Times," *Journal of Henan Normal University*, 2010: 2, p. 63.

② See also Xiang Yuqiao, *A Study of Postmodern Western Ethics*, Beijing: China Social Sciences Press, 2011, pp. 93–94.

the inherent connection and integrality of cosmic inventory, persevering in the ecological consciousness of "interdependency," "sustainability," "partnership," "flexibility," "diversity," etc. It persists in the viewpoints of Social Ecology, advocating to eliminate the oppressive social structure that man rules man and all the forms of government (including the form that man rules nature) derived and intensified by that structure, and establishing the relation of equality between man and nature on the basis of social justice. Postmodern Ethical Literary Criticism adheres to the monism of ecological unity of Deep Ecology, insisting high consistence of man's body and soul, action and cognition, calling on that man and nature co-exist harmoniously, share life and prosperity with each other, and making coordinative progress with nature.

In the discussion about artistic innovation of postmodernist literature, Postmodern Ethical Literary Criticism thinks that, to represent and deepen the themes of their works and to express their postmodern ethical propositions, postmodernist writers dispel the writer's authority and the narrator's center, observe from multiple angles, narrate by many voices, use carnival narration formed with various and mixed structures and techniques with multivariate changes, and use intertextual narration made up of parallel structures, parodies, and the direct citations from other texts. This postmodern ethical narrative forms and the postmodern ethical propositions represented in the works bring out the best in each other and thus the postmodernist writers have realized dialectical unity of deep themes and innovative artistic forms.

1. Discussing the Postmodern Ethical Thought in the Works of Postmodernist Literature

In the novels of Kurt Vonnegut, Jr. (1922–2007), one of the representative writers of postmodernist literature, from the perspective of postmodern ethics, we find that postmodernist literature deconstructs metaphysics of modernity, reconstructs the moral relationship that "self" esteems "the Other," emphasizes self's absolute responsibility for the Other, establishes "humanism for the Other," calls responsibility and friendliness, and rethinks and criticizes centralization of power and violence that cause social injustice. Meanwhile, postmodernist literature also reconstructs the moral relationship between self and nature that self respects nature, restores the integrality of interrelation between man and man, man and the world, constructs a sustainable ecological society, advocates to break the oppressive system in which man rules man, establishes the equal relationship between man and nature on the basis of social justice, insists on monism of ecological unity, insists on high consistence of man's body and soul, action and cognition, and finally appeals to human beings to follow the postmodern ecological morality to highly esteem, care for and protect nature to realize the purpose that man and nature co-exist harmoniously.

(1) Exploring the Development Pattern of Establishing a Future Society with Ecological Health

Vonnegut is a distinct postmodernist writer. Beginning from his first novel *Player Piano* (1952), he represented his proposition of humanism for the Other (that self respects the Other, shoulders absolute responsibility for the Other). In his novel *The Sirens of Titan* (1959), while deconstructing grand meta-narration, Vonnegut put forward the thought for the Other: "Our most sublime ideal is to love and serve the human race."① Vonnegut's every novel "represents the conflict between his humanism and the hollowness of postmodern life."② In his novel writing, always starting from his humanistic concern for the Other, Vonnegut exposed the absurd and terrible reality in the modern capitalist industrial society and presented his own ethical propositions to change this reality as well.

a. Calling on Dignity and Restoring Man's Integrality

In the modern times, mankind did not properly apply science and technology into the human society to serve it. On the contrary, the modern capitalist society "has subverted the traditional social combination—the integrality of human community, [and]capitalism has invaded and destroyed the territory of social life."③ In Vonnegut's novel, *Player Piano*, the reader sees that one of the consequences that the modern science and technology promote industry to rapidly develop is that machines have replaced people. Consequently, large quantities of workers have become useless parts of the large machine of capitalism and been thrown aside, thus out of work, caught in poverty, become valueless, and lost their human dignity and human integrality. Paul, a young engineer, leads a proletarian revolutionary movement to destroy automated factory, "return the world to people... let men and women go back to the factory, work, and be masters of machines."④ In court, he proclaims solemnly: "The main things of humanity is to do good things for mankind, rather than serve as appurtenance of machines, public institutions and systems."⑤ Through the characters in the novel, Vonnegut raised his ethical propositions to reject mechanization and restore human dignity and human integrality.

---

① Todd F. Davis, *Kurt Vonnegut's Crusade, or, How a Postmodern Harlequin Preached a New Kind of Humanism*, Albany: State University of New York Press, 2006, p. 51.

② Ibid., p. 116.

③ Murray Bookchin, *The Ecology of Freedom: The Emergence and Dissolution of Hierarchy*, trans. Huan Qingzhi, Jinan: Shandong University Press, 2008, p. 300.

④ Kurt Vonnegut, *Player Piano*, New York: Charles Scribner's Sons, 1952, p. 261.

⑤ Ibid., pp. 272–273.

b. Advocating Peace, Opposing Wars and Entering into Natural Humanization

According to social ecological point of view, we have once again entered into the process of natural evolution, "which is more of natural humanization rather than a naturalization of mankind."① Humanism advocates humanity, which is characterized by goodness instead of killing each other following the law of jungle. Advocating peace and opposing wars is one of the important themes represented in Vonnegut's novels. Vonnegut repeatedly emphasized that war gives rise to destruction and therefore it is villainous. The novel *Slaughterhouse-Five* (1969) uses a true slaughterhouse in Dresden, a German city, in the Second World War to suggest that the human world would become a place like a slaughterhouse in the worst situation. In the novel, the allied forces destroyed Dresden by using firebombing, which shows man's inhumanity and its ability of self-destruction. Through characters in the novel, Vonnegut gave out his humanistic calling: "Don't join massacre in any case; don't work for the company that manufactures massacring machines,"② called on peace, opposed wars, and hoped that human society will enter into natural humanization.

c. Constructing Extended Families That Concern and Love the Same Kind, and Constituting Human Nature Itself

As Social Ecology points out, "Human beings as animals are organized according to biological principles, thus live together with their kind, concern and love their kind in a broad and free social organization. These human characteristics are regarded not only as the characteristics of human nature but also as formation of human nature itself."③ In his novel, *Slapstick* (1976), Vonnegut revealed that the reason of isolation of individuals from society is that social members are seriously short of mutual concern and love among them. In the novel, President Wilbur gives every American a middle name by using the name of flowers, fruits or vegetables, uses a hyphen to connect it with a figure between 1 to 20, having thus formed several extended families, each of which has more than a thousand members. He has thus made every one become a member of a human community, which concerns and loves the same kind. Consequently, President Wilbur has established friendliness, removed loneliness, and helped people pull through with the support of fraternal love of the extended families. The important moral of the novel, *Slapstick*, is that human community's concern and love for human beings can help people eliminate loneliness and thereby

① Murray Bookchin, *The Ecology of Freedom: The Emergence and Dissolution of Hierarchy*, trans. Huan Qingzhi, Jinan: Shandong University Press, 2008, p. 375.

② Kurt Vonnegut, *Slaughterhouse-Five*, New York: Delacorte Press, 1969, p. 17.

③ Murray Bookchin, *The Ecology of Freedom: The Emergence and Dissolution of Hierarchy*, trans. Huan Qingzhi, Jinan: Shandong University Press, 2008, p. 375.

constitute human nature itself.

d. Creating New Community and Forming an Ecological Society

In Bookchin's opinion, "The sprout's structure of an ecological society is likely to be organized around a commune—This is an intimate connection which is freely created, consciously trained and suitable for the human nature... What an ecological society pursues is to create a new community which has rich creation and characteristics of liberalism."① In the novel, *Galapagos* (1985), Vonnegut, in the manner of black humor, revealed that the world today has already been destroyed by the human beings whose brains are well-developed, no longer suitable for mankind to exist; human beings can constitute a social organization with the people whose brains have degenerated and pursue community anew, and thus people can better realize ecological progress. Similar to the story of Noah's Ark, in *Galapagos*, those persons who have most developed brains and have high intelligence quotient are the origin of evils and do not suit for living on the earth. All evil men with high intelligence quotient die before the houseboat arrives at Galapagos. Finally, only one simple, honest, and kind-hearted man, Captain Adolf von Kleist and a few aborigine women survive and live on the Islands of Galapagos which helps mankind avoid extinction. For a million years, the offspring of the colonists are the only human survivors on the planet, and they evolve to fit their environment, with fur, flippers, and small brains for swimming and catching fish. Humanity has finally found paradise. Now, human beings have evolved into a kind of new state of coastal life with lower intelligence. Though a million years later, the brains of the inhabitants of the islands have degenerated and they "survive in the form of ceasing to be complete human beings,"② they have organized a community the members of which "have similar harmonious emotions, gender preference, intelligence and interests, etc.,"③ and thus established a kind of social relationship among the members of the society who concern and love each other and live in harmony, and has realized the creation of new community and formed a new ecological society.

e. Exploring Construction of Ecological Human Society Coexisting Harmoniously with Nature and Developing Sustainably

In his novels, Vonnegut represents ecological ethics of Ecological Postmodernism: what we perceive is an uninterrupted continuum formed by jointing the following links: the Universe /

---

① Murray Bookchin, *The Ecology of Freedom: The Emergence and Dissolution of Hierarchy*, trans. Huan Qingzhi, Jinan: Shandong University Press, 2008, p. 407.

② William Rodney Allen, *Understanding Kurt Vonnegut*, Columbia: University of South Carolina Press, 1991, p. 249.

③ Murray Bookchin, *The Ecology of Freedom: The Emergence and Dissolution of Hierarchy*, trans. Huan Qingzhi, Jinan: Shandong University Press, 2008, p. 407.

the Earth/mainland/nation/biosphere/community/neighborhood/family/individual. These are all bounds of the extended self. Our field, our foundation and our existence is precisely universe. We and all the other species in the universe have internal connections with each other, and we and all the other species are all integral parts of the whole universe, equally important and interdependent in existence.

(2) Establishing Ecological Postmodernist Ideology

Postmodernism stresses, "In the Earth community, every form of universal life comes to the world in its own way; however, none of them comes in isolation. Whether animate or inanimate, they are all our relatives and exist around us."① In his novel, *Breakfast of Champions* (1974), Vonnegut emphasized self's connection with everything around him and self's esteem for the Other and nature.

Vonnegut condemned capitalist industrial society that uses "human beings as machines"② and makes human beings in the modern society become robots that have no friendly emotions and that are not worth to be brought into any human family. This kind of mechanized persons cannot be kind to themselves and their neighbors, and they cannot respectfully treat nature, too. In the novel, Dwayne Hoover, an automobile dealer, regards himself as "the only creature in the entire Universe who has free will... Everybody else is a robot, a machine,"③ "unfeeling machines,"④ so that he can treat other people as he wishes, and consequently he beats all the people around him until 11 people are sent to the hospital. Along the road to Midland City to attend the Art Festival, what jumps into Kilgore Trout's sight is the landscape polluted and made very ugly by the extracted strip mine and all kinds of advertisements. In order to produce coal, capitalists, machines and explosive join up and have together destroyed the appearance of West Virginia and those mountains, which had once found it easy to stand by themselves, are sliding into the valley. Vonnegut angrily condemned the governments, "The demolition of West Virginia had taken place with the approval of the executive, legislature, and judicial branches of the State Government, which drew their power from the people."⑤

Vonnegut yearned for creating a multi-subject world in which every life can be taken

① Charlene Spretnak, *The Resurgence of the Real: Body, Nature, and Place in a Hypermodern World*, trans. Zhang Nini, Beijing: Central Compilation & Translation Press, 2001, p. 232.

② Kurt Vonnegut, *Breakfast of Champions, or Goodbye Blue Monday*, New York: Delacorte, 1999, p. 11.

③ Ibid., p. 259.

④ Ibid., p. 266.

⑤ Ibid., p. 123.

seriously. In the novel, Rabo Karabekian's painting "The Temptation of Saint Anthony" is constituted with only one vertical luminous orange tape that symbolizes life. Karabekian alleges that this painting "shows everything about life which truly matters, with nothing left out. It is a picture of the awareness of every animal. It is the immaterial core of every animal—the 'I am' to which all the messages are sent. It is all that is alive in any of us—in a mouse, in a deer, in a cocktail waitress. A sacred picture of Saint Anthony alone is one vertical, unwavering band of light."① This passage emphasizes our understanding of the concept about "interrelation and integrality of man and nature": "... human beings and our environment as being part of nature. Human life, too, is embedded in the life cycles of ecosystems."② Embracing this tape is just embracing the holiness in all life species including human beings.

(3) Establishing Relative Society

Vonnegut's novels reveal that in order to rescue human beings out of the situation of self-destruction, it is very important to enlighten people to correctly know the relationships between man and man, man and nature: "Not only all beings are linked together in a structure through the relation chain of the universe but also all beings are inherently constituted with the relations to Others,"③ and therefore all species are premises for each other's existence, should concern and love each other. The important theme of Vonnegut's novel, *Slapstick*, is to establish a relative society: "In this kind of relative society, all human beings accepted by this society are all treated as human beings;... nature is also treated as human beings... the elements of nature, the characteristics of landscapes, animals, and particularly anything in environment that hints human quality with its appearance or behavior—human quality is attributed to these species."④ In the novel, President Wilbur turns the United States into a relative society by establishing several extended families. On the road, wherever they are and meet difficulties, people have relatives to come out and rescue them; on the battlefield, when they find that they are relatives according to their middle names, soldiers of opposing sides immediately hug each other closely and leave the battlefield hand in hand.

---

① Kurt Vonnegut, *Breakfast of Champions, or Goodbye Blue Monday*, New York: Delacorte, 1999, p. 226.

② Fritjof Capra and Charlene Spretnak, *Green Politics*, New York: E. P. Dutton, Inc., 1984, p. 33.

③ Charlene Spretnak. *Postmodern Directions in Spirituality*, Wang Zhihe, "Spretnak and Her Ecological Postmodernism," Foreign Social Science, 1997: 6, p. 20.

④ Kurt Vonnegut, *Wampeters, Foma and Granfaloons*, New York: Delacorte, 1974, pp. 177–178.

(4) Restoring the Interrelated Integrality of Man and Man, Man and the World

The premise of realizing that human society recognizes differences, contains the Other, and co-exists harmoniously is the concept of restoring the interrelated integrality of man and man, and man and the world. As the constituent parts of the Earth community, the constituent parts of the universe, any part encountering destruction will affect the other beings. Vonnegut's novel, *Hocus Pocus* (1990), indicates that this sort of cognition is the key of constructing an ecological society.

In the novel, *Hocus Pocus*, Vonnegut criticized Americans' act of war in Vietnam in the 20th century—the evil act of a part of human beings' massacring another part of human beings. In Eugene's narrative, Vonnegut describes that during Vietnam War human beings used nightmarish modern technology and thus realized the darkest and the most evil desire—the destruction of another part of human beings. In Tarkington College, Eugene, employed as a professor of physics, by using the machine of perpetual motion left by the college founder, gives his students a lesson about the stupid act of war. He tells the students that the United States had lost the battle and knocks on the college's metal time bell, which releases a peaceful melody. Because of his speaking of such truth, Eugene is expelled by the college. Later, he teaches in a prison that locks black prisoners. Under his education, several black prisoners have obtained high school diplomas. Most black prisoners have realized that they are only cogs of capitalism, the meat-eating machine, deeply suffering the maltreatment of this system. Here, again, because of his speaking of truth, Eugene is accused of instigating black prisoners to break prison and becomes a criminal. The writer uses the word of Eugene Victor Debs, leader of American Labor Organizations and socialism, in the same name of Eugene in the novel, as the epigraph of the novel: "While there is a lower class I am in it. While there is a criminal element I am of it. While there is a soul in prison I am not free."① This passage very deeply reveals the close relationships between self and the Other and between self and the society. Eugene laments that in the modern world, on account of losing the interrelated integrality between man and man, and man and the world, people have lost sympathy, concern and love for each other.

In his description of the human beings in the 20th century, Vonnegut stresses that if they do not learn to respect each other irrespective of skin color, education status, religious belief, human beings will soon live in the post-apocalyptical age in which crimes are rampant, the days of the Earth can be counted on people's fingers.② In his novel, *Hocus Pocus*, Vonnegut indirectly

① Kurt Vonnegut, *Hocus Pocus*, New York: G. P. Putman's Sons, 1990, p. 9.

② See also Todd F. Davis, *Kurt Vonnegut's Crusade*, *or*, *How a Postmodern Harlequin Preached a New Kind of Humanism*, Albany: State University of New York Press, 2006, p. 361.

indicated that if we destroyed one life or one part of this planet, we would exactly hurt and destroy ourselves. We must learn to cherish all people around us irrespective of classes, ranks, and races, and then it is possible for the human society to exist persistently.

(5) Insisting on the Awareness of Human Beings' Living in the Universe—the Spirit of Ecological Postmodernism

In his novel, *Timequake* (1997), Vonnegut puts forward such an important concept of the awareness that we live in the universe.① Insisting on the integrality of the universe, social responsibility and decentralization is ecological postmodernist consciousness—postmodernist spirit. Ecological Postmodernism defines "spirit" as the consciousness of human beings which concentrates upon the subtlety of existence. This consciousness reveals for us the integrality and deep relation of all things in the universe, also means that existing with deep understanding of the interrelated integrality of everything in the universe is sharing "God's consciousness," and "this deep non-rational understanding of the interrelated experiences is... the true meaning of the graceful state of existence."②

In the novel, *Timequake*, Kilgore Trout, a science fiction writer, while looking up at the stars in the sky, comments on the vast expanding universe and the consciousness that mankind lives in the universe like this: "Your awareness is a new quality in the Universe, which exists only because there are human beings. Physicists must from now on, when pondering the secrets of the Cosmos, factor in not only energy and matter, but something very new and beautiful, which is *human awareness*."③ Trout's words show clearly the profound reality that we and everything in the universe interrelate to each other and form a whole. Trout goes a step further in thinking deeply and then corrects this term: "Let's call it *soul*."④ Trout and Vonnegut remind us that we live in the universe, that everything in the universe (including human beings) has right to exist, and has its intrinsic value, that we and they have close relation with each other in interdependence, and we must respect them and develop harmoniously together with them. This cognition is a sacred trust and this cognition is precisely the spirit of Ecological Postmodernism.

Though he writes down chaos and darkness in contemporary human society, Trout renames the consciousness that human beings live in the universe spirit, and this renaming is of great significance. In an age that people often seriously use specific choice of words such as "inhuman"

① Kurt Vonnegut, *Timequake*, New York: G. P. Putman, 1997, pp. 213–214.

② Charlene Spretnak, *The Spiritual Dimension of Green Politics*, Santa Fe: Bear & Company, Inc., 1986, p. 42.

③ Kurt Vonnegut, *Timequake*, New York: G. P. Putman, 1997, pp. 213–214.

④ Ibid., p. 214.

and "evil" etc. to describe human society, Vonnegut uses his novels to manifest that as long as human beings insist on the spirit of Ecological Postmodernism, the human society can develop towards the direction of continual existence.

2. Studying Postmodern Ethical Narrative Forms in the Works of Postmodernist Literature

Postmodern Ethical Literary Criticism interprets the texts of postmodernist literature from the perspective of postmodern ethics. This postmodern ethical criticism not only discusses postmodern ethical thought represented in the texts of postmodernist literature and the writers' postmodern ethical concerns for postmodern society but also studies the ethical narrative form of postmodernist literature used by the writers to represent such themes as postmodern ethical thought and the writers' postmodern ethical concerns for postmodern society. The postmodernist ethical narrative is in conformity with the values of postmodern ethics. It respects differences and the Other, eliminates the author's narrative authority and the narrative center of the text, adopts carnival narrative formed with multi-angle observation, multiple narrators, narration of multiple voices (or polyphony), hybridized structure, expressive techniques of multivariate changes, etc., and uses intertextual narration made up of parallel structure, parody, direct quotations, etc. This kind of centerless and diversified ethical narrative form and the postmodern West ethics respecting differences and the Other that it represents bring out the best in each other.

(1) Carnival Narrative

Mikhail Bakhtin, Russian philosopher, literary critic, semiotician and scholar who worked on literary theory, ethics, and the philosophy of language, earlier put forward the thought about the dialogue nature of fiction. He thought that "Any statement is dialogue in its essence,"① a novel "has numerous, independent respectively, and incompatible voices and consciousnesses, the true polyphony formed with different voices with full values."② Bakhtin's polyphonic fiction is a kind of fiction of composite dialogue and multi-voice. In the fiction, multi-angle observation, multiple narrators, multi-voice narration (or polyphony), hybridized structure, multivariate change techniques of expression, etc. form the postmodern carnival narrative mechanism of equal dialogue. This sort of postmodern ethical narrative form dismantles integrality and identity of traditional narrative which has the structure with central referent, and proclaims that meta-discourse and meta-narration have lost efficacy. James Patrick Donleavy, American

① Mikhail Bakhtin, *Poetic Problems of Fyodor Dostoyevsky*: *Theory of Polyphony in Fiction*, Beijing: Sanlian Bookshop, 1988, p. 177.

② Ibid., p. 29.

postmodernist novelist, in his novel, *The Ginger Man* (1955), a novel with Angry Young Man as its theme, through shifting points of view, stream of consciousness, symbol's jumping, time and space in disorder, language experiment, the polysemy of image, etc., breaks the narrative form of realism and modernism, puts up subversive and popular characteristics of postmodernist art, employs linguistic carnivalism in postmodern context to describe Dangerfield and his friends, representatives of the generation of Angry Young Man, and the actuality of their life in which they are pushed aside, wander around, helpless and repressed just because of their identity of nonconformists.

In his novel, *The Saddest Summer of Samuel S* (1967), with the Beat Generation as its theme, Donleavy integrated surrealistic artistic technique into his work, mixing with fantasy, imagination, stream of consciousness, contemplation, daydream, and reality together, masterly combining realistic detail description with art of postmodernism. Moreover, through internal focalization, covert narrator and flexibly handled narrative time, Donleavy uncovers a character's "psychological truth," and blends his own feeling of the world with the figures in his works together. This carnival narration reveals that the world that Samuel deals with is a garbled world with self as its center. In this chaotic world, as a patient, Samuel's noema is incomparably sober; a psychologist takes his patient's money to invest in filthy business; man longs for getting married while woman only wants to walk the world with a bag on her back, looking for her next travelling companion; finally, Samuel feels disillusioned in his life and chooses to commit suicide.

In his novels, *The Onion Eaters* (1971) and *Wrong Information Is Being Given Out at Princeton* (1998), Donleavy, through some postmodernist artistic techniques such as parody of genre, polyphony, juxtaposition of facts and fiction, anti-genre, etc., manifests his writing tendency towards "vulgarity" and "hybridization," as Hassan pointed out that, "in that plural present, all styles [are] dialectically available in an interplay between the Now and the Not Now, the Same and the Other."① By using such artistic techniques such as parody, anti-genre writing, etc., Donleavy strives to liberate the repression of modern civilization and power mechanism, and change the absurd reality in deathly still world, and makes deep interpretation and reconstruction of such metaphysical philosophical propositions as destiny, changeableness, death, etc. Under Donleavy's pen, there is a broken, unstable and absurd world, the characters in his novels become "clowns" in the carnival, and they perform a carnival ceremony of crowning and uncrowning.

In his works such as *The Beastly Beatitudes of Balthazar B* (1964), *A Fairy Tale of New*

① Ihab Hassan, *The Postmodern Turn: Essays in Postmodern Theory and Culture*. Columbus: The Ohio State University Press, 1987, p. 170.

York (1973), etc., Donleavy showed his unique style of dancing-together of Bacchus and Death, intertexture of love desire and death desire, and co-existence of comedy and tragedy. After his deconstruction of seriousness and authority of realistic fiction, subversion of the writing train of thought of "art for art" in modernist fiction, Donleavy innovatively made unique postmodernist language experiment and language games. In his textual world that represents love and death, sadness and happiness, and intoxication and insanity, Donleavy showed all kinds of life as much as he liked and exposed the tragic reality by using comic language.

In form, the postmodern ethical carnival narrative in Donleavy's novels break through tradition and is bold in innovation; in themes, it manifests the writer's postmodern ethical concerns for the contemporary society, exposes the contradiction between substance prosperity and man's spiritual inadequacy in Western society, and criticizes injustice in capitalist society.

(2) Intertextual Narrative

On the basis of Bakhtin's dialogue theory, Julia Kristeva, French semiologist and literary critic, put forward the concept of "intertextuality": "Any text is a knock-together of quotations, and any text is assimilation and adaptation of another text. Therefore, the concept of intertextuality should replace the concept of intersubjectivity."① About "intertextuality," Roland Barthes explains in this way, "Any text is intertext; in a text, do exist other texts to different extent and in more or less recognizable form: for example, the text of previous culture and the text of surrounding culture."② "Intertextuality" is a basic concept of deconstruction that aims at breaking the isolation and closure of structuralist texts. Deconstruction thinks that any text's composition is a dialogue triggered from this text with other texts, is assimilation and transformation from other texts, and forms its own value in differences. In his novel, *Nice Work* (1988), David Lodge (1935–), English postmodernist novelist, combines intertextual narrative with social criticism; the reader can discover the origin of discourse and can better appreciate the text as the symphony that constitutes social discourses. Lodge's intertextual narrative is formed mainly with three techniques such as parallel structure, parody and direct quotations.

a. Parallel Structure

The parallel structure refers to that when demonstrating certain viewpoint or thesis, a writer expounds it by disassembling it into several aspects that have certain connections, while

① Julia Kristeva, "Word, Dialogue and Novel," *The Kristeva Reader*, ed. Toril Moi, Oxford: Blackwell Publishers, Ltd., 1986, p. 35.

② Roland Barthes, "Theory of the Text," *Untying the Text: A Post-structuralist Reader*, London: Robert Young and Regan Paul, 1981, p. 39.

all these aspects pertain to a central thesis or a viewpoint, equal in status, appear in parallel relationship, and therefore are called parallel structure. In demonstration, the several parallel aspects are the revelations and elucidations of the attributes and the thought significance of the central viewpoint, and the results of the writer's pondering and understanding of a certain thesis. Bakhtin emphasized that a literary work is not "a unified objective world constituted with numerous personalities and destinies and unfolded layer upon layer under the control of the writer's unified consciousness; here is exactly the place where numerous consciousnesses equal in status together with their respective worlds are combined in a unified event but there is nonoccurrence of fusion between them,"① and advocated to endow all kinds of voices (that is, all kinds of ideas) with rights and freedom to burst out and right to appeal at the same time. The novel, *Nice Work* (1988), by David Lodge, English postmodernist novelist and literary critic, is mainly made up of two parallel structures, each of which is formed with two cross referencing texts. One parallel structure is constituted with a narrative about Rummidge University whose educational fund is abridged by the national government and where Robyn Penrose, the heroine in the novel, works and another narrative about J. Pringle Father and Son's Cast and General Engineering Firm of which Vic Wilcox holds the post of manager and whose production is stagnant; another parallel structure is formed with the narrative about Robyn who is going to lose her "nice work" of a university teacher being faced with job cut and the narrative about Charles whose job as a university teacher is stable but who resigns to be a moneychanger in order to make a lot of money. The bigger texts of the two parallel structures also refer to each other and further constitute even larger intertextual narrative. By using parallel structure, through his male and female protagonists that he described, Lodge not only expressed his own notions but also revealed all kinds of different senses of independence which have equal values. By using different senses of independence that are not mixed with each other and the different voices each having complete values, Lodge composed an intertextual novel, which exposes that in any historical period the nature of capitalism is precisely private interests and exploitation and that money is the master of the society.

b. Parody

Parody is one of the commonly used techniques by postmodernist writers. In their works, they make exaggerated, twisted, distorted, and jeering imitation of historical events and personages, some phenomena in everyday life, the subjects, contents, forms and styles, make

① Mikhail Bakhtin, *Poetic Problems of Fyodor Dostoyevsky: Theory of Polyphony in Fiction*, Beijing: Sanlian Bookshop, 1988, p. 29.

them absurd and funny, and thus realize the purpose to criticize, satirize, and negate the value and significance of tradition, history and reality as well as the past literary model. In his novel, *Nice Work*, Lodge parodied the Victorian novels that deals with industrial subjects in the 19th century, made them cross referencing with the novels which represent postmodern industrial subjects in the 20th century, and form intertextual narrative. Lodge, by using parody, realized the transforming, criticizing, and negating of the English novels representing industrial subjects in the middle of the 19th century, and exposed that this kind of novels are, at heart, still products of capitalist economic society, and that the novelists are capitalists who make a profit from highly commercialized form of literary production.

c. Direct Quotations

Quotations assemble reading and writing together and thus reveal the writing backgrounds of the texts or the preparatory work, the reading notes and the reserved knowledge needed for completing the texts.① Quotations become grafting of texts, the grafted texts take roots in the new environments and form organic relations with new texts, the relations produced in the new environments not only relate to original materials but are also compatible with the whole situation that they carry on.② In his *Nice Work*, Lodge used the direct quotations from the Victorian industrial novels in the 19th century such as Dickens' *Hard Times* (1854), Disraeli's *Sibyl* (1845) and Gaskell's *North and South* (1855) to form intertextuality with his own novel text and thus constituted intertextual narrative to represent the theme of capitalist industry. In his *Nice Work*, by using the intertextual narrative formed with direct quotations, Lodge made clear that whether capitalism was in the period of primitive accumulation of capital or in its monopoly stage or in its late stage (or transnational or multinational capitalism), its goal is the same: to seek profit, more profit. Its means to seek profit is common to implement ruthless exploitation of workers for their private interests. The consequences of competition between capitalist enterprises are only to constantly increase the exploitation of workers. With the direct quotations from the Victorian industrial novels, the theme of *Nice Work* becomes very clear to expose the ruthless exploitation and maltreatment of workers by capitalism in the postindustrial times.

In his novel, *Nice Work*, Lodge used postmodern ethical narrative forms to represent his postmodernist ethical concerns for the conditions of human beings in the postmodern times. In the intertextual narrative by making it mutually refer to with many other literary works, Lodge "destroyed all the barriers between different genres, all kinds of closed ideological

① Tiphaine Samoyault, *Intertextuality*, trans. Shao Wei, Tianjin: Tianjin People's Press, 2003, p. 37.

② Ibid., p. 131.

systems, and multiple different styles,"[①] and in the literary carnival, Lodge constructed an open, heterogeneous, fragmented, postmodernist ethical narrative text with numerous sounds clamoring, having effectively expressed the main ideas of postmodern Western ethics and his strong political criticism of capitalism and the capitalist society.

3. Conclusion

Postmodern Ethical Literary Criticism, as one of the methods of contemporary literary criticism, uses Marxist Historical Materialism as the basis for argumentation, the theory of Postmodern Ethics as critical perspective, makes deep and meticulous analyses of the texts of postmodernist literature, probes deep into postmodern ethical and moral concepts represented by the works of postmodernist literature and the writers' postmodern ethical concerns for postmodern society, focalizes on the reconstruction of the moral relationship between self and the Other that self admits differences and respects the Other, and emphasizes that self must shoulder infinite and absolute responsibility for the Other and humanism for the Other. At the same time, Postmodern Ethical Literary Criticism makes its focus on the reconstruction of the moral relationship between man and nature that man esteems nature, opposes the modern master-slave relationship between man and nature, stresses the fellowship between man and nature that man and nature are interdependent in existence, appeals to harmonious coexistence, common prosperity, and cooperation in progress of man and nature, opposes the mode of production and the mode of life that man calculates, exploits, and plunders nature, establishes ecological ideology, and constructs ecological human society that keeps sustainable development. While deeply discussing the themes of postmodernist literary works, Postmodern Ethical Literary Criticism also pays attention to the artistic innovation of postmodernist literary works, and probes deep into the postmodern ethical narrative forms constituted for presentation of postmodern ethical ideas, such as carnival narrative formed with multi-perspective observation, diversity-blending structure, multivariate-change techniques as well as polyphonic narration, etc. and intertextual narrative made up of parallel structure, parody, and direct quotations from other literary texts, etc., which are intended to dispel the author's authority, dislodge the narrative center from literary texts and effectively represent and deepen the themes in the postmodernist literary works.

① Mikhail Bakhtin, *Poetic Problems of Fyodor Dostoyevsky: Theory of Polyphony in Fiction*, Beijing: Sanlian Bookshop, 1988, p. 190.

Further Reading

Bauman, Zygmunt. *Modernity and the Holocaust*. Ithaca: Cornell University Press, 1989.

——. *Paradoxes of Assimilation*. New Brunswick: Transaction Publishers, 1990.

——. *Thinking Sociologically. An introduction for Everyone*. Cambridge: Basil Blackwell, 1990.

——. *Modernity and Ambivalence*. Ithaca: Cornell University Press, 1991.

——. *Intimations of Postmodernity*. London & New York: Routledge, 1992.

——. *Mortality, Immortality and Other Life Strategies*. Cambridge: Polity Press, 1992.

——. *Postmodern Ethics*. Cambridge: Basil Blackwell, 1993.

——. *Life in Fragments: Essays in Postmodern Morality*. Cambridge: Basil Blackwell, 1995.

——. *Alone Again—Ethics After Certainty*. London: Demos, 1996.

——. *Postmodernity and its Discontents*. New York: New York University Press, 1997.

Booth, Wayne. *The Rhetoric of Fiction*. Chicago: Chicago University Press, 1961.

——. *The Company We Keep: An Ethics of Fiction*. Berkeley: University of California Press, 1988.

Derrida, Jacques. *Specters of Marx: The State of the Debt, the Work of Mourning, and the New International*. Trans. Peggy Kamuf. New York: Routledge, 1994.

——. *The Politics of Friendship*. Trans. George Collins. London: Verso, 1997.

De Waal, Frans, *Good Natured: The Origins of Right and Wrong in Humans and Other Animals*. London & Cambridge: Harvard University Press, 1996.

Dickstein, Morris, The Undying Animal. *Columbia Magazine*, Fall 2008. 28–31.

Dutton, Denis. *The Art Instinct: Beauty, Pleasure, and Human Evolution*. New York: Oxford University Press, 2009.

Eldridge, Richard. *On Moral Personhood: Philosophy, Literature, Criticism, and Self-Understanding*. 2nd ed. Chicago: University of Chicago Press, 1989.

Gottschall, Jonathan & David Sloan Wilson. *The Literary Animal: Evolution and the Nature of Narrative*. Evanston: NorthWestern University Press, 2005.

Gregory, Marshall. Ethical Criticism: What It Is and Why It Matters. *Style* 32: 2, 1998. 194–220.

——. *Shaped By Stories: The Ethical Power of Narratives*, Notre Dame: University of Notre Dame Press, 2009.

Harpham, Geoffrey Galt. *Shadows of Ethics: Criticism and the Just Society*. Durham: Duke University Press Books, 1999.

Lentricchia, Frank. *Criticism and Social Change*. Chicago: University of Chicago Press, 1983.

Louden, Robert B. *Morality and Moral Theory: A Reappraisal and Reaffirmation*. New York:

Oxford University Press, 1992.
MacIntyre, Alasdair. *After Virtue: A Study in Moral Theory*. Notre Dame: University of Notre Dame Press, 1981.
Midgley, Mary. *Can't We Make Moral Judgments*? New York: St. Martin's Press, 1991.
Nussbaum, Martha C. *The Fragility of Goodness: Luck and Ethics in Greek Tragedy and Philosophy*. Cambridge: Cambridge University Press, 1986.
Pinker, Steven. *The Blank Slate: The Modern Denial of Human Nature*. New York: Viking, 2002.
Wilson, James Q. *The Moral Sense*. New York: Simon and Schuster, 1993.

Bibliography

Cuddon, J. A. *A Dictionary of Literary Terms and Literary Theory*. 5th ed. Malden: Wiley-Blackwell, 2013.
Rice, Philip & Patricia Waugh. *Modern Literary Theory*. New York: Oxford University Press, 2002.
Bressler, Charles. *Literary Criticism: An Introduction to Theory and Practice*. Beijing: Higher Education Press, 2004.
Richter, David H. *A Companion to Literary Theory*. Hoboken: Wiley Blackwell, 2018.
Habib, Rafey. *A History of Literary Criticism: From Plato to the Present*. Oxford: Blackwell Publishing, 2005.
泰勒，温奎斯特. 后现代主义百科全书. 章燕，李自修，等译. 刘象愚，校. 长春：吉林人民出版社，2007.
王治河. 后现代主义辞典. 北京：中央编译出版社，2004.
张中载，王逢振，赵国新. 二十世纪西方文论选读. 北京：外语教学与研究出版社，2002.
朱刚. 二十世纪西方文艺批评理论. 上海：上海外语教育出版社，2001.

Selected Readings

Zygmunt Bauman: *Postmodern Ethics* (a part of a chapter)

Jacques Derrida: *Specters of Marx: The State of the Debt, the Work of Mourning, and the New International* (a part of a chapter)

Emmanuel Levinas: *Humanism of the Other* (a part of a chapter)

Chapter Eighteen

Post-humanism

Post-human or post-human is a concept originating in the fields of science fiction, futurology, contemporary art, and philosophy that literally means a person or entity that exists in a state beyond being human. The concept addresses questions of ethics and justice, language and trans-species communication, social systems, and the intellectual aspirations of interdisciplinarity. Post-humanism is not to be confused with transhumanism (the nanobiotechnological enhancement of human beings) and narrow definitions of the post-human as the hoped-for transcendence of materiality. The notion of the post-human comes up both in post-humanism as well as transhumanism, but it has a special meaning in each tradition. In 2017, Penn State University Press in cooperation with Stefan Lorenz Sorgner and James Hughes (sociologist) established the *Journal of Post-human Studies* in which all aspects of the concept "post-human" can be analyzed.

In critical theory, the pos-thuman is a speculative being that represents or seeks to re-conceive the human. It is the object of post-humanist criticism, which critically questions humanism, a branch of humanist philosophy which claims that human nature is a universal state from which the human being emerges; human nature is autonomous, rational, capable of free will, and unified in itself as the apex of existence. Thus, the post-human position recognizes imperfectability and disunity within him or herself, and understands the world through heterogeneous perspectives while seeking to maintain intellectual rigour and a dedication to objective observations. The key to this post-human practice is the ability to fluidly change perspectives and manifest oneself through different identities. The post-human, for critical theorists of the subject, has an emergent ontology rather than a stable one; in other words, the post-human is not a singular, defined individual, but rather one who can "become" or embody different identities and understand the world from multiple, heterogeneous perspectives.

Critical discourses surrounding post-humanism are not homogeneous, but in fact present a series of often contradictory ideas, and the term itself is contested, with one of the foremost authors associated with post-humanism, Manuel De Landa, decrying the term as very silly. Covering the ideas of, for example, Robert Pepperell's *The Post-human Condition*, and N. Katherine Hayles's *How We Became Post-human* under a single term is distinctly problematic due to these contradictions.

The post-human is roughly synonymous with the "cyborg" of *A Cyborg Manifesto* by Donna Haraway. Haraway's conception of the cyborg is an ironic taking on traditional conceptions of the cyborg that inverts the traditional trope of the cyborg whose presence questions the salient line between humans and robots. Haraway's cyborg is in many ways the "beta" version of the post-human, as her cyborg theory prompted the issue to be taken up in critical theory.

Following Haraway, Hayles, whose work grounds much of the critical post-human discourse, asserts that liberal humanism—which separates the mind from the body and thus portrays the body as a "shell" or vehicle for the mind—becomes increasingly complicated in the late 20th and 21st centuries because information technology puts the human body in question. Hayles maintains that we must be conscious of information technology advancements while understanding information as "disembodied," that is, something which cannot fundamentally replace the human body but can only be incorporated into it and human life practices.

A. Development of Post-humanism

The roots of post-humanism can be traced in the first wave of postmodernism, but the post-human turn was fully enacted by feminist theorists in the 1990s, within the field of literary criticism—what will later be defined as critical post-humanism. Simultaneously, Cultural Studies also embraced it, producing a specific take which has been referred to as cultural post-humanism. By the end of the 1990s (critical and cultural) post-humanism developed into a more philosophically focused inquiry (now referred to as philosophical post-humanism), in a comprehensive attempt to re-access each field of philosophical investigation through a newly gained awareness of the limits of previous anthropocentric and humanistic assumptions. Post-humanism is often defined as a post-humanism and a post-anthropocentrism: it is "post" to the concept of the human and to the historical occurrence of humanism, both based, as we have previously seen, on hierarchical social constructs and human-centric assumptions. Speciesism has turned into an integral aspect of the post-human critical approach. The post-human overcoming of human primacy, though, is not to be replaced with other types of primacies (such as the one of the machines). Post-humanism can be seen as a post-exclusivism: an empirical philosophy of mediation which offers a reconciliation of existence in its broadest significations. Post-humanism does not employ any frontal dualism or antithesis, demystifying any ontological polarization through the postmodern practice of deconstruction.

Not obsessed with proving the originality of its own proposal, post-humanism can also be seen as a post-exceptionalism. It implies an assimilation of the "dissolution of the new," which Gianni Vattimo identified as a specific trait of the postmodern. In order to postulate the "new," the center of the discourse has to be located, so that the question "New to what?" shall be answered. But the novelty of human thought is relative and situated: what is considered new in one society might be common knowledge in another. Moreover, hegemonic perspectives do not explicitly acknowledge all the resistant standpoints which coexist within each specific cultural-historical paradigm, thus failing to recognize the discontinuities embedded in any discursive formation. What Post-humanism puts at stake is not only the identity of the traditional center of Western discourse—which has already been radically deconstructed by its own peripheries (feminist, critical race, queer, and post-colonial theorists, to name a few). Post-humanism is a post-centralizing, in the sense that it recognizes not one but many specific centers of interest; it dismisses the centrality of the center in its singular form, both in its hegemonic as in its resistant modes. Post-humanism might recognize centers of interests; its centers, though, are mutable, nomadic, ephemeral. Its perspectives have to be pluralistic, multilayered, and as comprehensive and inclusive as possible.

As post-humanism attracts more attention and becomes mainstream, new challenges arise. For example, some thinkers are currently looking to embrace the "exotic" difference, such as the robot, the biotechnological chimeras, the alien, without having to deal with the differences embedded within the human realm, thus avoiding the studies developed from the human "margins," such as Feminism or Critical Race Studies. But Post-humanism does not stand on a hierarchical system: there are no higher and lower degrees of alterity, when formulating a post-human standpoint, so that the non-human differences are as compelling as the human ones. Post-humanism is a philosophy which provides a suitable way of departure to think in relational and multi-layered ways, expanding the focus to the non-human realm in post-dualistic, post-hierarchical modes, thus allowing one to envision post-human futures which will radically stretch the boundaries of human imagination.

B. Emergence of Philosophical Post-humanism

As we mentioned before, by the end of the 1990s, critical and cultural post-humanism developed into a more philosophically focused inquiry, now referred to as philosophical post-humanism, in a comprehensive attempt to re-access each field of philosophical investigation through a newly gained awareness of the limits of previous anthropocentric and humanistic assumptions.

Ihab Hassan, theorist in the academic study of literature, once stated that humanism may be coming to an end as humanism transforms itself into something one must helplessly call post-humanism. This view predates most currents of post-humanism which have developed over the late 20th century in somewhat diverse, but complementary, domains of thought and practice. For example, Hassan was a known scholar whose theoretical writings expressly address postmodernity in society. Beyond postmodernist studies, post-humanism has been developed and deployed by various cultural theorists, often in reaction to problematic inherent assumptions within humanistic and enlightenment thought.

Theorists who both complement and contrast Hassan include Michel Foucault, Judith Butler, cyberneticists such as Gregory Bateson, Warren McCullouch, Norbert Wiener, Bruno Latour, Cary Wolfe, Elaine Graham, N. Katherine Hayles, Donna Haraway, Peter Sloterdijk, Stefan Lorenz Sorgner, Evan Thompson, Francisco Varela, Humberto Maturana and Douglas Kellner. Among the theorists are philosophers, such as Robert Pepperell, who have written about a post-human condition, which is often substituted for the term "post-humanism."

Post-humanism differs from classical humanism by relegating humanity back to one of many natural species, thereby rejecting any claims founded on anthropocentric dominance. According to this claim, humans have no inherent rights to destroy nature or set themselves above it in ethical considerations *a priori*. Human knowledge is also reduced to a less controlling position, previously seen as the defining aspect of the world. Human rights exist on a spectrum with animal rights and post-human rights. The limitations and fallibility of human intelligence are confessed, even though it does not imply abandoning the rational tradition of humanism.

Proponents of a post-human discourse, suggest that innovative advancements and emerging technologies have transcended the traditional model of the human, as proposed by Descartes among others associated with philosophy of the Enlightenment period. In contrast to humanism, the discourse of post-humanism seeks to redefine the boundaries surrounding modern philosophical understanding of the human. Post-humanism represents an evolution of thought beyond that of the contemporary social boundaries and is predicated on the seeking of truth within a postmodern context. In so doing, it rejects previous attempts to establish anthropological universals that are imbued with anthropocentric assumptions.

Michel Foucault, French philosopher, placed post-humanism within a context that differentiated humanism from enlightenment thought. According to Foucault, the two existed in a state of tension: as humanism sought to establish norms while Enlightenment thought attempted to transcend all that is material, including the boundaries that are constructed by humanistic thought. Drawing on the Enlightenment's challenges to the boundaries of humanism, post-humanism rejects the various assumptions of human dogmas (anthropological, political, scientific) and takes the next step by attempting to change the nature of thought about what it means to be human. This requires not only decentering the human in multiple discourses (evolutionary, ecological, technological) but also examining those discourses to uncover inherent humanistic, anthropocentric, normative notions of humanness and the concept of the human.

C. Core Ideas of Philosophical Post-humanism

We all know that humanism is a doctrine, attitude, or way of life centered on human interests or values; *especially*, a philosophy that usually rejects supernaturalism and stresses an individual's dignity and worth and capacity for self-realization through reason. Post-humanism, a trend of thought of philosophy, having occurred in the contemporary West, takes criticizing traditional humanism as its own duty. It exerts a considerable influence so that a significant minority of people claims that our age is "the age of post-humanism." As early as in the early 20th century, in his monograph *The Dehumanization of Art and Ideas About the Novel* (1925), Jose Ortega y Gasset (1883–1955), Spanish philosopher, asserted that being opposed to humanism is the main task of his contemporary artists. In his book *Structuralism* (1947), Jan M. Broekman, Belgian philosopher, also thought that many Paris philosophers, in order not likely to be all sorts of deliberately mystifying victims, endorse a sort of active anti-humanism. Here, the "active anti-humanism," obviously, is another name of post-humanism. Beyond doubt, having an indissoluble bound with humanism, anti-humanism is a sort of abnegating and transcending of humanism. Just in this sense, Ihab Hassan, American contemporary thinker, occasionally uses trans-humanism to replace "post-humanism."

The first key point for post-humanism to challenge is the concept of "man" as the theoretical cornerstone of humanism. Because in fact, at least since the 17th century, the so-called humanism had to rely on certain concepts of "man" borrowed from religion, science, and politics. Having deconstructed man's series of privileges with which traditional humanism endowed it, such as priority, centrality, absoluteness, transcendence, autonomy, etc., post-humanism has proclaimed that man divinized by traditional humanism has died. In terms of French philosopher Michel Foucault's words, the age that God had died has been replaced by the age that man has died. Claude Levi-Strauss (1908–2009), French anthropologist and philosopher, avowed that we must abandon subject (man), the rebarbative favorite, for it has occupied the philosophy stage too long. When receiving an interview from French weekly *Express*, Levi-Strauss pointed out that Sartre mainly developed a subjective philosophy. Actually, since Descartes, French philosophy has been all the time controlled by the concept of subject. If we want to acquire some other truth, we must choose another viewpoint, a different viewpoint. Then, post-humanism encircles and suppresses "man," the "favorite" in the following approaches.

Firstly, post-humanism launches an attack on man's centrality and superiority. We know that varied philosophical humanisms all take anthropocentrism as their hypothetical theory premises, all uplift humanity, esteemed man as supremacy, and put subject in the center of reality and history. According to post-humanism, this is a kind of megalomania which is a sign that yearns for changing man himself into God. In his book *The End of Humanism* (1981), Richard Schechner thought that the so-called the end of humanism is the end of the tradition of megalomania. This privilege of man is considered the privilege of idealism. To post-humanists, the subjectivity revered by humanism is not a deep-seated philosophical reality hiding under the surface acting, and studied by those sciences such as psychology, sociology etc. It is a superficial phenomenon having no deep structure or deep reason needing explanation. Using "decentralization" as its weapon, post-humanism has decentralized self. The traditional self as the center has been abandoned as an illusion, a product of belief. The conclusion of post-humanism is that we are non-unified and plural beings.

Relating to the attack on man's centrality, post-humanism has further destroyed man's apriority and autonomy. In this aspect, post-structuralist thinker Foucault's viewpoint was quite representative. Foucault, using his own method of archaeology, carried out archaeological studies of "man" and the result of his investigation astounds the world. According to his analysis, the respectable Western concept of "man" itself is not the eternal infinite existence but a conditional product of the specific age and the specific knowledge. As for Sartre's talk that Existentialism was the true philosophy in our age because Existentialism was a sort of humanism and it affirmed man's beingness, Foucault's response was that the so-called concept of man is no more than an epistemological construction in a given historical period. Not only is man finite but the so-called man's autonomy and creativity are of a "myth." For Foucault, man is not a dynamic creator as humanists thought to be and he is imaginary. On the contrary to the belief that man was the creator of codes in the scientific discourse, man is now exposed by Foucault to be only "a category" created by these codes. Individuals or human subjects that we always habitually consider something of primacy are nothing but superficial results of anonymous language or ideological system. As thus, for post-humanists, subjects are exiled and marginalized. Man originally considered to be of ultimate source and of constructivism in traditional humanism has been changed to be something deuterogenic, derivative, and constructed.

The crusade against various theories of human nature, constant human nature and human essence constitutes another important theoretical content. Foucault ever declared that all his analyses were aimed at opposing the universal inevitability of human existence. To post-humanists, the universal, general and constant human nature and human essence do not exist. They insist on thinking that the concepts of "human nature" and "human essence" of traditional humanism ought to be abandoned because man is not a deep-seated reason and an independent, self-existent thing as humanism thought to be but he is a product of history, a product of all kinds of societies, politics, economy, and cultures. According to Roland Bathes' radical positivism, people are no longer interested in the motivation of explaining but only pay attention to actions. People no longer try to make sure whether different persons are actually the same individuals in different forms but only admit the role as the unique truth about individuals that can be recognized.

In the relation between thinking and existence, humanism firmly believes that man had a natural and boundless cognitive ability and that man's thought could absolutely know the truth about everything. Post-humanism has overturned this self-confidence of humanism by means of skepticism. On this basis, post-humanism has further subverted the humanistic concept of human progress. This human self-confidence manifested itself mainly in the old aphorism that man was the measure of everything. Post-humanism challenges this belief and the challenge first starts with the measure. According to Ihab Hassan's analysis, the ideal pattern of measure is the counter closed in the vacuum but this instrument used to gauge length is also constantly changing. The change is reflected all the while by the early platinum, iridium, spectrum, light wavelength, and then orange line of 86 krypton. Its characteristics are more and more non-substantialized and dematerialized. Then, using Marcel Duchamp's drawing "Canned Chance" for example, Hassan again explained that we could have three views about the same ideal length. Now that the so-called objective precise "measures" are all mutative and various always, then the man as "measure" must be impossible to be absolute. His conclusion was that we live at the threshold that the man as measure begins to change. One important aspect of that change is the change from being absolute to being relative.

That is to say, mankind can only relatively know things and it is impossible for them to absolutely grasp things. Austrian philosopher Ludwig Wittgenstein ever said that really there were things that we could not tell. They themselves reveal themselves. This is a mysterious thing. Levi-Strauss once also talked about a world that nobody began and that nobody would end. Man is not as omnipotent as traditional humanism thought to be because everything is not given and everything is not known. As the theoretical precursor of post-humanism, Martin Heidegger, German philosopher, ever spoke of the unavoidability of an unthought thing. Heidegger criticized traditional humanism that wrongly understood the "unthought thing," regarding it either as the abstract form of the object or as the abstract form of the subject. That is to say, all traditional humanistic thinkers had made a simplistic mistake by artificially restoring the complex and multiple things into a simple and single nature. Hegel's "spirit," Schopenhauer's "will," Nietzsche's "power will," Freud's "libido," and Husserl's "intentionality," were all like this. In this sense, humanism was a sort of idealism. Post-humanism regards thought as a thing that further produces complexity, and thinks that there is not any self-evident thought. Knowledge is no longer a deterministic result of Descartes' type that a private person examines the content of thought but is socially produced. Descartes' "cogito" was not the premise of knowing but the result of knowing and the result of the simplified cognition of idealism. Moreover, the methods of introspection, self-examination, self-study of Descartes' type would no longer work because, for ourselves, we are "no longer self-transparent." On the contrary, in most instances, we do not know how we will know and what we will know.

Broekman pointed out that humanism is exposed as a philosophical method with an overrich ideological aspect. Similarly, Louis Althusser, French philosopher, also revealed that the essence of humanism is ideological just because it is established on the basis of the general non-scientific problem of "man" and "subject." According to Foucault's analysis, the dignity of humanism could come down to a jugglery of ideology. For Foucault, all these inner voices and these demands proposed to man and to the existence of man are all abstract, namely dissevered from the world of science and technology, which is, after all, our real world. He objected humanism because it is the screen that hides reactionary ideas and behind which an outrageous and inconceivable alliance is formed. To post-humanists, humanism has already become an excuse that covers up other inhuman objectives and viewpoints.

It seems to post-humanists that another fallacy of humanism is blind optimism. The theoretical basis of this blind optimism is placing man in God's position and equating the progress of human freedom with the progress of human reason. This optimism is doomed to be out of the wits to the following questions raised by post-humanism: Mankind has civilization, but why do they feel more worried and lonely day by day? Mankind possesses science, but why are they unceasingly puzzled? Mankind's knowledge is continuously enriched, but why freedom has become remoter? The pessimism of post-humanism is obviously the negation of the low-priced optimism of traditional humanism. This negation is not fallacious but has deep historical contents. Associated with this negation is disillusionment of the concept of progress. All sorts of stories about the mankind's continuous improvement ever told by the thinkers of humanism are now regarded by post-humanism only as a fiction, an artificial fiction.

D. Post-humanist Thought in Contemporary Literature and Culture

The post-humanist literary criticism reveals that the postmodernist writers criticize the traditional humanist thought based on "human-centered theory" and "subjective-object dualism" and the various modern crises caused by it. At the same time, the writers actively advocate and construct the thought of post-humanist harmonious society in their works, which is mainly reflected in the following three dimensions: firstly, building an ecological society that respects nature and in which different species are interdependent; secondly, human beings must guide and normalize scientific and technological practice with postmodern ethics, policies and regulations, and make rational use of high technology; and thirdly, human beings should care for the non-human world, treat the intelligent robot Cyborgs equally—the companions of human beings, and build a harmonious and symbiotic post-human society.

Post-humanism can be crucial in the examination and interpretation of contemporary and postmodernist literary and cultural works. Fictions such as William Gibson's *Neuromancer* (1984), Bruce Sterling's *Crystal Express* (1989), Richard Powers' *Galatea 2.2* (1995), and China Miéville's *Perdido Street Station* (2000)—along with television series such as *Star Trek: The Next Generation* and films such as *Blade Runner* (1982), *Tetsuo: The Iron Man* (1989), *Ghost in the Shell* (1995), and *eXistenZ* (1999)—depict humans and machines interfacing with and reshaping each other in new, complex, and often, provocative ways. To encounter such narratives is to see the certainties of humanism fade and to find bodies, minds, desires, limits, knowledge, and being itself reimagined in ways for which traditional anthropocentrism cannot possibly account.

Specifically, for example, in his works, Richard Powers (1957–), American postmodernist novelist, explores the impact of modern technology and advocates: 1) building an ecological society that respects nature and in which all species are interdependent: Daniel in *The Echo Maker* (2006) and Laura in *Gain* (1998) see their bodies as part of nature, people and all things in nature are harmonious and symbiotic, and nature has irreplaceable precious value to human beings, so humans must physically contribute to the integrity, balance and beauty of nature; 2) constructing a high-tech society that benefits mankind and develops sustainably: in *Prisoner's Dilemma* (1988), Powers argues that human beings should not give up eating because of various crises brought about by the abuse of high-tech development. The key lies in reasonable planning to prevent the abuse of science and technology; in *Generosity: An Enhancement* (2009), Powers proposes the necessity of genetic engineering to preserve human nature in a high-tech society and the ethical appeal of respecting the dignity of life; 3) building a post-human society in which humans and Cyborgs are interdependent and symbiotic: in *Galatea 2.2*, Powers describes the post-human living conditions in which humans and Cyborgs, intelligent robots, interact and depend on each other, and points out the future trend of human society: a post-human society full of artificial technology and man-made objects, a post-human society in which humans and Cyborgs live in harmony, and a post-human society that respects the happiness of the Other.

In conclusion, post-humanism is not a product of a few thinkers' work behind closed doors, who are carried away by a whim, but is a philosophy of the epoch, a philosophical cultural thought with broad influences that set itself afoot in the contemporary West. It is both the reflection of free capitalism and the response to the post-industrial society. It is both a philosophical rethinking of the reality and a self-introspection of philosophy itself. To see from the perspective of philosophy, the main contribution of post-humanism is compelling us to know again man's position in the world and reality, reexamine man that was ever considered "the measure for all things on earth" and "the center," and re-recognize the world ever thought to be known clearly. To be specific, post-humanism has made man's existence at one time thought to be absolute but now "relative," plural, and complicated. Relevant with this is that the world has also become relative, plural, and complicated. Here, an important method or an enlightenment that post-humanism has given us is that we should refuse looking at things simply because things themselves are complicated. A famous saying of post-humanists is that: No! Don't understand me all too easy. It is just through abandoning the idealistic "concept of subject" that post-humanism has done like this. At the point to criticize the idealistic and abstract human essence, the classical writers of post-humanism and Marxism tread different paths that lead to the same destination. The "death of man" that post-humanists said does not indicate the death of mankind that animatedly lives on the earth, but means the death of "man" understood subjectively. Once all sorts of "essence" and "privilege" (that can be said to be an encumbrance of thought) artificially added to man by idealistic humanistic thinkers are denuded, man is given back his original, relative, plural, complicated, and true face. Unlike classical humanism, post-humanism rejects any claim to domination based on anthropocentrism by reducing humanity to one of many natural species. On the basis of the understanding that human rights, animal rights and post-human rights all exist in one scope, post-humanism has formed the idea of constructing a harmonious post-human society.

Further Reading

Badmington, Neil. *Post-humanism* (*Readers in Cultural Criticism*). London: Palgrave Macmillan, 2000.

Braidotti, Rosi. *Post-human Knowledge*. Cambridge: Polity Press, 2019.

Cecchetto, David. *Humanesis: Sound and Technological Post-humanism*. Minneapolis: University of Minnesota Press, 2013.

Hassan, Ihab. Prometheus as Performer: Toward a Postmodern Culture? // Michel Benamou & Charles Caramello. *Performance in Postmodern Culture*. Madison: Coda Press, 1977.

Hayles, N. Katherine. *How We Became Post-human*: *Virtual Bodies in Cybernetics*, *Literature*, *and Informatics*. Chicago: University of Chicago Press, 1999.

MacFarlane, James. Boundary Work: Post- and Transhumanism, Part I, James Michael Mac Farlane. *Retrieved* 25, August 2016.

Miah, A. A Critical History of Post-humanism. Gordijn, B. & Chadwick R. *Medical Enhancement and Post-humanity*. Berlin: Springer, 2008, pp. 71–94.

Schechner, Richard. *The End of Humanism: Writings on Performance*. New York: Performing Arts Journal Publications, 1982.

Herbrechter, Stefan. *Post-humanism, A Critical Analysis*. London: Bloomsbury, 2013.

Winner, Langdon. Resistance Is Futile: The Post-human Condition and Its Advocates // Harold Bailie & Timothy Casey. *Is Human Nature Obsolete*? Cambridge: Massachusetts Institute of Technology Press, 2004: 385–411.

Wolfe, Cary. *What is Post-humanism*? Minneapolis: University of Minnesota Press, 2009.

Bibliography

Cuddon, J. A. *A Dictionary of Literary Terms and Literary Theory*. 5th ed. Malden: Wiley-Blackwell, 2013.

Rice, Philip & Patricia Waugh. *Modern Literary Theory*. New York: Oxford University Press, 2002.

Bressler, Charles. *Literary Criticism: An Introduction to Theory and Practice*. Beijing: Higher Education Press, 2004.

Barry, Peter. *Beginning Theory: An Introduction to Literary and Cultural Theory*. Manchester: Manchester University Press, 2017.

Selden, Raman, Peter Widdowson & Peter Brooker. *A Readers Guide to Contemporary Literary Theory*. 5th ed. Great Britain: Pearson Longman, 2005.

泰勒，温奎斯特. 后现代主义百科全书. 章燕，李自修，等译. 刘象愚，校. 长春：吉林人民出版社，2007.

王治河. 后现代主义辞典. 北京：中央编译出版社，2004.

张中载，王逢振，赵国新. 二十世纪西方文论选读. 北京：外语教学与研究出版社，2002.

朱刚. 二十世纪西方文艺批评理论. 上海：上海外语教育出版社，2001.

Selected Readings

Francesca Ferrando: "Post-humanism, Transhumanism, Antihumanism, Metahumanism, and New Materialisms: Differences and Relations"

N. Katherine Hayles: *How We Became Post-human: Virtual Bodies in Cybernetics, Literature, and Informatics*

Rosi Braidotti: (a part of) *Post-human Knowledge*

图书在版编目（CIP）数据

当代西方文艺批评理论要义 / 陈世丹等著. -- 2版
. -- 北京 : 中国人民大学出版社, 2023.9
高级英语选修课系列教材
ISBN 978-7-300-32140-0

Ⅰ. ①当… Ⅱ. ①陈… Ⅲ. ①英语—阅读教学—高等学校—教材 ②文艺批评—理论—西方国家 Ⅳ. ①H319.39：I

中国国家版本馆 CIP 数据核字（2023）第 165927 号

高级英语选修课系列教材
本成果得到中国人民大学“研究生精品教材建设经费”支持
当代西方文艺批评理论要义（第二版）
陈世丹　史岩林　张东芹　王小会　黄　贺　著
Dangdai Xifang Wenyi Piping Lilun Yaoyi (Di–er Ban)

出版发行	中国人民大学出版社		
社　址	北京中关村大街 31 号	邮政编码	100080
电　话	010–62511242（总编室）		010–62511770（质管部）
	010–82501766（邮购部）		010–62514148（门市部）
	010–62515195（发行公司）		010–62515275（盗版举报）
网　址	http:// www. crup. com. cn		
经　销	新华书店		
印　刷	天津鑫丰华印务有限公司	版　次	2017 年 10 月第 1 版
开　本	787 mm×1092 mm　1/16		2023 年 9 月第 2 版
印　张	15.75	印　次	2023 年 9 月第 1 次印刷
字　数	325 000	定　价	68.00 元